D1006709

Juvenile Delinquency

VIEWPOINTS IN SOCIOLOGY

NORMS AND HUMAN BEHAVIOR
Arnold Birenbaum and Edward Sagarin

A SENSE OF SOCIOLOGY
Lee Braude

WORK AND WORKERS: A SOCIOLOGICAL ANALYSIS
Lee Braude

MARRIAGE AND ITS ALTERNATIVES
Lucile Duberman

CRIME AND CRIMINALIZATION
Clayton A. Hartjen

ANALYZING SOCIAL PROBLEMS
Jerome G. Manis

JUVENILE DELINQUENCY
William B. Sanders

METHODOLOGY AND MEANINGS: VARIETIES OF
SOCIOLOGICAL INQUIRY
George V. Zito

Juvenile Delinquency

William B. Sanders
University of Florida

Praeger Publishers • New York

To My Parents

Published in the United States of America in 1976
by Praeger Publishers, Inc.
111 Fourth Avenue, New York, N. Y. 10003

Second printing, 1976

© 1976 by Praeger Publishers, Inc.

Library of Congress Cataloging in Publication Data

Sanders, William B.
  Juvenile delinquency.

  Bibliography: p. 217
  Includes index.
  1. Juvenile delinquency. 2. Juvenile justice,
Administration of. I. Title.
HV9069.S25   364.36   74–15685
ISBN 0–275–22360–4
ISBN 0–275–85440–X (pbk.)

Printed in the United States of America

Foreword

Arthur J. Vidich

The Viewpoints in Sociology Series is designed to present to the beginning student a sense of the sociological attitude and an appreciation of a significant sociological problem. Each of the studies in this series has been selected because it offers a fresh approach and a new viewpoint to the analysis of a basic subject of sociological inquiry.

In *Juvenile Delinquency* Professor William Sanders' approach to his subject is informed by an awareness of the ambiguous status of the juvenile in industrial civilization. The juvenile, as we know that category now, did not exist in the preindustrial world. Then, the child moved from childhood directly to adulthood without an intervening period of juvenility. Now, we think of the juvenile as someone who is capable of adult behavior but does not have the legal status of an adult. The development of this interim period in the life cycle is related to two factors closely bound to the economic and occupational requirements of industrial society. First, the time of entry of youth into the labor market has progressively moved from childhood to early adulthood, and, second, compulsory formal schooling has been extended to include the entire period of adolescence. Thus, youths today are regarded as neither ready for economic independence nor educationally prepared to enter the world. The "juvenile" lives in a state of limbo between childhood and adulthood. It is a station in life that is inexactly defined as being too old to be a child, but not adequately prepared to be an adult.

Because of the ambiguousness of the juvenile status, a vast and complex body of law and legal institutions has developed as part of society's apparatus to control and set limits to juvenile conduct. Juvenile delinquency has its origins in violations of the law, or as Professor Sanders more precisely states it, "Juvenile delinquency is the characterization of an act as a violation of delinquency laws." By anchoring his analysis of juvenile delinquency to a sociolegal definition, he has opened the way for a genuinely objective sociological treatment of a problem that has long been burdened in the sociological literature with unnecessary ideological bias or a commitment to the values of specific agencies which are themselves part of the delinquency process.

Like other fields of sociological inquiry that have had their origins in a moral or legal attitude toward the behavior being studied, students of juvenile delinquency have frequently been unable to respond to the vast changes that in recent years have taken place in the role of the juvenile in our society. Age of entry into the labor market has been extended to the post-teenage period. The educational system into which youth is absorbed is not usually connected to occupational training or to job opportunities. Yet large numbers of them have access to sources of income from allowances, part-time work, and irregular jobs, which allow them to behave like adults in the economic marketplace. American business, including drug distributors, give full recognition to the consumption power of youth. In addition, youths have participated in some of the important political issues of our times: antiwar demonstrations, draft resistance movements, busing strikes, and the racial integration of schools. We can no longer look at juvenile delinquency as something that will "go away" if only it is properly treated. The juvenile and juvenile delinquency are part of the social and legal fabric of our society, and a whole host of cultural, legal, social, and class institutions are identified with this status and its maintenance.

In *Juvenile Delinquency* Professor Sanders shows himself to be a keen and precise observer of the juvenile world. In his analysis, he moves with ease between the concrete ethnographic data on which his work rests and a theoretically informed attitude that is derived from a heuristic response to the works of authors such as Robert Merton, Albert Cohen, Gresham Sykes, David Matza, Richard Cloward, Donald Cressey, Edwin Sutherland, Stanford-Lyman, Marvin Scott, Harold Garfinkel, Edwin Lemert, Erving Goffman, and Karl Marx. He has written an excellent book, one which brings a fresh set of viewpoints to the study of a problem that up to now has not received the integrated sociological treatment it has deserved.

Preface

This book was written with two goals in mind. First, I wanted to give the reader a basic understanding of the phenomenon of juvenile delinquency. In so short a work on so complex a subject, any understanding provided is necessarily *basic* in a literal sense. Second, I wanted to bring into sharper focus certain areas of delinquency that are all too often ignored or given only passing mention. I refer particularly to juvenile-status offenders, the group comprising "predelinquents," "runaways," "truants," "promiscuous girls," and others who have committed no crime for which an adult would be arrested. I have also given what some might consider an unusual amount of attention to the juvenile justice system, including the role of the police, the juvenile courts, and juvenile corrections. This was done to emphasize the intimate relationship between delinquency and the juvenile justice system. The reasons for my somewhat nontraditional emphasis are elaborated in the text; I believe it to be justified, and I mention it here only to give the reader a foretaste of what follows.

Much of the material presented here is the product of my own research and experience. At one time I worked with a group of juveniles from wealthy families who were labeled "emotionally disturbed." Later, when I worked with juveniles from poor families who were labeled "delinquent," I found that there was no difference between the two groups other than the economic one. Those families that could afford to have their children called "emotionally disturbed" did so, and those who either could not afford it or were unaware of this alternative did not. I found, also, that a number of the kids in the latter group were locked up for things I had done during my own adolescent years. Most of them were not hoodlums in any sense, and the rich kids, who had to get into serious trouble before any official notice was taken of their misbehavior, were often a lot wilder than the poor kids, who are usually blamed for all the delinquency. These experiences led me to question my own preconceptions about delinquency.

In later years, as a sociologist, I had the opportunity to check out a number of these questions. In several research projects—on juvenile drug use, juvenile-status offenders and diversion programs, and the police and juvenile offenses—what remained of my earlier conceptions melted away. My sympathies for the so-called delinquent increased, but I also found myself in sympathy with those who were responsible for controlling delinquency, especially the police. No one was happy about the situation, and each understood it from his or her own point of view—which means no understanding at all. The multiple dilemmas posed by delinquency have clearly affected the style and content of this book, and my personal feelings often show through. The more one becomes involved with the problem of delinquency, the more likely it is that one will abandon all pretense to objectivity. However, without the involvement, there is little hope of understanding. In any event, I have attempted to minimize my own prejudices, and where I have failed, I hope the reader will realize that they are a product of frustration.

As is true of all works of this sort, a number of people have contributed in one way or another. However, any shortcomings in the work are not their responsibility but mine.

Charles Frazier of the University of Florida offered helpful criticisms and suggestions concerning the chapter on theory. Those who have read Dr. Frazier's work will readily see what advice I followed and what I did not. George Muedeking of California State College, Stanislaus, provided a number of helpful suggestions for organizing the material at the outset of the project.

My mentor, Donald R. Cressey, had a great deal of influence on the theoretical direction and organization of material, and he provided the opportunity to participate in a research project dealing with juvenile-status offenders and diversion programs. Don Zimmerman and D. Lawrence Wieder were also important influences in the direction I took. Professor Albert Hess enabled me to gather the European data presented in this book.

Elmo Innocenti provided me with the opportunity to observe at first hand what happens to juveniles when they are locked up. His humanity and genuine concern for the juveniles who came under his care were evident despite the limited means at his disposal. Others in this area provided both positive and negative images—both heroic efforts and sadistic manipulations aimed at children in their control. They will not be named for obvious reasons.

The data on juvenile-division detectives were made available by members and former members of the juvenile detail of the Santa Barbara County Sheriff's Office, including detectives Anthony Baker, Moorman Oliver, Jr., "Sully" Skehan, Chip Marchbanks, Frank Wright, James Taylor, and Fred Holderman. Their jobs were at best a difficult and unrewarding, and at worst painfully impossible. Without their compassion and tolerance for frustration, they could not have done their jobs.

I am extremely grateful to Professor Arthur Vidich, whose editorial comments, support, and overall enthusiasm served as a needed electricity to complete this project.

Secretarial and library assistance was provided, always effectively, by Jackie Moore, Peggy Dever, and Esperanza Vera. Gladys Topkis of Praeger Publishers made the manuscript bearable, intelligible—in short, readable. My wife, Eli, and my sons, Billy and David, hung in there while I made noises in the house. Finally, I am grateful to my parents, who, like all parents, provided the juvenile but not the delinquent.

W.B.S.

Contents

Foreword by Arthur Vidich   v
Preface   ix

1. THE PHENOMENON OF JUVENILE
      DELINQUENCY   1
   What Is Juvenile Delinquency?   3
   The Amount, Distribution, and Measurement of Delin-
      quency   11
   Delinquency as a Phase of Growing Up   20
   Conclusion   22

2. WHY ARE THERE DELINQUENTS?: Theories of Juvenile
      Delinquency   23
   Deviance, Crime, and Delinquency   23
   The Social Deprivation Theory   26
   The Availability of Crime: The Development of Delinquent
      Subcultures   32
   The Generation Gap: Value Conflict   41
   Whom You Hang Around With: Differential Association
      45

Only If You Get Caught: Labeling Theory   51
Where the Action Is: Character and Delinquency   55
Conclusion   61

3. JUST FOR KIDS: Juvenile-Status Offenses   64
Young and in Love: Juvenile Sexual Offenses   67
Gotta Get Out of Here: The Runaways   73
You're Too Young: Waiting to Be an Adult   80
Conclusion   83

4. RIPOFF: Juvenile Property Crimes   84
Boosting   86
Joy Riding   92
Trashing   95
Conclusion   105

5. DOPE: Drug Use by Juveniles   107
Trends in Drug Use by Juveniles   109
"Everyone Smokes Pot"   116
Higher and Higher   122
Juvenile Junkies   127
Drug Use as a Social, Medical, and Legal Problem   131
Conclusion   132

6. HANGING TOGETHER: Juvenile Gangs   134
The Structure of Juvenile Gangs   137
Types of Gangs   141
Gang Violence   148
Turf   153
Conclusion   155

7. BUSTED: Juveniles and the Police   157
Encounters with the Man   158
The Kiddie Kops   168
Conclusion   174

8. DUBIOUS SALVATION: Juvenile Justice   176
Juvenile Court: The Child-Savers   176
"We're Only Here to Help You": The Assumption of Guilt   179

The Process of the Juvenile Courts   184
"Who's Your P.O.?": Juvenile Probation   187
Conclusion   196

9. SPARE THE ROD: Juvenile Corrections   197
Probation   199
Juvenile Jails   201
Street Work with Gangs   207
Diversion from the Juvenile Justice System   211
Conclusion   215

References   217
Index   229

1 The Phenomenon of Juvenile Delinquency

A fifteen-year-old boy walked into a bank and robbed it of almost two thousand dollars. The first time I saw him was in a photograph published in the papers that had been taken by the bank's security cameras, and he appeared to be between twenty and twenty-five years old. The second time I saw him was when two detectives brought him into the juvenile custodial facility where I was working part-time while in graduate school. He told me that he had been captured only because a friend had "finked" on him, and judging from what he told me of the sophisticated plan carried out in the robbery and from what the police had said, there was every reason to believe him. During this stay at the juvenile hall, as the detention center was called, I learned that the boy planned to become a "gentleman criminal." In order to show me that he could carry out his intentions, he taught me a number of con games, explained in detail how to commit various other cons, and demonstrated a rich vocabulary of rationalizations for breaking the law instead of following it. From this association I am convinced that he probably will become some kind of adult criminal, "gentleman" or otherwise.

At the same juvenile facility, I met another boy, aged seventeen, who was in custody for being "out of control." On the advice of his hometown police chief and with a note from his parents, the boy had left home to hitchhike to the northern part of the state. When he arrived in "Mountainbeach," the town where I met him, he was arrested for being out of his parents' control. He showed the police the note permitting his travel, but he was arrested anyway. When they brought him in, he had to call his parents to come pick him up from their home two hundred miles away.

Another "runaway" I met at the juvenile hall was a girl aged sixteen, who had been bounced from one foster home to another. The court decided that she was not being cared for properly by her mother, who was separated from her husband, so the girl was made a ward of one set of foster parents after another. She generally did not like her foster parents, so she would leave them and return to her mother, who would call the authorities and have her sent to juvenile hall while a new temporary home was located. We used to talk about her life, and she said that there was one foster home she had really liked, but she knew that she could stay there for only a year before she would be sent to another home. To avoid becoming too attached to this family, she left before the year was up. Her real home, she came to believe, was the streets, where she had friends with whom she could talk and relate. As a result, she drifted away from any semblance of organized family life into the street life.

A fourth resident of the juvenile hall was a fifteen-year-old boy who had been arrested for attempted murder. He had come from the East for the summer and had fallen in with other unattached adolescents in the community. They had taken on a hip life style that centered around drug use. This particular boy had less money than his friends, but he wanted the same things they had. He took a pair of jeans to a tailor to be altered according to the prevailing fashion of his group. When the pants were ready, he tried to take them without paying. The tailor attempted to stop him, and the boy knifed him and ran out of the store. This was the first time he had ever been in trouble with the law.

These cases illustrate the wide range in the behavior that is termed "juvenile delinquency." Popular images of juvenile delinquency portray young "hippies" freaked out on dope or gangs of youths in black leather jackets hanging around street corners, brandishing switchblades, or competing in illegal drag races. Some of these images are accurate, but juvenile delinquency covers a far broader range of activities, is more complex than it is typically believed to be, exists in many distinct forms, and varies from state to state. It has been a major source of national concern over the past few decades and continues to be a problem and cause for concern. Simple panaceas citing "permissiveness" as the cause and claiming that "putting 'em to work" will "cure" juvenile delinquency reflect ignorance more than understanding. In this book I will attempt to convey the varied facets of juvenile crime rather than feed popular myths.

WHAT IS JUVENILE DELINQUENCY?

As the cases presented earlier suggest, "juvenile delinquency" covers a wide range of activity. Merely to define the term by fiat cannot convey the complexities of juvenile offenses and offenders.

To begin, let us consider the legal nature of delinquency. Some statutes apply only to juveniles, and thus a whole group of illegal acts can be committed only by juveniles ("juvenile-status offenses"). For instance, someone who is over the age legally defined as juvenile cannot be arrested for running away from home or being truant from school. The legal age, however, varies among states. Four state jurisdictions define juvenility as under twenty-one years old; at the other end of the continuum, eight states set the age of possible juvenile delinquency at under sixteen (Sellin and Wolfgang, 1964:73). A twenty-year-old who runs away from home in a state where the juvenile age is set at under twenty-one can be arrested, while a sixteen-year-old can legally run away from home if he happens to live in a state where the legal adult age is sixteen. The twenty-year-old can be considered legally to have committed a delinquency and judged to be a juvenile delinquent, while the sixteen-year-old cannot commit a delinquency or be judged a delinquent.

It may appear to be advantageous for young people to live in states with a low age limit for delinquency treatment, and this is certainly true where juvenile-status offenses are concerned. However, in those states youths who would be treated as juvenile in other states are treated as adults. For example, if a sixteen-year-old who lives in a state where the juvenile age is under sixteen commits a burglary, he will be thrown in with adult offenders and will receive the more severe treatment generally meted out to adults—possibly a prison sentence. But if a twenty-year-old in a state where he is considered a juvenile commits a burglary, he will be treated as a juvenile and will not have to suffer the same fate as an adult burglar.

The modal age for being treated as a juvenile is under eighteen years old. In twenty-eight states, when a person reaches eighteen, he or she is considered an adult as far as most criminal matters are concerned (Sellin and Wolfgang, 1964:73). One of these states is California, and offenders who are under eighteen are treated under the statutes of the Welfare and Institutions Code instead of the Penal Code, which applies to adult offenders. At the same time, however, California law states that the legal age for possession of alcohol is twenty-one. Therefore, a twenty-year-old in California will not be given the leniency awarded to juveniles if he is arrested for drinking beer even though the law stipulates that he is under age! California youths between the ages of eighteen and twenty-one are in limbo, neither juveniles nor full-fledged adults. This "limbo" category exists in several other states as well and is especially wide in range in states with relatively low age limits for delinquency.

The category of juvenile-status offenses is broad and vague. For example, Section 601 of the California Welfare and Institutions Code provides that

> Any person under the age of 18 years who persistently or habitually refuses to obey the reasonable and proper orders or directions of his parents, guardian, custodian or school authorities, or

who is beyond the control of such person, or any person who is a habitual truant from school within the meaning of any law of this State, or who from any cause is in danger of leading an idle, dissolute, lewd, or immoral life, is within the jurisdiction of the juvenile court which may adjudge such person to be a ward of the court. [Amended Ch. 1748, Stats. 1971. Effective Mar. 4, 1972]

This definition could include everything from a juvenile on a vacation away from his parents to an incorrigible runaway. The seventeen-year-old boy who was arrested for being "out of control" because his parents lived two-hundred-miles away, even though they approved of his travels, demonstrates how arbitrary the application of this section can be. As the criterion of being "out of control," the police used being "out of county," even though the statute did not define "out of control" in that way.

The other major California statute regulating the treatment of juvenile delinquents groups all other possible offenses together. Section 602 of the California Welfare and Institutions Code reads:

Any person who is under the age of 18 years when he violates any law of this state or of the United States or any ordinance of any city or county of this state defining crime or who, after having being found by the juvenile court to be a person described by Section 601 [see above], fails to obey any lawful order of the juvenile court, is within the jurisdiction of the juvenile court, which may adjudge such person to be a ward of the court. [Amended Ch. 1748, Stats. 1971. Effective Mar. 4, 1972]

Juveniles who commit any illegal act, from malicious mischief to homicide, are cited under this section. Of course, young murderers receive stiffer penalties than young mischief makers, but the juvenile record cites the same legal code for both offenses.

Other states have equally broad statutes regulating juveniles, although these statutes may differ from the juvenile laws of California in specific wording and in the age limits. For example, the Pennsylvania law for juveniles (Public Law 1433) states:

(2) The word "child," as used in this act, means a minor under the age of eighteen years. . . .

(4) The words "delinquent child" include:

   (a) A child who has violated any law of the Commonwealth or ordinance of any city, borough, or township;

   (b) A child who, by reason of being wayward or habitually disobedient, is uncontrolled by his or her parent, guardian, custodian, or legal representative;

   (c) A child who is habitually truant from school or home;

   (d) A child who habitually so deports himself or herself as to endanger the morals or health of himself, herself, or others.

As can be seen, subsection 4a is essentially identical to the California Welfare and Institutions Code Section 602, and subsections 4b through 4d are the same as the California Section 601.

Now that we have an idea of the range of behavior covered by the laws regulating juvenile delinquency, can we evolve a realistic definition of juvenile delinquency and juvenile delinquents? Can we say, for example, that delinquency is any act that violates delinquency laws (cf. Gibbons, 1970:7) and that a juvenile delinquent is anyone of juvenile age who engages in such acts?

Considering the broader aspects of the delinquency laws, it is difficult to imagine any young person who could *not* be said to have violated some part of the law. In other words, if we examined any single juvenile's biography, it is likely that we would find some act that could be characterized as a violation of the delinquency laws. For example, if a boy and girl go fishing on a farmer's land without his permission, this could conceivably be construed to be a violation of antitrespass laws. Hence we could say that the boy and girl had committed a delinquent act.

Now, if a juvenile who commits a delinquent act is a juvenile delinquent (as is explicitly stated in the Pennsylvania law), then the boy and girl who went fishing are delinquents. And if, as we pointed out, it is unlikely that anyone can grow up without doing something that can be assessed as being in violation of the law, then by this purely legal definition, most if not all juveniles are also juvenile delinquents.

This view is unrealistic for two reasons. First, it assumes that delinquent acts exist in the world independent of social interpretations of these acts. But it is the assessment of an act as delinquent, not the act alone, that makes the act delinquent (Hartjen, 1974:5–8). Using our example of the boy and girl who went fishing without asking permission, we can identify various assessments by those who might be involved. The children may or may not see the action as a violation of the law. If they see it as a violation, they may simply regard it as "wrong," "naughty," or "sneaky" but not as illegal. Similarly, the farmer may assess the children's action in any number of ways. He might recall his own boyhood, when he did the same thing, and disregard the children's trespass, or he might worry about the possibility of a civil suit should something happen to the children on his land and might therefore call the police to arrest them. If they are called to take action against the trespassing children, the police may not see the children's actions as in any way delinquent and may simply tell them to go home, or they may arrest them and take them to a juvenile detention facility. Once the children are booked into the detention center, the probation department may or may not see their action as warranting court action. It is clear that numerous assessments of the action must be made for it to be treated as "really delinquent." Delinquency, therefore, is not something that is legally defined but is assessed and characterized as such in social interaction.

The second problem with the purely legal view is in the notion of a juvenile delinquent. Let's suppose that the boy and girl who went fishing were sent to juvenile court and placed on probation for violating delinquency laws. If their fishing expedition is the only thing for which they have ever been brought to court, it is unlikely that they will be considered "juvenile delinquents" by most people, even though they might be so considered "legally." Their friends, parents, teachers, and probably even their probation officer would see them as "just a couple of kids who got in trouble," but not as "bad kids" or "delinquents." Similarly, the seventeen-year-old boy picked up for being "out of control" because he was in a different county than his parents was seen to have broken a delinquency law but was not characterized as a delinquent. Like the assessment of delinquent actions, the assessment of juvenile delinquents is an interactive, social process, not simply a legal one.

Having examined some of the legal and social aspects of delinquency, we are now ready to provide a *sociolegal* definition of delinquency based on these conceptions: *Juvenile delinquency is the characterization of an act as a violation of delinquency laws.*

The person who takes an action that might possibly be characterized as delinquent will be referred to here as the *actor,* and those who assess the action as delinquent or not as *others.* Since the actor may assess his or her own behavior, the actor can be both actor and other simultaneously (Blumer, 1969). That is, if an actor characterizes his own behavior as violating the delinquency laws even though nobody else is around, the act can be considered delinquent. For instance, the youngsters who went fishing without permission might take steps to avoid detection for fear of being arrested on trespassing charges. They would thus be characterizing their action in terms of the delinquency law. But the farmer who owns the land might see the situation as an innocent fishing expedition, and the notion that the children are violating the delinquency laws may never enter his mind. However, by our definition, since at least some of those involved in the situation characterized the act in terms of a violation of the delinquency laws, we can speak of the act as delinquent.

Often the assessment of an act as delinquent or not is vague for all involved. This is especially true of judgments of intentions. For instance, let's say that some juveniles are hiking along an embankment and accidentally start a landslide, which hurtles rocks onto the roadway. A police officer witnesses the act and believes that the juveniles did it intentionally; that is, he views the act as a violation of the laws prohibiting malicious mischief. When he catches the hikers, he tells them that he is going to arrest them for malicious mischief. The hikers say the act was an accident, and they volunteer to clear away the rocks. If the policeman believes them, he reassesses the act retrospectively as not being a violation of the law; thus, even though the act was initially characterized as a violation, it is reformulated as an accident. Even though the act was seen for a while to be delinquent, the final assessment was something else. So, by our definition, the act would not be considered delinquent.

In order to understand "real" or "actual" delinquency, we must suspend the commonsense notion that delinquency is some objective action that takes place in the world. This is an "idealistic," not a "realistic," notion. We are tempted to say that a delinquent act can occur even though nobody characterizes it as a violation of the delinquency laws. But what is the actual status of an act other than the way we talk about it? If a juvenile takes a candy bar from a store without paying for it and no one, including the juvenile, characterizes the act as a legal violation, how can we say that a delinquent act has occurred? We could characterize the act as delinquent, but then instead of studying delinquency, we would be creating delinquency where *socially* no delinquency occurred. This would be like saying that the headhunters of the Amazon should be arrested for homicide even though they have broken none of *their* laws. The sociologist's data are based on the social understandings of the world, and our task is to come to terms with these understandings, not to create understandings that do not exist in social reality and then study *them.*

Now that we have defined a delinquent act, we can define a juvenile delinquent in much the same way. As we pointed out earlier, it would be naive to offer a purely legal definition, saying that anyone who has been characterized as having violated delinquency laws is a delinquent. It would be equally naive to say that for a youth to be considered a delinquent, he must have broken the law. A member of a juvenile gang is regarded by the police to be a delinquent even though he may never have been observed breaking a law. His association with others who are characterized as delinquents is generally sufficient for him to be viewed as a delinquent. And if a juvenile is judged to be delinquent because of the company he keeps, this assessment of his character is no less real than if it were based on his commission of delinquent acts.

Kai Erikson (1962) has pointed out that the amount of time dedicated to deviant or criminal activities by people labeled deviant or criminal is very small compared to the amount of time they spend in noncriminal activities. A boy judged to be delinquent may spend the great majority of his time going to school, obeying his parents, and in similarly nondelinquent actions. However, if he is known to spend as little as one hour a week going for "joy rides" in stolen cars, he is likely to be considered a delinquent. Our definition of a juvenile delinquent, then, must recognize that someone does not have to spend the majority of his or her time breaking the law to be considered a delinquent.

A juvenile delinquent is anyone whose character, biography, and actions are assessed in terms of his/her having committed delinquent acts. Note that a juvenile does not have to commit delinquent acts to be considered a delinquent. As long as a juvenile is *assessed in terms of delinquent acts,* he or she is considered to be a delinquent whether or not any delinquent act was actually committed. By the same token, a juvenile may have committed numerous delinquent acts, but as long as his character is not judged in terms of such acts, he will not be considered a delinquent by our definition.

Consider, for example, a girl who is caught shoplifting. If the store manager calls the girl's parents instead of reporting the incident to the police, the act will not be considered an "official" delinquency but an "informal" delinquency; although the store may keep a record of the girl's action, it will not be an "official" record. The girl's parents might say that the shoplifting "isn't like her" or otherwise deny that the act and their daughter's character have anything in common. Therefore, they do not assess their daughter's past and future behavior in terms of her being a delinquent.

On the other hand, the store manager might call the police. The police will then be likely to set up an official record of the delinquent act, attaching the act to the person. The girl's parents may speak of their daughter's delinquent act as "just like her" or may say, "We're not surprised." Future activities by the girl, such as getting poor grades or staying out late, may be judged in terms of her "being a delinquent," and this second course of action by others—unlike the first course of action, where the parents denied their daughter's delinquent identity—transforms the girl into a delinquent. The mere act of delinquency was insufficient for the girl to be judged "a delinquent."

THE AMOUNT, DISTRIBUTION, AND MEASUREMENT OF DELINQUENCY

How much delinquency is there? Who commits delinquency? Who are the delinquents?

Each year the Federal Bureau of Investigation publishes the *Uniform Crime Reports,* with statistical compilations of crimes reported to the police. Some of the crimes are juvenile-status offenses; the rest are general crimes of various types. The juvenile-status offenses, by definition, must be committed by juveniles. How many of the other crimes are perpetrated by juveniles? In 1965 over half the arrests for major property crimes involved people under twenty-one (President's Commission, 1967:55), and from the arrest rates for general crimes we can estimate that many are committed by juveniles. However, if we rely solely on these figures we will miss all unreported and undetected juvenile crimes as well as unapprehended juveniles who have committed delinquent acts. Moreover, we will link our analysis to the complex processes of the juvenile and criminal justice systems, and instead of deriving an accurate estimate, we will merely reflect the record-keeping practices of these agencies.

Black and Reiss (1970), for example, found that white victims were less likely than black victims to demand that an arrest be made in delinquency situations. Since the victims of crimes are typically of the same race as the suspects, it is possible that more black youths are arrested than white youths in part because black victims are more likely to demand that arrests be made. Furthermore, Piliavin and Briar (1964) found that juveniles who look "tough" were more likely to be arrested than "clean-cut" youths, so there are probably more lower-class and working-class youths arrested than middle-class juveniles on the basis of appearance alone. And since arrest records of the police list only those who were actually taken into custody, it would be a mistake to assume that these records reflect the actual patterns of those committing delinquent acts.

One strategy we can take in estimating the frequency and distribution of delinquency is to examine the number of crimes typically attributed to juveniles, other than juvenile-status offenses. Unfortunately, in order to estimate these "typically juvenile crimes" we must rely on police records, but even with the shortcomings we have pointed out, these records give us something more than sheer speculation. If we limit our examination to those crimes that arrest rates indicate are overwhelmingly committed by juveniles, we can estimate the amount of juvenile crime with greater assurance.

For example, motor vehicle theft, which includes joy riding, is a typical juvenile crime. In 1965, 61.4 percent of those arrested for stealing cars were between eleven and seventeen years of age, only 26.4 percent were between eighteen and twenty-four and 11.9 percent were over twenty-five (President's Commission, 1967:56). Moreover, because juveniles often steal cars only for joy rides and soon abandon them, many juvenile car thieves are not caught; therefore, the arrest rate may be lower than the actual rate of juvenile involvement in car theft. In 1965 there were almost a half million car thefts; on the basis of juvenile arrests, we can estimate that some 300,000 of these automobiles were taken by juveniles. However, if we concluded that 300,000 youths had stolen cars, we would be wrong. First, some of those arrested may have taken more than a single car or may have been arrested more than once for stealing cars. Secondly, it has been found that juveniles are likely to commit crimes in groups of two or more (Reiss and Rhodes, 1964), so that several juveniles may be arrested for the same crime. Thus, while we can make rough guesses as to the amount of juvenile crime, it is difficult to assess the number of juveniles involved in delinquency. What we *can* do, though, is point out that car theft is a typical juvenile crime.

Another means of establishing typical juvenile crimes is to look at police organization in handling crimes. Several police departments have special divisions to deal with juvenile problems. By examining what these divisions understand to be typical juvenile crimes, we can estimate what types of crime other than juvenile-status offenses are generally committed by juveniles.

In one study (Sanders, 1974:208–36), it was found that the juvenile division handled all petty thefts—that is thefts of items or money totaling less that two-hundred dollars (e.g., shoplifting) and all malicious-mischief cases (e.g., vandalism). Of course, not all such crimes were committed by juveniles, but since most of those arrested for these crimes were juveniles, the police allocated their investigative resources for these crimes to juvenile officers. The police generally assumed that a vandalized school or broken window was likely to be the work of juveniles, and there was little evidence that these assumptions were inaccurate, for when the police caught a vandal, the culprit was typically a juvenile.

Police and court records may give us some idea of how many acts are characterized as delinquent and what type are committed by juveniles, but they still leave us with the results of bureaucratic record keeping and really nothing more. In order to obtain a more accurate view of the extent of crime, two other methods have been employed. One is the victimization survey, in which a population is surveyed to learn what proportion has been victimized in crime. The other method is the self-report survey, in which people are asked whether or not they have been involved in criminal or delinquent activities.

The victimization survey does not differentiate between delinquent and criminal activities; however, by looking at typical juvenile crimes, such as car theft and petty larceny, we can get a better idea of the actual amount of juvenile delinquency. Since there is little difference in the rate of car theft revealed by comparing police records and victimization surveys (Ennis, 1967), we will look at larceny, another crime with heavy juvenile involvement. According to police reports, there were 267.4 larcenies involving fifty dollars or more per 100,000 population in the area surveyed by Ennis. However, a victimization survey revealed that the rate was 606.5, more than twice what had been reported to the police. Another victimization survey found that all larcenies, both petty and grand, were vastly underreported. While the rate of larcenies reported to the police was about 15 per 1,000, the rate reported by the survey respondents was about 80 per 1,000 (President's Commission, 1967:21) —over five times as high! If we use the FBI estimate that some 50 percent of larcenies are committed by juveniles, the vast majority of juvenile larcenies are not even reported to the police.

Victimization surveys provide a way of setting up a ratio of known to unknown crimes. With the information that the ratio of known to unknown larcenies is one to five (1:5), for example, if we know that 378 larcenies were reported to the police in a week, we can estimate that five times that number, or 1,890 larcenies, actually took place. Further, by estimating the proportion of juveniles typically involved in various crimes, we can come up with a more realistic idea of how many delinquent acts have been committed. Thus, if we estimate, on the basis of victimization-survey ratios, that 1,890 larcenies were committed in a week and that 50 percent were delinquent acts, we have a more nearly accurate figure—945 juvenile involvements in crime.

Now that we have a way of estimating the amount of delinquency, we need to have a way of knowing how many juveniles are involved in delinquency. As we pointed out, court and police records reflect only those who were caught and so are of little use. To overcome this limitation, a number of studies have been done in which juveniles were given questionnaires and asked to report whether or not they have committed various delinquent acts. The President's Commission Report (1967:55) found on the basis of these self-report studies that 90 percent of all young people have committed at least one act for which they could have been brought before juvenile court. Some of the offenses to which youths admit are relatively trivial; however, they are still serious enough in the eyes of the juvenile courts to require court action.

The exact form and content of the offenses vary, ranging from skipping school to feloneous assault. As can be seen in tables 1 and 2, which compare two high school groups (M.W. and West) with a correctional school group (Tr.S.) for both boys and girls, there is a good deal of juvenile delinquency committed by the respondents.

The two high school groups (M.W. and West) had lower rates than the groups incarcerated in a training school (Tr.S.), but in several categories the boys in the high school groups had engaged in more delinquency than the girls in the training school. Most important, however, is that virtually all juveniles engage in at least some activities that can be characterized as delinquent. Admittedly, most delinquencies are juvenile-status offenses and would not be against the law if the actors were older, but since juveniles can be arrested and turned over to juvenile court for these types of offenses, they are no less consequential in their impact.

From examining the data, another lesson should be driven home. As noted in our definition, the amount of delinquent behavior does not reflect the number of people considered to be juvenile delinquents. All those incarcerated in a training school are probably judged to be delinquents, but even though almost all in the high school group had committed a delinquent act, it is unlikely that more than a few are considered delinquents. Thus, even though just about all the juveniles engage in delinquency, only a few are considered delinquents, and even fewer are ever brought before juvenile courts.

Another pattern in the rates of self-reported delinquency is the general trend toward male overrepresentation, especially in instances of theft and fighting. In the high school groups, twice as many boys as girls admitted having taken something that did not belong to them. Similarly, over 80 percent of the boys in the high school groups had been in fights as compared with less than a third of the girls. The same overrepresentation of boys is found in juvenile arrests.

But patterns of delinquency are not static; they change over time. During the 1950s and early 1960s, the status symbol of youth was the automobile. Proportionately more delinquencies

Table 1: Reported Male Delinquency Behavior in Three Samples

Type of Offense	Percent Admitting Commission of Offense			Percent Admitting Commission of Offense More than Once or Twice		
	M.W.	West	Tr.S.	M.W.	West	Tr.S.
Driven a car without a driver's license or permit	81.1	75.3	91.1	61.2	49.0	73.4
Skipped school	54.4	53.0	95.3	24.4	23.8	85.9
Had fistfight with one person	86.7	80.7	95.3	32.6	31.9	75.0
"Run away" from home	12.9	13.0	68.1	2.8	2.4	37.7
School probation or expulsion	15.3	11.3	67.8	2.1	2.9	31.3
Defied parents' authority	22.2	33.1	52.4	1.4	6.3	23.6
Driven too fast or recklessly	49.7	46.0	76.3	22.7	19.1	51.6
Taken little things (worth less than $2) that did not belong to you	62.7	60.6	91.8	18.5	12.9	65.1
Taken things of medium value ($2–$50)	17.1	15.8	91.0	3.8	3.8	61.4
Taken things of large value ($50)	3.5	5.0	90.8	1.1	2.1	47.7
Used force (strong-arm methods) to get money from another person	6.3	—	67.7	2.4	—	35.5
Taken part in "gang fights"	24.3	22.5	67.4	6.7	5.2	47.4
Taken a car for a ride without the owner's knowledge	11.2	14.8	75.2	4.5	4.0	53.4
Bought or drank beer, wine, or liquor (include drinking at home)	67.7	57.2	89.7	35.8	29.5	79.4
Bought or drank beer, wine, or liquor (outside your home)	43.0	—	87.0	21.1	—	75.0
Drank beer, wine, or liquor in your own home	57.0	—	62.8	24.1	—	31.9
Deliberate property damage	60.7	44.8	84.3	17.5	8.2	49.7
Used or sold narcotic drugs	1.4	2.2	23.1	0.7	1.6	12.6
Had sex relations with another person of the same sex (not masturbation)	12.0	8.8	10.9	3.9	2.9	3.1
Had sex relations with a person of the opposite sex	38.8	40.4	87.5	20.3	19.9	73.4
Gone hunting or fishing without a license (or violated other game laws)	74.0	62.7	66.7	39.6	23.5	44.8
Taken things you didn't want	15.7	22.5	56.8	1.4	3.1	26.8
"Beat up" on kids who hadn't done anything to you	15.7	13.9	48.7	3.1	2.8	26.2
Hurt someone to see them squirm	22.7	15.8	33.4	2.8	3.2	17.5

Source: James F. Short and F. Ivan Nye, "Extent of Unrecorded Juvenile Delinquency: Tentative Conclusions," *Journal of Criminal Law,*
Criminology, and Police Science 49, no. 4 (1958). Copyright © 1958 b. Northwestern School of Law

Table 2: Reported Female Delinquent Behavior in Three Samples

Type of Offense	Percent Admitting Commission of Offense			Percent Admitting Commission of Offense More than Once or Twice		
	M.W.	West	Tr.S.	M.W.	West	Tr.S.
Driven a car without a driver's license or permit	60.1	58.2	68.3	33.6	29.9	54.4
Skipped school	40.3	41.0	94.0	10.1	12.2	66.3
Had fistfight with one person	32.7	28.2	72.3	7.4	5.7	44.6
"Run away" from home	9.8	11.3	85.5	1.0	1.0	51.8
School probation or expulsion	2.7	3.7	63.4	0.3	0.2	29.3
Defied parents' authority	33.0	30.6	68.3	3.7	5.0	39.0
Driven too fast or recklessly	20.9	16.3	47.5	5.7	5.4	35.0
Taken little things (worth less than $2) that did not belong to you	36.0	30.0	77.8	5.7	3.5	48.1
Taken things of medium value ($2–$50)	3.4	3.9	58.0	1.0	0.6	29.6
Taken things of large value ($50)	2.0	1.3	30.4	1.7	0.9	10.1
Used force (strong-arm methods) to get money from another person	1.3	—	36.7	0.3	—	21.5
Taken part in "gang fights"	9.7	6.5	59.0	1.7	1.1	27.7
Taken a car for a ride without the owner's knowledge	5.4	4.5	36.6	1.0	0.6	20.7
Bought or drank beer, wine, or liquor (include drinking at home)	62.7	44.5	90.2	23.1	17.6	80.5
Bought or drank beer, wine, or liquor (outside your home)	28.7	—	83.9	10.8	—	75.3
Drank beer, wine, or liquor in your own home	54.2	—	71.1	16.4	—	42.2
Deliberate property damage	21.7	13.6	65.4	5.7	1.6	32.1
Used or sold narcotic drugs	1.3	0.5	36.9	0.3	0.3	23.8
Had sex relations with another person of the same sex (not masturbation)	5.4	3.6	25.0	1.7	0.5	12.5
Had sex relations with a person of the opposite sex	12.5	14.1	95.1	4.1	4.8	81.5
Gone hunting or fishing without a license (or violated other game laws)	20.6	20.3	27.5	5.7	3.9	21.3
Taken things you didn't want	6.4	3.6	43.0	0.7	0.6	13.9
"Beat up" on kids who hadn't done anything to you	5.7	3.1	37.8	1.0	0.9	18.3
Hurt someone to see them squirm	10.4	9.3	35.4	1.0	1.1	20.7

Source: James F. Short and F. Ivan Nye, "Extent of Unrecorded Juvenile Delinquency: Tentative Conclusions," *Journal of Criminal Law, Criminology, and Police Science,* 49, no. 4 (1958). Copyright © 1959 by Northwestern School of Law.

involving automobiles, especially drag racing, existed then than in a later period, when drug use became more popular. The Short and Nye data were collected sometime before 1958, when their findings were published, and consequently do not reflect the rise of the "drug culture." Less than 3 percent of all the boys and girls in the two high schools had ever sold or used a narcotic drug of any type. In a more recent study of two Midwestern high schools (Sanders, 1970) it was found that almost 20 percent had used marijuana at least once (table 3).

Table 3:   Marijuana Use in Two Midwestern High Schools, 1970

Amount of Use	N	Percent
Never	375	80.6
Experimented	51	10.9
Every now and then	19	4.0
Weekends and parties	8	1.7
Smoke whenever possible	12	2.5

The same study found that the use of other drugs was also higher in this group than in the group Short and Nye studied in the late fifties.

Table 4:   Use of Other Drugs in Two Midwestern High Schools, 1970

Type of Drug	N	Percent
LSD	25	5.4
Amphetamines	35	7.5
Mescaline and peyote	10	2.1
Opium and cocaine	7	1.5
Heroin	9	2.0

Thus, by examining data collected over a period of time, we are able to see the changes in patterns of delinquency. Not only the amount of delinquency but the forms of delinquency vary. Just as youthful fashions in clothing, hair styles, and other habits and attitudes are different today than they were in the 1950s and 1960s, so styles of delinquency have changed. These changes clashed with the traditional legal and cultural patterns in ways that redefined the patterns of delinquency. The massive shift to drug use in the mid-1960s was in no way a "group psychosis" or "mass insanity" but instead was merely (or significantly) a change in fads. Perhaps few Californians recall the widespread distaste for surfers with their sun-bleached hair, bare feet, and single-minded devotion to riding waves. Yet many southern Californians in the early 1960s were terribly upset about the "surf bums," and the police, business people, and everyone else of a traditional bent saw them as dangerous. However, if the surfers were disconcerting, they were not so shocking as the later "hippies" who smoked dope, grew long hair, and wore wild outfits; in retrospect the surfers probably seem tame, if not healthily athletic. But like all sudden changes with tradition, new fads and styles bring on a panic reaction.

In summarizing this section, the answer to the question "How much delinquency?" is not a simple one. As we saw, we cannot rely on police and court records, for they reflect only crimes reported and youths arrested. Only about 5 percent of the juvenile population appears in court in any given year (Gibbons, 1970:3), but we find that in examining self-reported delinquency, almost all youths engage in delinquent acts for which they could be brought to juvenile court. Further, the victimization surveys show that far more crime is committed than is reported, but we can only guess, on the basis of arrests, at the proportion committed by juveniles. We know that juveniles in general are likely to commit at least some delinquent acts, and the nature of the acts as well as the volume changes over time; however, we still cannot say exactly how much delinquency exists. What we can say, though, is that almost everyone commits a delinquent act during the time of being a juvenile and that only a minute proportion are brought before the courts. Therefore, there is a massive amount of activity characterized as delinquent, of which the police and court records reflect very little.

DELINQUENCY AS A PHASE OF GROWING UP

Having examined the extent of juvenile delinquency, we are left with the sobering fact that virtually everyone commits some type of delinquent act during the ages defined by the law as juvenile. If we subtract the juvenile-status offenses from the total amount of delinquency, we would have a great deal less juvenile crime and certainly fewer youths defined as delinquents, but Short and Nye (1958), who did perform this subtraction, still found that two-thirds of the high school boys and one-third of the girls in their study had stolen. Most boys commit battery in the form of a fistfight, and it is hard to imagine a youth who has never been guilty of trespassing. During the time that one is a juvenile, delinquency, including acts that would be against the law if committed by an adult, is very likely.

We might well ask, then, Is delinquency, like acne, simply a phase of growing up, something we all grow into and out of? In certain respects it is, for the law defines certain ages as juvenile, and age is something we all flow through without any choice in the matter. If a girl leaves home in California the day before her eighteenth birthday, she can be arrested for running away, but the next day she will have grown out of her delinquent status. Similarly, if a boy steals a car the day before his "adult birthday," he will go to juvenile court, but if he does the same thing the next day, he will be taken before the adult criminal court. In this sense, then, delinquency is a phase of growing up.

Adolescence might also be characterized as a "waiting age" during which a person waits to become an adult. A 16-year-old must attend school in order to prepare himself or herself for college or a vocation. Juveniles typically cannot get married or work full time but must wait until they are "ready," socially and legally, to accept the responsibilities of marriage and to exercise certain minimum survival skills. The more ambitious, who seek high social status and highly complex abilities, have a longer wait until they can break free and end their waiting stage.

What is there to do during this waiting stage? Some occupy themselves with school, social groups, athletics, and other activities that are legal. For others, there are all kinds of not so legal activities. Many young people love to travel, as do adults, but until a youth is of legal age, traveling can be interpreted as being "out of control." Others enjoy going to parties and drinking as their parents may, but if youths are caught drinking at a party they are sent to juvenile court. Juveniles, again like adults, enjoy being in love and making love. Young girls who do so are brought to court and generally humiliated and judged as being in danger of leading an "immoral life." If a girl's lover is over eighteen and she is under that age, he may be charged with statutory rape. So, while waiting to be an adult, as defined by law, juveniles are forbidden to practice a great many of the activities that they are free to practice on their eighteenth birthday. They are not given the legal opportunity to prepare for certain aspects of adult life. Ironically, while our educational system and other socialization institutions put a great deal of effort into preparing youths for adulthood, juveniles are denied the opportunity to prepare for, much less practice, some of the most important aspects of adult life.

In this sense, juvenile delinquents are no more than young people preparing for adulthood. Juvenility is a stage in growing up during which the law defines preparatory activities as delinquent. Perhaps it would be unfair to ask why the law doesn't deem it delinquent for juveniles to prepare for other aspects of adult life. Is it any less important to know how to handle oneself when drinking than it is to know various career skills? Wouldn't it be better to instruct youths in how to make love and how to avoid unwanted pregnancies than to brand a young girl delinquent for having sexual intercourse? It is one thing to protect the young from the pitfalls of life in the hope of preserving them until they can survive on their own; but they cannot be prepared if we punish them for attempting to learn. We might ask ourselves whether the juvenile-status laws really protect the young or are simply artifacts that lawmakers preserve to foster the myth that a now defunct moral code still exists.

Is the high rate of juvenile larceny due to the fact that child labor laws and mandatory school attendance prevent young people from making enough money to buy the things they want? Or is it due to some other cause, such as the thrill of getting away with breaking the law? What about youthful assaults? Why do gangs constantly engage in wars? Are they doing anything more or less than what the government does when it wages war? What about dope? Is smoking marijuana an imitation of getting high on liquor? Is juvenile amphetamine and barbiturate use a reflection of taking aspirin or some other legal drug that is common in our society? How do we come to terms with the myriad activities defined as delinquent and the massive number of juveniles who engage in these activities?

In chapter 2 we will try to come up with answers to a number of these questions. We will address the question of why some juveniles commit delinquent acts while others do not, first considering several theories of delinquency. Not all of them are satisfactory, and some account for only some delinquencies. In our examination, therefore, we will not only answer the questions but also question the answers.

CONCLUSION

Juvenile delinquency is not a simple matter of kids breaking the law but a highly complex phenomenon. To understand it, we must deal not only with statutes that officially spell out what can legally be considered delinquent behavior but also with the social context of the behavior.

When we attempt to identify patterns of delinquency, we find many kinds of frequencies and distributions depending on the data we examine. If we look at the court records, we find that most delinquents are poor and belong to minority groups; if we look at the self-report surveys, it appears that almost every adolescent, regardless of class, has been involved in some kind of delinquency. Therefore we ask, Is delinquency a phase in growing up? In the following chapters we hope to unravel some of these problems and to raise still more, in the hope of at least clearing away simpleminded misconceptions.

2 Why Are There Delinquents?

Theories of Juvenile Delinquency

DEVIANCE, CRIME, AND DELINQUENCY

To understand why some juveniles engage in delinquency and others do not, we will need to examine not only theories of delinquency but also theories of deviance and crime. We have already defined "delinquency," but in order to appreciate fully why some young people break the law we will also have to understand what is meant by "deviance" and "crime" and how these concepts are related to delinquency.

When lay people think of deviance and deviants, they generally conjure up images of weirdos and sexual perverts. But sociologists use these terms simply to refer to some form of rule violation and those who have been labeled rule violators (Becker, 1963). This conception of deviance, not to be confused with crime or delinquency, stresses social processes, for it assumes that others must identify behavior as violating a rule and must label an actor as a rule breaker.

Rule violation occurs in the context of specific groups, not necessarily in terms of society as a whole. What is deviance in one group may be perfectly normal in another group. For example, in the context of membership in the Ku Klux Klan, it would be deviant *not* to hold racist attitudes. In contrast, it would be a violation of expectations for members of a civil rights group to voice or display racist attitudes. When we talk about deviance, we must specify the rule violation in terms of group orientation.

Secondly, deviance must be defined in the context of specified activities. An act that might possibly be assessed as a rule violation is not deviant unless others define it so. For example, suppose a man is observed breaking into a car that is known not to belong to him. If others approach him and charge him with engaging in a deviant act, the man may offer an account (cf. Scott and Lyman, 1968), perhaps explaining that he was simply trying to unlock the car for a friend, who had locked herself out. Even though the act was initially assessed as deviant, the account that he was helping someone in need would probably allay suspicions of deviance. Furthermore, it is only in certain contexts that such an act would be noticed at all. In a high-crime area, breaking into a car would probably not be seen as deviant, except possibly by outsiders such as the police, even if it were known to be in violation of the law.

A crime, on the other hand, is the violation of a criminal statute. As noted above, criminal behavior is not deviance if those assessing the situation do not regard lawbreaking as a rule violation. This may seem to be a contradiction, because laws are a form of rules; however, if people are judged in the context of their group, and their group does not share the legal view of rules and rule violation, in this context no rule has been broken. On the other hand, if the police assess the act, they must do so in terms of the criminal law and not necessarily in terms of a breach of expectations. Thus, even though the police may consider a breach of certain laws as normal in certain areas and therefore nondeviant for the area's residents, they may nonetheless arrest the actor for violating the law.

Finally, as we noted in chapter 1, "delinquent" is a title reserved for those below a certain age. Some delinquencies are not crimes if committed by adults and therefore are not crimes. And some delinquencies are normal behavior for juveniles and therefore are not considered deviant by other juveniles. Under-age drinking, for example, is a delinquency that is not judged to be deviant. In a study of high school students, it was found that three-quarters of the students had used alcohol without their parents' knowledge (Sanders, 1970). Similarly, although premarital sex among minors is seen as deviant by some segments of the youth population, it is not uncommon and is generally not considered a violation of youthful norms even though it is against juvenile statutes. Violating curfew, ditching school, and misrepresenting one's age are other delinquencies that are nondeviant in the context of most juvenile subcultures.

We have noted that while all criminal acts are also violations of juvenile statutes, not all crime is deviance, for in some social circles criminal behavior is approved and expected. Conversely, not all deviance is criminal or delinquent. In certain contexts it may be deviant to obey the criminal and delinquent laws. Finally, not all delinquencies are criminal or deviant, for, on the one hand, some delinquent acts are not against the law if committed by adults and, on the other hand, delinquency, like crime, is considered appropriate in certain groups.

In considering theories of delinquency, crime, and deviance, we need to know why conformity to the norms of certain groups leads to delinquent (or nondelinquent) behavior. Moreover, since all crimes are delinquencies, to understand delinquency we need to understand crime. For example, if conformity to group norms means committing delinquent acts, we need to know what leads to conformity and thus to delinquent behavior. Delinquent gangs expect delinquent behavior from members, but if we understand theories of deviance we can explain why certain delinquencies do not take place, since nonconformity, in this case, is *not* committing delinquent acts. That is, if we understand why some segments of society take on norms in opposition to those of the dominant society, we not only will understand "deviant subcultures," in which lawbreaking is normal, but will come to appreciate the context of crime and delinquency in a setting where it is deemed normal.

There are various patterns in delinquency—boys are more likely to be involved than girls; only certain types of delinquencies are popular; a given delinquent activity may be prevalent at one time but not at another time. We need to understand these general repetitive forms of juvenile delinquency; and at the same time, we need a theory to account for *individual* involvement in delinquency, or the social-psychological processes of becoming a delinquent, so as to explain why certain forms of delinquency exist and why some people become involved in some forms of delinquent activity. For example, one form of delinquent behavior is gang activity. Our theory should account not only for the delinquency of the gang but also for the participation of the individual.

Another consideration is criminalization, the process whereby someone comes to be seen by himself and others as a criminal (Hartjen, 1974:8). In the context of juvenile delinquency, we will refer not only to acts assessed as criminal but to other assessments reserved for juveniles. Perhaps we should say the "delinquentization" process, but since that is somewhat awkward, we will use the term "criminalization" to include all acts that can be characterized as delinquent.

Thus, we will evaluate various theories in an attempt to determine whether each theory accounts satisfactorily for (1) patterns of delinquency, (2) the social-psychological processes of becoming one who commits delinquent acts, and (3) the sociolegal processes of making a delinquent.

THE SOCIAL DEPRIVATION THEORY

Early attempts to explain delinquency centered on biological and psychological factors, seeking to explain crime and delinquency in terms of some deficiency or imbalance within the individual who engaged in the behavior. Noting that criminal and delinquent behavior patterns were found under certain conditions and in certain areas more frequently than in others, sociologists began to look at the social milieu in which the acts took place. Could it be that the problem lay not with the individual but in the social conditions under which the individual lived? Would a biologically and psychologically sound person placed in the same social conditions turn out to be a delinquent? One of the first theories that looked to problems in social conditions as the source of delinquency comes under the umbrella term "structural frustration."

A factor that seemed promising in explaining delinquency was the home of the delinquent. In homes where one or both parents were absent because of death, divorce, or desertion, the child was seen to be deprived relative to those who had the advantages of a complete, stable family life. The amount of delinquency "caused" by broken homes was not specified, but since a number of studies showed that delinquents were likely to come from broken homes (Johnson, 1974:107), it was believed that broken homes must have something to do with delinquency. Glueck and Glueck (1950) found that 60.4 percent of the delinquents and 34.2 percent of the nondelinquents they studied came from broken homes. The Gluecks' study was based on matched pairs of delinquents and nondelinquents: the sample of delinquents was selected on the basis of juvenile records. Since the courts consider a juvenile's home life in making decisions about the disposition of delinquents (Cicourel, 1968), those who come from broken homes are more likely to be made wards of the court. Therefore, it is possible that the Gluecks' study was based on a self-fulfilling prophesy. The courts believe that juveniles from broken homes are more likely to be delinquents; therefore, they are more likely to make them wards of the court. Hence, in a sample based on those judged delinquent by the courts, one is likely to find an overrepresentation of juveniles from broken homes, because of court practices.

In an examination of the data on delinquents from broken homes, Toby (1957) found that the broken home had a greater impact on younger (preteen) juveniles than on older ones. Poorly integrated families did not provide the control over the younger juveniles that well-integrated families did, but neither type of family had much control over older, more mobile youths. According to Toby, young juveniles who lacked the control and direction that can be offered by a complete family were more likely to drift into delinquent activity. In summarizing numerous studies of family cohesion and delinquency, Rodman and Grams (1967) point out that family control is the most significant factor in preventing delinquency. If the parents lack control of their children because they pay little attention to the children or because the children regard them as unfair, the socialization of the children is incomplete, and instead of taking on the general social values, they come to take on delinquent values.

Writers have also attributed delinquency to poor home life defined on the basis of the disciplinary techniques used. The Gluecks (1950) found that families that used firm but kind techniques in disciplining their children produced the fewest delinquents, while families using either lax and erratic measures or overstrict techniques were more likely to produce delinquency. Parents who provided affection for their children had the fewest delinquent offspring, while the children of parents who were indifferent or only sporadically affectionate were likely to develop a poor image of authority figures, insecurity, and overall frustration with family values—conditions that tend to foster delinquent values and activities.

While the "broken home" explanations of juvenile delinquency clearly left a great deal to be desired and were never developed into a full-scale theory, they did pave the way for an examination of the social conditions of delinquency. The fact that the studies on home life and delinquency found relationships between external social conditions and the conduct of juveniles showed that delinquency did not stem merely from biological or psychological factors and prompted researchers to look still more closely at the social milieu of the delinquent.

A more ambitious and theoretically sophisticated explanation of crime and delinquency was developed by Robert Merton (1957), who pointed out how the structure of social values leads to a high rate of property crimes in the working class. According to Merton, just about everyone wants the "good things in life," as identified by the society. The mass media, especially television, present us with a cornucopia of material things which we are told we must have. Success and "happiness" are often measured in terms of whether or not we have these material things, which Merton calls "culturally prescribed goals."

At the same time that society's members are directed toward these goals, they are given a set of rules, or "socially sanctioned means," for the achievement of these goals. For example, we are told that it is good to become rich, and we are also told that only certain avenues should be taken to gain wealth. It is socially correct to get a job and save money to buy material things, but it is wrong to rob a bank even though the money from the bank robbery will be used to realize the culturally prescribed goals.

The problem is that the social structure blocks certain members from attaining these goals in acceptable ways. Certain occupations provide only enough income for the essentials, leaving little or no surplus for the "good things in life." Groups whose occupational status and overall situation prevent them from attaining the necessary resources are "blocked" from realizing these goals. The American social structure has room for only a limited number of people to reach a position where they can begin to attain the culturally prescribed goals. Even though the American ideology and mythology stress equal opportunity to "make it," there are only just so many niches in the social structure that allow goal attainment. For example, in a large corporation, there are so many executive positions, so many staff positions, and so many assembly line positions. Even if everyone in the corporation is of equal ability and works equally hard, there are only a few who will fill the executive positions.

Furthermore, equal opportunity is a myth. Those from higher socioeconomic backgrounds typically have far more opportunity to go to college and learn the necessary skills for higher-paying jobs. Many lower- and working-class members cannot afford to send their children to college, and even if they can, the children are less likely to have been brought up with the idea that college is important. Moreover, a person from a wealthy family, whether or not he goes to college, is more likely to get a good job since his parents are in a position to know the "right" people to help him. Many of the sons and daughters of the wealthy are assured of positions in the family business no matter what their educational background is.

Merton outlines a number of possible responses to this state of affairs. A person can try to stay within the socially provided boundaries in attempting to realize the culturally prescribed goals, by working, saving, and so on. This line of adaptation, called *conformity*, represents the ideal adaptation in a stable society.

Secondly, an individual can accept the culturally prescribed goals but reject the institutionalized means of achieving them. This adaptation is typical of societies where there is an overemphasis on success goals and structural barriers to reaching the goals for certain segments. Merton refers to this mode of adaptation as *innovation*, a term that generally denotes positive action but here refers to not following the rules for goal attainment. This mode of adaptation is especially relevant to a study of delinquency, for essentially it refers to breaking the law. For example, a juvenile may steal (rejection of institutionalized means) a car (cultural goal) or commit some other property crime to get money.

A third adaptation, *ritualism*, refers to one who accepts the institutionalized means while rejecting the cultural goals. Some individuals scale down their expectations below the cultural standards while holding onto the socially correct means. In this way, they don't risk getting into trouble for breaking the rules, and at the same time they're not frustrated by failure to meet the high expectations of the cultural goals. Examples are the frightened bureaucrat who plays it safe but never rises in the bureaucracy. He holds tenaciously to what he has, rigorously conforming to the rules, but he has no expectations of advancement.

Retreatism, the fourth mode of adaptation, applies to individuals who reject both the culturally prescribed goals and the means. In a sense these individuals are aliens, for they do not feel themselves a part of the society in which they live. Skid row bums and chronic heroin users (junkies) examplify this mode of adaptation. They do not expect to attain cultural goals, nor do they conform to the institutionalized norms. Young dropouts who give up the values and norms of the Establishment are the juvenile counterparts of these bums and junkies and constitute a significant segment of the delinquent population.

In the final adaptation, *rebellion,* cultural goals and social norms are rejected and new ones are established in their stead. The difference between retreatism and rebellion is that in the latter the goals and norms are replaced while in the former they are merely rejected. The rebel substitutes new ideologies for the old and strives toward the new goals by new means. Among the young, the counterculture, hippie movement, and radical movement represent rebellion.

Conformity and ritualism are relatively unimportant for our analysis since they involve law-abiding behavior, but the other three adaptations are useful in examining juvenile delinquency, for each represents a form of activity that can be characterized as delinquent. Merton's main point is that the social structure gives rise to these different adaptations. Various deviant adaptations emerge because of the frustrations produced by the social structure. Thus, delinquency has a pattern and is not merely a set of random responses to frustration by individuals. People in certain parts of the social structure experience more frustration than others, and when we compare those who are deemed delinquent with those who are not, we find an overrepresentation of the underprivileged, disadvantaged, and poor. In other words, those who are most likely to experience frustration because of their position in the social structure are most likely to be judged delinquent. Self-reported crime surveys also show that while almost everyone commits some crime, crimes are more prevalent among the lower socioeconomic strata (Wheeler and Cottrell, 1966:12–13).

This theory explains why more crime is committed by the disadvantaged but does not account for the various types of delinquency or for the patterns of delinquent behavior; it explains "too much" delinquency. Given that structural frustration causes delinquency, why is it that only a relatively few members of the lower socioeconomic strata commit delinquent acts frequently? Why are boys ten times more likely to engage in delinquent acts than girls in the same social position?

Further, while Merton's theory of structural frustration does explain why some may adopt innovation (e.g., shoplifting) and others choose retreatism (e.g., drug use) as a mode of adaptation to frustration, it does not explain why some innovators choose shoplifting, for example, and others choose armed robbery, or why some retreaters prefer to use drugs and others alcohol. It does not show why drug use replaced alcohol use as the most popular form of retreatism for the young.

Richard Cloward (1959:312–31) provided a "repair" of sorts for structural-frustration theory by pointing out that for some youths illegitimate means as well as legitimate means may be blocked. As Cloward notes, a boy may be denied membership in a delinquent gang because the gang members don't think he is tough enough or that he has some other defect. Thus, the boy is denied access to the delinquent activity generated in the gang. Other illegitimate means are similarly limited. Those who are blocked from both legitimate and illegitimate means are considered to be "double failures," unable to make it either way.

Cloward's contribution to Merton's theory helps to explain why not all lower-class members and other structurally frustrated individuals turn to illegitimate means. "Double failures," he claims, are likely to take on a retreatist mode, rejecting *both* legitimate and illegitimate means *as well as* the culturally prescribed goals. Without access to any means of achievement, they tend to abandon goals and simply sink into the apathy of retreatism.

THE AVAILABILITY OF CRIME: THE DEVELOPMENT OF DELINQUENT SUBCULTURES

Cloward's insight that there is a delinquent opportunity structure in addition to a legitimate one led to his development, with Lloyd Ohlin, of a theory of delinquent gangs (Cloward and Ohlin, 1960). The Cloward-Ohlin theory puts its main emphasis on the structural conditions that lead to *lower-class* gang delinquency, but it also explains the development of other delinquent subcultures. A delinquent subculture, in this context, is a group that fosters beliefs legitimizing delinquent activities. When the experience of frustration is a collective one, as is the case with lower-class juveniles, the response to the socially created condition is likely to be collective as well; thus Cloward and Ohlin saw delinquent gangs arising out of blocked opportunities to cultural goals. The gangs are "forced" to take illegal measures to realize these goals because their opportunities to use legitimate means are limited or nonexistent. In lower-class enclaves, therefore, in addition to adult criminal rackets, juvenile reactions to blocked opportunities develop in the form of delinquent gangs.

As the gangs develop, they come to rationalize their activities. Instead of seeing their delinquency as "bad" or "wrong" they evolve their own beliefs and values, which do more than merely reduce guilt. Risk-taking in the form of delinquent behavior comes to be seen as a sign of manliness, and those who will not engage in delinquency are characterized as "sissies" and "punks." Since there are positive connotations associated with "manliness" and negative images with "sissies" and "punks," the illegal actions that show "manliness" have social rewards in addition to any crime payoff there might be. Likewise, those who abide strictly by the law are given negative status. Thus, in delinquent subcultures both the norms for achieving status and the goals are different from those of the larger social order. What is considered proper and decent in the larger society is turned on its head, and numerous illegal activities are seen as intrinsically good.

In addition to spelling out how criminal subcultures begin and flourish, Cloward and Ohlin explain how different types of delinquent subculture develop in lower-class areas. They identify three types—criminal, conflict, and retreatist—each based on the integration of supporters of conventional and deviant values as well as on the integration of people at different age levels. In all three subcultures legitimate channels to success goals are closed, but in the *criminal subculture* there is a good deal of opportunity through illegal routes. Racketeers, pimps, and others who have achieved success illegitimately are regarded by lower-class juveniles with admiration. To a youth who has little hope of becoming a banker, lawyer, or doctor, the racketeer is impressive, as the following statement makes clear:

> Every boy has some ideal he looks up to and admires. His ideal may be Babe Ruth, Jack Dempsey, or Al Capone. When I was twelve, we moved into a neighborhood with a lot of gangsters. They were all swell dressers and had big cars and carried "gats" [guns]. Us kids saw these swell guys and mingled with them in the cigar store on the corner. Jack Gurney was the one in the mob that I had a fancy to. He used to take my sis out and that way I saw him often. He was in the stick-up rackets before he was in the beer rackets, and he was a swell dresser and had lots of dough. . . . I liked to be near him and felt stuck up over the other guys because he came to my home to see my sis. [Shaw, 1933]

The boy's conception of and relationship with the racketeer illustrates how those who hold deviant values are used as role models by youth. The relationship is not unlike that between a nondelinquent youth and an adult in a legitimate pursuit to which the youth aspires.

The criminal subculture requires a stable community organization; wild juveniles engaging in gang conflict and other destructive activities are likely to be strongly disapproved of in such a subculture. Beginning in apprenticeship criminal positions, juveniles are required to discipline themselves and work their way up in the rackets in much the same way that a young businessman is required to work his way up in a company.

Where stable community organization does not exist, a *conflict subculture* is likely to emerge. If the local criminals are disorganized and cannot provide an orderly route to success through crime, there is little chance that the transition from young delinquent to adult criminal can be made. A disorganized, unstable community cannot provide the illegitimate opportunities that a criminal subculture can, and at the same time it cannot provide legitimate opportunities as can a stable middle- or upper-class community. Because of community disorganization, there is little direction, and the conflict subculture emerges.

In part, conflict subcultures have developed because of the government's attempts to clean up the slums. When old tenement houses are bulldozed and housing projects for low-income people are set up, a community is often scattered and thereby disorganized. The stability provided by the network of neighborhood relationships is distributed as different families are bureaucratically allocated new housing in the projects.

Without the opportunity structure provided in the criminal subculture, such virtues as self-discipline and conformity to community standards are no longer valuable. Frustration due to lack of opportunity is often vented in the form of violence. The status of having either legitimate or illegitimate "connections" is replaced by individualistic status based on personal bravery and a willingness to demonstrate "heart." Typically "heart" is realized through risk-taking behavior such as fighting or breaking the law. In this context, violent gangs emerge and juvenile gang warfare increases. As long as the opportunity structures remain closed the violence is unchecked.

Finally, the *retreatist subculture* is exemplified in the drug-using cultures of the lower class and, more recently, the middle class. As in Merton's definition of retreatist behavior, both cultural goals and legitimate means are abandoned. While retreatism initially appears to be an individualistic mode of adaptation, Cloward and Ohlin show that much retreatist behavior is a collective phenomenon. A good example is the middle-class drug subculture that emerged in the 1960s, in which a collective life style centered around the use of psychedelic drugs and rejection of the established values.

As we have pointed out, Cloward and Ohlin explained that many of those who joined retreatist subcultures of lower-class drug users were "double failures" who had not been able to attain success goals through either legitimate or illegitimate means. In the conflict subcultures, only some were able to attain a good "rep" (reputation) and the status that went with it. Those who failed, having also failed to achieve status through legitimate channels, withdrew and turned to drugs. In conflict subcultures, sometimes violent gangs would shift from fighting to drug use, thereby taking on a collective retreatist adaptation.

Those who entered the retreatist subculture entered an organized world of drug traffic and connections in addition to a world view supporting drug use.

While this seems to be an accurate description of lower-class drug-using groups, the process of "double failure" does not appear to describe the development of the middle-class drug subculture. Those who entered the "hippie" subculture were highly educated and had access to legitimate means to success goals. During the 1960s jobs for college graduates were plentiful and material comfort was virtually guaranteed, yet they were more likely to become "hippies" than the lower-class youth who were denied these advantages. Many who joined the youth subculture centered on drug use were disillusioned with material success goals and sought something more meaningful. They were not "failures" in the sense of not having access to means of achieving cultural goals.

Techniques of Neutralization

Sykes and Matza (1957) contend that delinquents do not create a separate set of values but instead develop "techniques of neutralization" by which they rationalize and justify actions that in some circumstances they would condemn. Essentially, delinquents believe in the laws they violate, but they neutralize potential feelings of guilt by means of various techniques that justify their lawbreaking.

Five techniques of neutralization are identified. Delinquents may adopt a *denial of responsibility,* blaming their activities on conditions over which they have no control, such as their social position, family, or associates. They may become adept at using psychological and sociological theories in denying their responsibility. For example, a juvenile may claim that he did not have a father and because of this turned to a delinquent gang for a masculine identity. Secondly, they may adopt *denial of injury,* claiming that their delinquent acts are not really harmful. Gang violence, for example, may be defined as a private quarrel not harmful to innocent bystanders in the same sense that boxers in a match do not strike out at the audience. A third technique of neutralization is *denial of the victim*. The victim is characterized as having deserved whatever happened to him, perhaps because he is a homosexual, an unfair teacher, or a storekeeper who engages in shady business practices. Delinquents may also *condemn the condemners*, shifting the focus of their wrongdoing to those who condemn them. Thus they charge that the police accept bribes, teachers engage in favoritism, and others are pious hypocrites. This technique changes the subject and the impact of accusation, functioning to relieve the assault on the juvenile's self-image. Finally, delinquents may *appeal to higher loyalties*, claiming that they are sacrificing the demands of the larger society to higher loyalties to friends and neighborhood solidarity. They come to characterize themselves as caught between the loyalty they owe the legal order and the more immediate allegiance they owe to those close to them.

The techniques of neutralization attest to the delinquents' acceptance of general social values and do not stand as a set of subcultural values. They develop as a means of coping with the guilt generated by violation of the internalized norms and values of the larger society. However, the collective acceptance of these techniques as justification for delinquency does suggest the development of a delinquent enclave in society. Sykes and Matza point out that these techniques do not always succeed in relieving delinquents of guilt, for they may not be sufficiently isolated from conforming society to accept such techniques as valid. Those who are isolated from the values of larger society may not need to employ any techniques of neutralization at all. What is important about the Sykes-Matza thesis is that it explains how the mechanisms of social control may lose their effectiveness in compelling compliance with the social norms. The extent to which such techniques are employed with social support points to some type of delinquent cohort and collective world view. At the same time, the absence of techniques of neutralization among delinquents suggests the existence of a delinquent subculture, for it is the internalization of conventional social norms and values that makes such techniques necessary.

Delinquency as Nonutilitarian Behavior

Another theory that attempts to explain the emergence of delinquent subcultures was put forth by Albert Cohen (1955). Like Cloward and Ohlin, Cohen pointed out that lower-class juveniles were denied opportunities to achieve middle-class goals and came to see their failures in terms of various social barriers. However, whereas Cloward and Ohlin emphasized utilitarian goal-seeking through illegitimate means, Cohen's main focus was on nonutilitarian behavior by lower-class juveniles.

Cohen explained that working-class juveniles were aware of the legitimate success paths in American society; however, they were equally aware of their limited chances of obtaining the goals implied in middle-class values. Instead of taking illegitimate means to achieve success goals, they turned the middle-class values and norms upside down. Such violent acts as unprovoked beatings and school vandalism achieved no ends in terms of middle-class success goals, but they did give the delinquents status. Status deprivation was the main problem working-class boys had to cope with, since they were denied the opportunity to achieve status in the conventional system. In the same way that illegal activities allowed boys in the conflict subculture described by Cloward and Ohlin to achieve a "rep," so nonutilitarian acts gave working-class youth a way of "being someone," of achieving *some* status even though it was not recognized as such by the larger society.

What is important about Cohen's theory is that it accounts for delinquent activities that appear to have no purpose. By providing something other than a middle-class measuring rod, Cohen was able to show that seemingly "senseless" acts of destruction and violence do have a purpose in terms of the subcultural values available in the lower and working class. Instead of being nonutilitarian, these "hell-raising" activities serve to achieve status for the juveniles who engage in them.

Like the Cloward-Ohlin theory of the retreatist subculture, Cohen's theory is based on lower- and working-class delinquency and does not adequately account for middle-class delinquency. The conditions described by Cloward and Ohlin as well as the social situation and reaction explained by Cohen fit only disadvantaged youths and do not explain the drug-using subculture consisting largely of middle-class youth.

In order to deal with the growing delinquency among middle-class youths, Cohen (1967) formulated a theory of middle-class juvenile subcultures that promote delinquent values and activities. As in his explanation of lower-class subcultures, he looked to the social structure and the structure of opportunities for his explanation. After World War II the opportunity structure for middle-class youths expanded as never before. In the prewar years, even middle-class youths had to work hard and defer gratification in order to obtain success goals, but in the postwar period youths from middle-class backgrounds could successfully pursue success goals without deferring gratification. As opportunities for success increased, there was no need to wait until one had attained a secure position to begin enjoying the fruits of the American dream. Juveniles in growing numbers had access to automobiles or even had cars of their own. Thus they were no longer tied to the home or under the supervision of their parents. Like their parents, young people were beginning to find new adventures and were exploring innovations in having fun. Premarital sex became increasingly common, and the introduction of birth-control pills banished or at least diminished the fear of unwanted pregnancies. All the while, there was little concern over "making it" in American society, for the opportunities appeared to be unlimited.

At the core of the youth culture was the hedonistic pursuit of fun, excitement, and enjoyment with peers. With the new affluence to provide the resources for this pursuit and with parents' desire to display this affluence by giving their children the status symbols previously reserved for independent adults, there was a breakdown in the traditional insulators against delinquency. Additionally, as the economy entered a phase dependent on huge consumption, the mass media encouraged the hedonistic values of the youth culture, not only for youths but for their parents as well. The Protestant ethic of compulsive hard work, which had dominated America in an earlier day, came to be rivaled if not replaced by the "have fun–stay young" ethic of Madison Avenue. Parents who did not allow their children or themselves the pleasures of an affluent society were characterized as old-fashioned and "square"; thus the breakdown of the traditional barriers against nonproductive free-time activity was also effected among parents. The urge to direct their children toward single-minded productive activity lessened as parents were encouraged to loosen up and enjoy themselves more as well.

The delinquency generated by this hedonistic pursuit of happiness did not involve an intentional reversal of values, as did the lower-class delinquency described by Cohen. Instead, by imitating and exaggerating adult values as depicted in the mass media, youth transformed adult resources into toys, and their playful handling of adult status symbols was seen as delinquent (England, 1967). For example, automobiles were used not only for functional transportation but also for the thrills of racing and speeding. Furthermore, juveniles were subjected to,legal sanctions for indulging in such pastimes as drinking and sex, which were not illegal for those holding adult age status. Thus, unlike lower-class youths, who often believed in the laws they broke, (Sykes and Matza, 1957), middle-class youths were more likely to see their violations of the law as a mere imitation of their parents' behavior; in their view, their actions were not bad, the laws were unjust.

The development of subcultural theories has several important implications for understanding delinquency. First, it set the stage for further theories about delinquency. Later in this chapter we will discuss theories of conflict and of differential association, both of which interact with subcultural theories in explaining delinquency. Secondly, subcultural theories pointed out the normal social processes involved in delinquent activities. Some subcultures were in no way delinquent or criminal, and participation in these subcultures led to law-abiding behavior. To speak of subcultures is simply a way of talking about values and norms, and deviant subcultures constitute only one type of subculture (Arnold, 1970). By examining normal social phenomena we can better appreciate and understand delinquency.

THE GENERATION GAP: VALUE CONFLICT

As subcultures develop, the likelihood increases that they will evolve norms that diverge from and conflict with conventional values. The extent to which there are different values among cohorts, in turn, points to the development of distinct subcultures. For example, as young people come to see themselves as a unique group with its own norms and values or even an entire life style dissimilar from their parents', a youth culture forms. Slogans such as "Don't trust anyone over thirty" suggest a distinct separation between young and old and also show that some conflict exists between the age cohorts.

According to Simmel, some conflict is an attempt to achieve an end, but other disputes are merely expressions of frustrations with no other end than to vent aggression (Coser, 1956: 171–79). The first type of conflict is termed *realistic* in that the conflicting parties are clashing with a goal in mind. For example, if two rival gangs fight over the right to a piece of territory, we can call the conflict realistic in that it is directed toward a specific result—namely, control of the territory. In contrast, when two parties are in conflict simply because one of the groups is using the other to release its frustration the conflict is *unrealistic*. Hitler's use of the Jews as a scapegoat for Germany's problems is an example of unrealistic conflict, for there the aggression had no true object.

In examining the conflict between the youth culture, especially those involved in the life style that emerged around drug use, and the larger society, do we find it to be realistic or unrealistic? The laws contain negative sanctions for marijuana use, and anyone who uses marijuana therefore comes into conflict with the larger society in the form of the juvenile and criminal justice systems. On the one hand we can say that the conflict is realistic in that one side is attempting to maintain the drug laws and the other side is attempting to flout them. On the other hand, the conflict is unrealistic in that goals for maintaining the laws are unclear. Similarly, when young men began to wear long hair, they found themselves in conflict with the bulk of the adult population, and there appeared to be no reason for the dispute. The same was true with the music of the young. Initial reactions to rock 'n' roll were extreme; many adults claimed that it signaled the downfall of Western civilization. The styles and fads of the young frequently evoke conflict between young and old.

Criticism and conflict were not in a single direction, however. During the civil rights movement of the fifties and throughout America's involvement in Vietnam, adult values and life styles came under violent attack by the young (Yankelovich, 1974: 3–5). The American dream of material affluence and the values of the Establishment were rejected by the emerging philosophy of youth. Adults were characterized as hypocritical and shallow, voicing the values of a Judeo-Christian heritage while engaging in racial, social, and economic discrimination, and compulsively pursuing material affluence at the cost of humanistic values. Thus, not only did adults attack the new values developing among the young, the young assaulted the old values of their parents.

In their desire to express the new freedom, the young often came into conflict with the delinquency laws. As we pointed out, the marijuana laws were violated with increasing frequency, and the life style of youth came into conflict with other laws as well, especially those reserved for the young. For example, numerous youths were leaving home without their parents' permission or knowledge, thereby breaking the laws pertaining to parental control over children. Juveniles who left home to join the youth culture in such rallying points as Haight-Ashbury in San Francisco, the Sunset Strip in Los Angeles, the East Village in New York City, and Oldtown in Chicago were subject to control by the juvenile court. Likewise, since the young no longer saw sex as something to be postponed until marriage, a number of female juveniles came under the jurisdiction of the juvenile courts.

It would seem initially that this reaction by the adult institutions might hinder the development of the youth culture; however, many theorists believe that conflict creates solidarity among the emerging outgroup—in this case youth. According to Karl Marx (1910), conflict creates cohesion within each warring faction. As the conflict increases, members of each group become increasingly aware of their common situation in relation to their adversary. That is, they come to identify with one side or the other rather than adopt an individualistic orientation. Since the battle lines were drawn between the young and the old, age status put people in one camp or the other. Furthermore, individual problems come to be interpreted in terms of group troubles, or, to paraphrase Marx and Engels (1888), each collective moves from being a *class in itself* to a *class for itself.* A class in itself is a group of people who share a similar fate in life but are unaware of their common interest. They have no class consciousness. However, as members of the classes come to see their common interest, they come to act in terms of their unique class status. They see the problems of those in like circumstances as their own problems, and the source of their problems are identified in terms of their adversary's actions. In the case of youth, when they attempted to exercise their new values, they were subjected to the sanctions of the adult establishment, and this was seen as a threat to all youth. Thus, rather than perceiving individualistic violations of basically just laws, the youth culture interpreted the laws as a means of maintaining the status quo by keeping youth in line. Law violations were therefore regarded not as delinquency but as a consequence of adult repression of the values of the youth culture.

The development of the youth-adult conflict along the lines suggested by Marx was destined to some form of cooptation, however. As youths become older, they move socially and economically into the adult world and eventually come to be part of that world. Many of them bring the new life styles along with them, and some of the conflicts of values and norms are thus dissipated. At the same time, as they grow older the laws regulating juveniles no longer apply to them. If a young man wishes to travel, for example, he can do so after he reaches legal age without becoming a ward of the court. Youth, as a class, is something one "grows out of," and the conflict between the youth and adult cultures, unlike racial conflict, has the feature that one group inevitably joins the other after a certain period of time.

One of the signals of the death of a strong and active youth culture was the apparent end of the war in Vietnam in 1974. When American soldiers left Vietnam, the protest movement more or less fizzled out. The war had been a rallying point for young people, and when it ended, so too did much of the spirit of solidarity among the young. The war's end also coincided with an economic slump, and job opportunities declined for college graduates, and even more so for high school graduates. Students sunk into apathy and thereby left a void in youth leadership, which had been provided by college-age youths. Young people came to see one another as competitors in a depressed job market and lost the sense of identity that was generated during the antiwar movement.

Another event that lessened the conflict between young and old came from an unexpected quarter. A major aspect of the youth culture had been disillusionment with the government's willingness to respond to the needs of young people. They distrusted governmental institutions and saw little input in decision making. When the Watergate scandal broke and grew, more and more people came to share this view of government. However, instead of inciting new mass demonstrations by the young, it merely confirmed what they had believed all along. As the adult world came to the same conclusion, young and old joined in their distrust of government. Instead of increasing conflict, the Watergate affair came to reduce conflict between young and old.

A key point for understanding conflict explanations of juvenile delinquency is that differences in the treatment of cohorts lead to different conduct norms as well as different values and life styles (Sellin, 1938). The implication, of course, is that to the extent that there is social differentiation, there will be conflict.

Juveniles are differentiated from adults in numerous ways, and this differentiation leads to conflict. The process of social differentiation for juveniles has two sources: the restriction placed on juveniles by adults, and the life styles and interests developed by the youths themselves. Special juvenile laws designed to protect and control the young set them off from the adult world, and this discrimination puts juveniles in a position to develop their own independent interests and norms. Schools, especially junior high schools and high schools, serve as collection points where youth can develop a unique identity apart from the adult world. Ironically, schools are supposed to be places where youth is prepared for the adult world, but because educational institutions for the young keep them apart from the adult world, they function to socialize juveniles into the youth culture and therefore into conflict with adults.

In summary, the conflict perspective points to the differences in the norms, values, and life styles developed by different groups as the source of crime and delinquency. By recognizing the process of social differentiation in society, we can understand why some groups commit more crime than others as well as why some groups tend to commit certain types of crime. The differentiation between young and old in America leads to the development of separate and distinct norms and values for the young, and these come into conflict with adult expectations. By acting in terms of their unique norms and values, young people break juvenile laws.

WHOM YOU HANG AROUND WITH: DIFFERENTIAL ASSOCIATION

A common assumption by laymen and social scientists that hindered the development of theories of crime and delinquency was that anyone who had the notion to do so could commit a crime. In a way, assuming that anyone can commit a crime is like assuming that anyone who wants to can build a house, perform surgery, or do anything else requiring a good deal of knowledge. But the fact is that safecracking, for example, requires the actor to know what kind of explosive to use, how much, where to get it, and the penalties for cracking a safe with and without explosives. If the safe the burglar plans to rob contains valuable jewels, he must know how to go about selling the jewels, whom to contact, and how much to ask for. In fact, if you took the notion to rob a safe, you would probably have to spend almost as much time learning how to rob it properly as you would have to spend learning how to do something legal that was equally profitable.

Differential association theory assumes that crime, like any other behavior, is learned, and it is learned in social interaction (Sutherland and Cressey, 1974). The learning of criminal behavior, however, involves learning more than the techniques, for many crimes, such as shoplifting, require little substantive knowledge. More important is learning the attitudes that favor breaking the law. By associating with others whose attitudes favor law violation, individuals come to learn these attitudes. Thus, if most of an individual's associations are with people who habitually break the law and who express attitudes that justify their activities, he is more likely to become delinquent than is someone who associates with people who do not break the law and who disapprove of law violation.

Given this theory, why don't all police and prison guards engage in criminal and delinquent activity, since they associate so frequently with law violators? As Sutherland and Cressey point out, the nature of the association is as important as the fact of social contact. Whether a person will take on criminal or anticriminal behavior patterns depends on certain variables describing the association. Some associations are more *frequent* than others. If a person spends most of his time with delinquent gangs and very little with law-abiding juveniles, he is more likely to take on the attitudes of the delinquent gang members. The *duration* of the association is also important: the longer the asociation, the more likely one is to pick up the attitudes of the others. The third factor is the *priority* of association—how early in life the individual is exposed to criminal or noncriminal attitudes. The earlier his exposure to criminal behavior patterns, the more likely the person is to engage in criminal activities.

Finally, the *intensity* of a relationship determines whether the association is close or casual. If a juvenile has close ties with delinquents and casual ties with nondelinquents of the same duration, he is more likely to take on the attitudes of the delinquents.

It is important that differential association theory points to the availability of criminal (or delinquent) *behavior patterns* in a given social milieu. These behavior patterns exist independent of any single cohort that may engage in the activity. For example, a delinquent gang may exist for several generations (Miller, 1969); while the people who occupy the various positions in the gang change, the behavior pattern of the gang may persist. Through differential association, a given juvenile is more or less likely to come into contact with the pattern of delinquent gang activity. Depending on his peers, he will come to see the delinquent activity in the gang as a good or a bad thing. If a boy lives in a neighborhood where membership in delinquent gangs is taken for granted as an aspect of growing up, he is more likely to take on a positive orientation to gang activities and attitudes than if he grows up in an area where nondelinquent peer relationships are available.

Additionally, differential association theory points out that delinquency is very much a social as opposed to an antisocial activity. In an area where there is massive delinquent activity, a youth who shuns social relationships and acts as a loner is less likely to become delinquent than a more gregarious youth. If a boy wants to pursue his own interests alone, he is less likely to join a delinquent gang and engage in delinquent activity than is a peer-oriented youth.

To get a thorough idea of differential association theory, we should look at all of its propositions, set forth by Sutherland and Cressey (1974:75–76):

1. Criminal behavior is learned.
2. Criminal behavior is learned in interaction with other persons in a process of communication.
3. The principal part of the learning of criminal behavior occurs within intimate personal groups.

4. When criminal behavior is learned, the learning includes (a) techniques of committing the crime, which are sometimes very complicated, sometimes very simple; and (b) the specific direction of motives, drives, rationalizations, and attitudes.
5. The specific direction of motives and drives is learned from definitions of the legal codes as favorable or unfavorable.
6. A person becomes delinquent because of an excess of definitions favorable to violation of law over definitions unfavorable to violation of law.
7. Differential associations may vary in frequency, duration, priority, and intensity.
8. The process of learning criminal behavior by association with criminal and anticriminal patterns involves all the mechanisms that are involved in any other learning.
9. While criminal behavior is an expression of general needs and values, it is not explained by those general needs and values, since noncriminal behavior is an expression of the same needs and values.

It appears that most of the theory is accounted for in terms of learning and associations, and the various propositions elaborate the manner in which learning takes place. However, the last proposition appears to stand by itself, and further explanation of this very important postulate is necessary. To explain it let us consider an example. Let's say that some boys want to go fishing (a value) and require fishing poles and tackle. In order to obtain the necessary gear there are a number of tactics they can employ. They can ask their parents for the money to buy the fishing equipment, they can work and earn money to purchase it, or they can engage in some illegal activity to acquire it. Whatever activity they choose will be for the *same* value and need (the wish to go fishing and the need for the gear); therefore, if they engage in delinquent behavior to realize their goals, we cannot say that the desire to go fishing *caused* the delinquent behavior, for the same desire presumably could have been realized through nondelinquent means. That is, we cannot explain delinquent behavior by pointing to the ends of the activity, for there are legal routes to the same ends. Similarly, it is tempting to explain bank robbery by saying that the robbers wanted the money. Well, everyone wants money, but not everyone robs a bank. We must ask, rather, why given individuals choose criminal or delinquent means to realize their needs and values. In this way we explain the delinquent activity instead of general social needs and values.

There have been a number of criticisms of differential association theory, which have generated several empirical tests of the theory's propositions and a good deal of debate as well as insight. We will look briefly at some of the criticisms of the theory, examine empirical studies, and discuss the theory's importance in accounting for juvenile delinquency.

Criticisms of differential association spring from numerous sources. Some criticisms, such as the charge that the theory neglects individual differences (Nettler, 1974:196), are aimed at sociological theories in general, but since the theorists are attempting to account for *patterns* of crime and not individual criminals this charge is not relevant. A second criticism is that while differential association theory accounts for a good many criminal patterns, there are several types of crimes which it does not adequately explain. For example, embezzlers appear to act alone in the commission of their crimes (Cressey, 1971) and do not appear to associate with other violators of financial trust. In many respects this criticism appears to be valid, especially since Donald Cressey, who was instrumental in the development of the differential association theory, carried out the research on financial trust violation. However, some other crimes that at first appear to be exceptions to differential association theory are found, upon closer examination, to be consistent with the theory. So-called compulsive crimes such as criminal homicide were thought to be exceptions to the theory; however, the "compulsive" nature of these crimes appears to be simply another theory of crime (Cressey, 1954). Luckenbill (1974) found that, far from being compulsive, homicides follow a consistent pattern of development. Further, they occur only on certain kinds of social occasions, and only when the sequence that leads to homicides is available and appropriate to the occasion (Sanders and Luckenbill, 1974). Thus, this criticism of the differential association theory was found to be based on a mis-conception of certain types of crime, or, as Cressey (1971:147–51) pointed out in the case of embezzlers, a partial understanding of the theory. Even though embezzlers act alone, they learn in social interaction the rationalizations, techniques, and everything else necessary for committing their crime. Finally, differential association theory has been criticized for not accounting for the origin of crime. While the theory shows how crime is passed on from one cohort to another, it does not explain how the criminal behavior pattern began. This is true: it is necessary to couple differential association theory with subcultural theories to explain how criminal behavior patterns originate. By the same token, however, the subcultural theories are dependent on differential association to explain the maintenance of the subculture.

The research designed to test differential association has had mixed results. In a self-report survey of juvenile drug use, the researchers found that the reason most often given by juveniles for trying illegal drugs was the desire to be "in" with their peers (Bowers and White, 1974). This supports the contention implicit in differential association theory that delinquent behavior is dependent on peer group attitudes. Similarly, in another self-report survey of high school students, it was found that almost 99 percent of those who had smoked marijuana had a close friend who had used the drug (Sanders, 1970:15). Furthermore, a number of studies have found that delinquent activities are typically committed by groups of two or more juveniles (Shaw and McKay, 1931; Eynon and Reckless, 1961). Reiss and Rhodes (1964) attempted to find out whether boys in close friendship groups share the same specific patterns of delinquent behavior. In their study, which focused on the *intensity* variable in differential association, they found that the probability that an individual will commit a specific delinquent act depends upon the commission of the act by his friends. This supports differential association theory. However, they also found that the salience of association as a variable itself varied with social class and with types of crime. Working-class delinquents were more likely to have associates who committed similar crimes than were mid-

dle-class delinquents. Also, those who committed the more serious crimes (e.g., robbery) were less likely to have close friends
who had done the same thing.

We could spend a great deal of time on differential association
theory as it relates to juvenile delinquency. However, it is sufficient here to point out that it is an extremely powerful theory
in accounting for delinquency. When we discuss the various
substantive areas, in later chapters, we will see numerous appli-
cations of this theory.

ONLY IF YOU GET CAUGHT: LABELING THEORY

In the discussion of an adequate definition of delinquency and
delinquents (chap. 1), I indicated that unless someone defines
an activity as delinquent, no delinquency exists. Similarly, when
we talk about a delinquent, we refer to someone who has been
labeled as such by the juvenile justice system. Once a person has
been labeled, he is often forced to play the role he has been
given even though he may prefer another course. Labeling
theory focuses on the *interactive* aspects of deviance in that it
takes into account not only the delinquent activity and per-
former but also the others who come to define the situation and
the actor as delinquent.

To understand this theory, it is important to know a little
about *symbolic interactionist theory.* First, labeling theory assumes that all reality is grounded in the symbols we use to talk
about it, or, as W. I. Thomas (1923) put it, "If men define situations as real, they are real in their consequences." For example,
if some juveniles are playing in front of a house when a bird flies
against a window and breaks it, then flies away, the juveniles
may be blamed for the broken window. If the juveniles are
believed to be responsible for the act, the police may be called,
and as a consequence of this definition of the situation the
juveniles may be labeled delinquents. Now, we might say that
they were falsely accused, but the point is that their innocence
of the act does not alter the consequences. They have been
defined as delinquents, on the basis of this definition, they are
treated as such.

A second important concept is that of the "looking-glass self." Essentially, this concept, developed by Cooley (1902), holds that people come to see themselves as they are defined by others. Thus, if a juvenile is seen by others as stupid and lazy, he is likely to come to see himself in the same way. Furthermore, since people act in terms of their self-identity, the definition of self is instrumental in determining behavior. A juvenile whose self-conception is that of a stupid and lazy student is more likely to act stupid and lazy than one who sees himself as intelligent and hard-working. Similarly, a juvenile who has been labeled delinquent is more likely to commit acts that are consistent with this identity than a youth who has not been so labeled.

Now we can appreciate some basic tenets of labeling theory. First, Lemert (1951) has distinguished between primary and secondary deviance. *Primary deviance* is the original act that is defined as deviant by others. Any number of social, cultural, psychological, and physiological factors can cause this original offense (Lemert, 1967 a:40). More important is *secondary deviation,* an adaptation to the societal reaction to primary deviation in terms of social roles, social identity, and processes in fixing a person in a deviant category. For example, let's say a girl is caught shoplifting. She enters a transformation process from a nondelinquent to a delinquent. First, the juvenile justice system judges her delinquent and places her in a social category along with all other delinquents. Goffman (1963) refers to the label of "delinquent" as a *stigma* and to the process by which a person is discredited as stigmatization. This process serves to separate the stigmatized individual from nonstigmatized others, and it also puts those with a like stigma into social contact with one another. That is, stigmatized individuals are isolated from everyone except others who are stigmatized. The girl who has been stigmatized for shoplifting will be cast in the role of a delinquent, and her parents, friends, and teachers may come to treat her somewhat differently than before. Sometimes this treatment is blatant and sometimes subtle, but when it exists the stigmatized individual can sense it. For example, as one convicted criminal noted:

You know, he didn't see this as an insulting remark at all: in fact, I think he thought he was being honest in telling me how mistaken he was. And that's exactly the sort of patronizing you get from straight people if you're a criminal. "Fancy that!" they say. "In some ways you're just like a human being!" I'm not kidding, it makes me want to choke the bleeding life out of them. [Parker and Allerton, 1962:111]

As labeled delinquents are gradually isolated from nondelinquents, they are forced into association with other delinquents. Parents tell their children not to associate with "bad kids," images of delinquents are exaggerated so that association with them is undesirable, and what began as a social sanction for norm violation becomes a force making it extremely difficult for the delinquent to avoid further deviation. The extent to which an individual is caught up in this process suggests secondary deviation.

It should be noted that the process beginning with official labeling does not inexorably lead to secondary deviation. Depending on his social status and resources, the individual can fight even repeated attempts to fix a stigma. For instance, one young man who was charged with first-degree burglary and arson had considerable resources behind him to fight off the stigma of a criminal (Sanders, 1974). His mother hired an expensive criminal attorney who was able to have the charge reduced to second-degree burglary and to have the arson charge dropped completely. The young man was placed on probation and fined even though he had been in trouble with the law on several other occasions. Someone with fewer resources may not have been able to avoid imprisonment and the stigma of a convict. Additionally, friends and relatives of the young man called the victim and berated her for having brought the charges and thus caused the burglar's problems! No one in the young man's circle saw him being delinquent because of his actions: instead they somehow redefined the event to emphasize the victim's willingness to report the crime.

Labeling theory at first may seem to tell us not so much about the patterns of delinquency as about the process whereby one comes to be seen as delinquent. However, as Becker (1967b) points out, the power to label people criminal is the power to determine their fate. As we have noted, almost all juveniles commit delinquent acts, but only a few are officially judged to be delinquent. Members of minorities and the poor are more likely to wind up in the official statistics as being delinquent. Lacking power in the form of either financial clout or knowledge, the disadvantaged in society are less able to fight the official labeling process. Because of this lack of power, and not necessarily because of their greater delinquent activity, the disadvantaged are overrepresented in the official statistics. Moreover, given the process of secondary deviation, since members of minorities and the poor are more likely to be labeled delinquent, they are more likely to be forced into the role of a delinquent and thereby actually be involved in more secondary deviation. Thus, there is a self-fulfilling prophesy. The minorities and poor may not commit any more primary deviance than the affluent, but they are more likely to be labeled delinquent. The labeling process leads to secondary deviation, which leads to further delinquency, and thus the disadvantaged come to commit more delinquent acts.

The labeling perspective is limited in explaining initial deviance. By linking this theory with other theories that share the symbolic interactionist framework, such as differential association, we can account for more delinquency. The most significant contribution of labeling theory is that it forces us to examine the input of others in creating delinquency instead of regarding delinquency as something that exists in a vacuum. Labeling theory shows that those who define the situation, either officially or unofficially, have an important role in creating the social reality of delinquency. It thereby further demonstrates the social nature of delinquency in society and refutes the notion that something must be pathologically wrong with juveniles for them to commit delinquent acts. Finally, labeling theory accounts not only for the patterns of delinquency and the social-psychological process of becoming delinquent but also for the role of the juvenile justice system in delinquency.

WHERE THE ACTION IS: CHARACTER AND DELINQUENCY

The theory of character and delinquency also has its roots in the symbolic interaction school, but it is significantly different from both differential association and labeling theory. Like labeling theory, it is centered in the process of identification, but it regards the individual as an active participant, not a passive agent. To understand this theory, we will need a basic appreciation of the works of Erving Goffman, who developed it.

To Goffman (1959), people are actors and the world is a stage. Using the resources available to them, men and women carry on performances, and on the basis of these performances, others make judgments about their moral character. On the one hand, we come to see ourselves according to how others treat us, but this treatment can be manipulated through impression management in our performances. Our appearance, including our dress, gestures, and posture, tells others who we are, and they are obliged to treat us in terms of the claims we make through this appearance. By the same token, if we put on any given performance, we are expected to back it up with certain other activities. For example, if a student wants to be seen as intelligent he may carry certain books with him, use a polysyllabic vocabulary, and present all the other props associated with being a scholar. However, if he does poorly on exams and papers, others will come to see him as a phony who cannot back up his claims. The incongruity between his appearance and his ability calls into question his moral character, and his claims to future identities may be difficult to make convincingly.

In the context of Goffman's dramaturgic framework, identities are made (and unmade) in social situations. Instead of being something that follows a person around as a constant, identity has a situational character. For example, a juvenile may be seen in school and classroom situations as "dull," "slow," or, in the parlance of educational newspeak, "educationally handicapped." The same juvenile, however, may be a gang leader in his neighborhood, and when he's with his gang, engaging in gang activities, he is seen as "tough," "brave," and full of "heart." His appearance and even his general performance may not be substantially different in the two situations, but the different audiences and contexts dictate the sense that is to be made of the performance.

As the youth grows up, his situational performances and the identity he develops in those situations come to be increasingly consequential, for more and more others are making judgments about his moral character (Goffman, 1967; Werthman, 1967). That is, each situational performance is assessed in terms of who and what the juvenile *really* is. Is the kid who talks tough *really* tough, or is he just a bigmouth? Does he have the heart to pull if off, or is it just talk? What kind of stuff is this person made of? These questions are not only asked by others who make judgments as to moral character but they are asked by the individual of himself. The problem is how to establish and maintain character.

In conventional middle-class society, juveniles' moral character is established by doing well in school, and the character tests are administered by teachers. Similarly, the tennis court, ski slope, surfing beach, and bedroom are settings where young men can prove themselves. The gang boy, on the other hand, does not have the resources or the interest to go skiing or surfing. Further, only a limited number of young men will be chosen to play on the varsity football team and to participate in other groups where membership is evidence of a strong character. In other words, there are limited resources in middle-class settings for character building by lower-class juvenile males.

Since identities are made in situations, it is necessary to create and enter into situations where moral character can be established. To show courage, one needs a situation where courage can be demonstrated. Likewise, other attributes prized by gang boys, such as "coolness" (Lyman and Scott, 1970) and "smartness," require situations where one can show others unequivocally that he is "cool" and "smart" (Werthman, 1967). It is not enough to tell others of one's courage, as we have shown. What is difficult about making identity claims is having others honor them, especially when the claims involve moral character. Furthermore, the situation must be a real test of these attributes and not one where the attributes are questionable. For instance, it is not difficult to maintain "coolness" and composure when one is not threatened, and if a youth performs coolly in any number of safe situations it tells us little of his ability to carry off the same performance when there are strong urges to the contrary. It is one thing to remain calm and cool during a normal class period but quite another matter when the school catches fire and everyone is beating a hasty retreat to the exits.

If juveniles waited around until their school caught fire to demonstrate those prized attributes, there would be few opportunities to establish character. However, by creating and seeking out risky situations in which conduct is seen to be a reflection of one's character, they have not only greater opportunity to show what they are made of but the added status that comes from searching for trouble instead of merely waiting until it comes along. Goffman (1967:185) uses the term *action* for situations that are created and entered into for the purpose of establishing moral character.

Now, action can exist and be created just about anywhere. Familiar places include gambling houses, racetracks, and roller derbies. However, these places are typically reserved for adults, and even though gang boys have no problem gaining access to such settings, they do not have the same character-establishing possibilities as situations the boys can create for themselves. Likewise, certain occupations promise action, notably police work, firefighting, and the military, occupations in which one's mettle is routinely tested and demonstrated. However, these occupations too are reserved for adults.

On the other hand, stealing cars, gang fights, and similar risk-taking activities provide lower-class youths with situations in which they can show the world that they have real courage, coolness, and smartness. The resources for creating action are those that happen to be available, and since opportunities to commit theft and engage in fights are the most readily available to lower-class youths, these are the situations they enter to establish moral character. Unlike their professional counterparts, however, who commit theft and violence as a source of income and take precautions to avoid detection, gang boys who engage in these same activities knowingly make them risky (Werthman, 1967:156). For example, when asked if he did much joy riding, one gang boy responded as follows:

> Yeah. When I was about thirteen, I didn't do nothing but steal cars. The guy that I always stole with, both of us liked to drive so we'd steal a car. And then he'd go steal another car and we'd chase each other. Like there would be two in our car, two in the other car, and we'd drive by and stick out our hands, and if you touch them then they have to chase you. Or we'd steal an old car, you know, that have the running boards on it. We'd stand on that and kick the car going past. Kind of fun, but, uh, it's real dangerous. We used to have a ball when we'd do that other game with the hands though. [Werthman, 1967:157]

Obviously, no professional car thief in his right mind would engage in this kind of behavior. Thus, gang boys not only transform their resources into props for demonstrating character but also transform normal criminal activities, in which there is a good deal of risk to begin with, into even riskier situations.

Attempts by the criminal and juvenile justice system to put a stop to these character-building events typically have the effect of making them more enticing. "Getting tough" with juveniles makes the risks of engaging in delinquencies even greater. As the risks increase, so does the value of the delinquent activity, for one must demonstrate greater courage, coolness, and smartness in order to pull it off. This logic is direct contradiction to the theory of law enforcement, which contends that increasing the risks reduces the likelihood of risk-taking activity. If there is a high value placed on character and if character is best demonstrated by taking risks, then the higher the risks, the better they are for showing off moral character. Hence, in the context of the high subjective value or utility placed on "action," the juvenile justice system provides not a deterrent to delinquency but a spur.

The delinquent behavior generated by the attraction of action situations is by no means limited to theft and fighting. During the youth movement of the 1960s, which included the free speech movement, antiwar protests, and the civil rights movement, there was a good deal of action (Scott and Lyman, 1970). College students, and to a lesser extent high school students, engaged in pitched battles with the police, not only risking their freedom but putting their physical welfare and their careers on the line. Leaders of the movement were not above challenging dithering followers to show that they had the "balls" to engage in civil disobedience or outright revolution. Moreover, in campus turmoil, the presence of the police was more likely to incite riot than to quell it. For example, at San Francisco State College, most of the students were politically apathetic. However, when the police department brought the tactical squad to the campus to put down a demonstration, many uncommitted students joined in the protest. Most accounts of the troubles at San Francisco State tended to blame the police for harassing innocent students, thus forcing them into the ranks of the protesters. However, it can also be said that the police activity provided an opportunity for students to demonstrate that they were courageous and willing to protect "their" territory. Moreover, as was amply shown in the mass media, a number of reputations were made during the movement, and in no small way the situations generated by the movement provided the necessary social ingredients for character building.

Another arena of character building for the young was the drug culture. "Acid trips" came to be an adventure in which one could "show his stuff," and the real and imagined dangers of using LSD provided the necessary risks for demonstrating moral character. As Goffman (1967:201) has noted:

> Interestingly, there is currently available through LSD and other drugs a means of voluntarily *chancing* psychic welfare in order to pass beyond ordinary consciousness. The individual here uses his own mind as the equipment necessary for action.

The challenge of "try it if you're not chicken" may not have led legions of youth to drugs, but it was incentive enough for a substantially large number of juveniles.

Besides the possibility of showing off character, a further feature of action is the excitement of the situations. To demonstrate coolness as well as other valued character attributes it is necessary to be at least somewhat agitated. This inner agitation provides a thrill that is not available in mundane activities. Finestone (1957) describes the "kick" as

> .any act tabooed by "squares" that heightens and intensifies the present moment of experience and differentiates it as much as possible from the humdrum routine of daily life. Sex in any of its conventional expressions is not a "kick" since this would not serve to distinguish the "cat" from the "square," but orgies of sex behavior and a dabbling in the various perversions and byways of sex pass muster as "kick." Some "cats" are on an alcohol "kick," others on a marijuana "kick," and others on a heroin "kick."

By transforming the everyday routine into an adventure, young people are not only able to say something about themselves as unique individuals but can also have fun. Delinquency occurs in these situations to the extent that the kicks are characterized as breaches of delinquency laws. In part the kick comes from the fact that delinquency violations are seen as exciting, and in part it is due to the fact that many exciting activities, pursued merely for excitement, happen to be against the law. This is not to say that delinquency is necessarily sustained, although it certainly can be, through action-seeking, for some adventures that begin as a kick may become a habit or a necessity. What is important to understand is that youths in their quest for action may (or may not) engage in delinquencies and that these acts are more likely to be expressive and thrill-provoking than instrumental.

Studies of gang violence have found not only that gang members enhance their moral character or "rep" by seeking out action-type situations (Miller, 1969) but also that maintaining individual as well as collective honor is an ongoing concern for gang members. This leads to situations in which character is made or reaffirmed. Horowitz and Schwartz (1974) found that when a gang member or a gang as a whole was verbally or otherwise derogated, the gang felt that it had to fight the detractors or lose face. Typically, this meant a gang fight between the gang whose honor and moral character were questioned and the gang that derogated it. In turn, the gang fight situation provided an occasion on which members of the warring gangs could demonstrate individual strength of character. Therefore, two purposes are served by clashes between gangs. The collective honor of the gang is defended, and at the same time individual members can build their "rep." All this is provided by gang rumbles in addition to the excitement they generate.

In summary, Goffman's framework provides a useful analytical tool for the student of juvenile delinquency. It highlights the position of juveniles in the social structure in terms of the resources available for developing a self-concept and thereby accounts for the effect of the social structure on delinquent activities. At the same time it brings in the subjective element of utility, enabling us to understand the value of, and thus the reason for, certain delinquent activities that are often described as "senseless" or "irrational." It accounts for the high rate of crime among juveniles and for the fact that as juveniles move into adult roles, where legitimate character claims are available to them, they tend to stop breaking the law. All in all, it offers a fresh and innovative view of juvenile crime.

CONCLUSION

At the outset of this chapter we outlined three criteria that any theory must meet to account adequately for juvenile delinquency. First, the theory must explain the patterns of delinquency. Secondly, it must explain why any single individual comes to engage in delinquency. Thirdly, it must come to terms with the sociolegal processes of criminalization.

In reviewing several theories, we find that while all three criteria are met by a combination of the theories, no single theory satisfies all three. Structural frustration theory explains the patterns of delinquency but it cannot explain either individual actions or the sociolegal process. Subcultural theories and conflict theories explain the patterns of delinquency but are limited in accounting for the social-psychological processes in individual delinquency. While differential association theory provides an excellent explanation of delinquent patterns and the social-psychological process of becoming delinquent, it does not explain the criminalization process. Labeling theory offers the first good explanation of the sociolegal input in the process of making delinquents and also a good social-psychological explanation of delinquency, but it is weak in accounting for primary deviance and patterns of delinquency that have not been labeled. Finally, Goffman's theory of delinquency is an outstanding formulation of primary deviance, patterns of delinquency, and the social-psychological process whereby a person is attracted to delinquent activity, but it gives only limited consideration to the sociolegal processes.

It is tempting to try to meet the criteria by combining all these theories. However, a "melting pot" theory not only would yield contradictions but would not offer an adequate explanation of delinquency. Instead we would have a hodgepodge of statements with no direction, and rather than clarification, there would be confusion.

On the other hand, if we could locate a single theoretical framework for some combination of explanations, we would be able to maintain theoretical consistency and provide a direction for further efforts to explain delinquency. In examining differential association, labeling, and Goffman's theory, we find that all three have what might be termed an "interactionist" philosophical and theoretical orientation (Rubington and Weinberg, 1968). This perspective holds that delinquency is the product of the processes of social interaction, and that by examining the processes of social interaction we can explain both normal and delinquent forms of action. Differential association accounts for the associations in interaction, labeling explains the process of defining the situation and the people in the situation, and Goffman shows how the pursuit of identity and character leads to involvement in certain kinds of situations. This combination, under the umbrella of the interactionist theory, meets all our criteria. We can account for patterns of delinquency in terms of the likelihood of interacting with others who engage in delinquency, explain the various forms of delinquent activity in terms of the resources available to juveniles for establishing character, and account for an individual's involvement in delinquency by examining his association patterns and the value he places on establishing himself in terms of his peers. Finally, the sociolegal process is simply one form of the labeling process, in which situations and people are socially defined as delinquent or nondelinquent.

The focus of this book, then, will be on delinquency in terms of social interaction. In looking at various aspects of delinquency, we will pose such questions as: How do the occasions arise on which delinquency is seen as the appropriate line of action? Why are some juveniles labeled delinquent and others not? What kind of interaction occurs between the criminal and juvenile justice systems and juveniles? What forms of interaction are likely to be defined as delinquent?

3 Just for Kids
Juvenile-Status Offenses

As we pointed out in chapter 1, delinquency has many faces, and one is that of the juvenile has been judged delinquent even though no crime has been committed for which an adult could be convicted. Nothing has been stolen, no one has been assaulted, no illegal drug has been used, but still the juvenile finds himself or, more frequently, herself incarcerated or placed on official probation. Such youngsters have committed so-called juvenile-status offenses, transgressions for which no adult could be brought to court; they are just for kids.

[Juvenile-status offenses fall into two categories. They may involve the violation of certain ordinances that apply only to juveniles, such as curfew, truancy, or alcohol and tobacco laws. Some cities have ordinances that prohibit juveniles from being out after certain hours in the evening even though it's perfectly legal for adults to stay out all night. The other category of juvenile-status offenses involves youths who are charged with being "out of control"—runaways, children who will not obey their parents, young people who are experimenting with sex. An unmarried seventeen-year-old girl who sleeps with her boyfriend is subject to legal sanction under the juvenile statutes, but the girl's eighteen-year-old sister who does the same thing with *her* boyfriend will be left alone since she is beyond the age of a juvenile in most states.*⌡

Now we might ask if juvenile-status offenders (JSOs) should be included in a study of juvenile delinquency since they have committed no crimes. Moreover, we might suspect that the courts are more lenient with JSOs than with other delinquents and that JSOs are therefore less likely to be officially labeled delinquents and incarcerated or placed on probation. Surely a girl or boy who commits an "adult crime" is more likely to receive harsh punishment than one who merely runs away from home or experiments with sex. We would expect that most of the "hard-core" delinquents who are placed in reformatories would be from the ranks of juveniles who commit crimes such as burglary, assault, and drug use.

When we look at the data, however, we find that a large proportion of those labeled delinquent are JSOs. Between a quarter and a third of the delinquent children in correctional institutions are there for juvenile-status offenses (Sheridan, 1967). More than half of the girls and about a fifth of the boys in detention programs are JSOs. Thus, by conservative estimate, juvenile-status offenders constitute one-third of the overall delinquent population and the majority of female delinquents.

If we expected juveniles who commit only juvenile-status offenses to be treated more leniently by the courts, we would be wrong again. According to Lerman (1973), juvenile-status offenders are more likely to be sent to an institution than juveniles who are found guilty of committing a crime for which an adult would be arrested. Of those juveniles who were convicted of Part I crimes, which include robbery, rape, burglary, and grand theft, 23 percent were placed in some controlled setting. Only 18 percent of the juveniles convicted of the less serious Part II crimes, such as petty theft and malicious mischief, were sentenced. However, 26 percent of the juvenile-status offend-

---

*Some states have antifornication laws for adults, but these laws are rarely enforced. However, juvenile statutes that merely *imply* antifornication sanctions are used vigorously against female juveniles.

ers, who had committed neither Part I nor Part II crimes, were sent away. There appears to be no logic to these figures. If Part II crimes are less serious than Part I crimes, and if juveniles who are convicted of Part II crimes are less likely to be incarcerated than those who commit Part I crimes, it would seem to follow that juveniles who have committed *no* crime for which an adult could receive punishment would be the least likely to be placed in or committed to a detention facility. However, they are the most likely to be committed.

Similarly, if we examine the length of incarceration, we find that JSOs receive more severe treatment than delinquents who have committed an adult-status crime (Lerman, 1973:250–51). For the latter, the length of institutional stay ranged from two to twenty-eight months, but for JSOs it was from four to forty-eight months. Those who were sentenced for a Part I or Part II crime were incarcerated for a median of 9 months and a mean of 10.7 months; the JSOs institutional stay was for a median of 13 months and a mean of 16.3 months. No matter how we look at it, juvenile-status offenders end up in a detention setting for a longer period than juveniles who commit adult crimes.

The number of juvenile-status offenders officially judged to be delinquent and the severity of punishment for these youths seem to indicate that society is more concerned about a juvenile's willingness to go to school, mind his parents, and refrain from experimenting with alcohol or sex than about his tendency to commit rape, robbery, or assault. However, there is evidence that juvenile-status offenses are believed by the general public to be less serious than almost all other types of crime. In a study by Rossi and others (1974), respondents ranked repeated runaways as 137th in seriousness out of 140 crimes, repeated truancy 136th, repeated refusal to obey parents 130th. Compared to these typical juvenile-status offenses, all ranked near the bottom of the list, almost all crimes for which an adult could be arrested were ranked as more serious. Why is it that the juvenile justice system uses so many resources to punish children for acts that society as a whole sees as relatively inconsequential?

In order to unravel this tangle, we will need to examine features of various juvenile-status offenses and the court's reaction to them. In this chapter our main emphasis will be on activities that are characterized as juvenile-status offenses. In chapter 8 we will concentrate on the juvenile justice system. There will be some overlap, since there is an intrinsic relationship between the juvenile justice system and laws and juvenile-status offenses and offenders.

YOUNG AND IN LOVE:
JUVENILE SEXUAL OFFENSES

One of the most ambiguous types of juvenile-status offenses is the sexual offense. First of all, heterosexual intercourse between consenting juvenile couples, like most sexual liaisons, is usually private and undetected. Therefore, unlike the number of runaways and other noticeable juvenile offenses, the extent of sexual offenses is unknown. Second, when the juvenile court adjudicates a sexual offense, it often masks the transgression under the category of "ungovernability," "loitering," "immoral or indecent conduct," or even "runaway" in order to protect the youthful defendants. We can only guess at the number of juveniles incarcerated for having sexual relations and must rely on self-report surveys to determine how many juveniles engage in sexual behavior of some sort. Short and Nye (1958) found that 95.1 percent of the girls committed to training schools and 14.1 percent of the high school girls (in West High) admitted to having had sexual intercourse. Since the Short and Nye study, sexual morality has undergone a significant change, and the incidence of adolescent sexual activity is probably higher today (Yankelovich, 1974:91). In 1970 Gibbons found in a self-report study that 33.2 percent of the females and 36.6 percent of the males had had heterosexual relations.

These statistics tell us very little beyond the fact that sexual chastity does not seem to be valued as much as it used to be. It is more important to understand sexual activity in the context of society and, more specifically, in the context of the juvenile justice system.

A dominant theme in American sexual relations is the "double standard"—the belief that sexual relations are a good thing for men and a bad thing for women. Among adolescent males, there is peer pressure to have sex with as many girls as possible, and there is pressure for girls to remain virgins until marriage. If the boys meet their goals, then at least some girls will fail to meet theirs, and vice versa. It is true that this double standard is now widely regarded by youth as stupid and hypocritical, but premarital sex is still frowned upon by most parents (Reiss, 1970), and many juveniles still believe that on the whole they should go along with their parents' views. Of course, the parental frown on premarital sex is directed toward daughters, not sons; a father may be distraught over his daughter's loss of virginity but secretly applaud the same transition for his son.

Albert Reiss, (1960) explains the double standard in terms of role expectations. Boys are taught to treat sexual intercourse as an *end*. By promising love, affection, dates, or even marriage, boys attempt to convince girls to have sex. Girls, on the other hand, are expected to use sex as a means to entrap some boy and not as an end. Implicit in this arrangement is the Victorian dictum that for women sex is something to be tolerated but that for men it represents conquest and, almost incidentally, enjoyment. Thus, a girl who has sex with a boy she loves is seen to be using sex as a means of keeping him, while a boy who has sex with just about any girl is behaving in terms of role expectations, since sex to him is merely an end.

According to Reiss, problems occur for juveniles when these role expectations are upset.

> An extremely important element determining public reaction to acts of sexual deviation is the *degree to which the status and role of the participants in the sexual act depart from the status and role expectations for these persons apart from the sexual act itself.*

In sexual matters aggressive females and passive males are reversals of role expectations. Females who treat sex as an end and actively seek out sexual partners simply because they enjoy sexual intercourse are considered promiscuous. Males who do not act aggressively toward females sexually are suspected of being "sissies" or effeminate. Thus, it is not sexual activity per se that is likely to bring a juvenile's status into question but also the role expectations. It is unlikely that a girl who had sex with a boy "because she was in love" would be treated in the same way as a girl who had sex "because she was horny." The former has treated sex as a means and the latter as an end, and it is the latter girl who is more likely to be considered delinquent.

The consequences of role expectations for young men and women can be seen in the differential treatment they receive in the juvenile justice system. Chesney-Lind (1974) pointed out that the police were more likely to arrest girls than boys for a sexual offense, although obviously in most cases there is an equal number of boys and girls engaged in a single heterosexual act (other than "gang bangs," in which several boys have intercourse with one girl). However, since boys are fulfilling role expectations in having premarital relations, they are not seen to be deviant. In terms of the double standard of sexual morality, it is not surprising that more girls are arrested for sex offenses.

Interest in young women's sexual activity by the juvenile justice system does not stop with those girls who are arrested specifically for sexual offenses. In New York, when a girl is brought before the juvenile court for any reason, a vaginal smear is taken to determine whether she has venereal disease (Chesney-Lind, 1974:45–46). Originally, vaginal smears were taken to determine whether girls had had intercourse, but now officialdom justifies them in terms of the rise in venereal disease among young people. A girl arrested for offenses other than sexual is subject to a vaginal smear in the name of preventive medicine; one arrested for shoplifting, say, is as likely to be examined as is a girl picked up for sexual promiscuity. Hence, either there is an assumption that all female delinquents are sexually promiscuous or the juvenile justice officials have a perverted interest in young women's sexual behavior. Either way, these practices smack of sexism, for only rarely are boys questioned about their sexual activity or examined for venereal disease, while girls routinely suffer the indignity and degradation of a compulsory vaginal examination. The wish to reduce venereal disease among the young is understandable, but the right of the juvenile justice system to usurp public health functions is questionable, and the exclusive focus on girls is indefensible.

Cavan (1962:105–7) characterizes the sexual activity of young females in terms of socioeconomic status, differential values, and problem solving. Lower-class girls, she says, have the same aspirations for marriage as middle-class girls, but they do not engage in the same temporal planning or sexual restraint. Sexual activity is more likely to be viewed as fun by these girls, and even though they are interested in maintaining a respectable reputation, they are not willing to postpone sexual activity until marriage. By having sexual liaisons with boys who are not from their town or neighborhood, they are able to preserve their reputations and at the same time enjoy sexual activity. These sexual contacts are not intimate, nor do they involve obligations; they are treated as ends. When the lower-class girls reach their middle and late teens, they enter more serious relationships with boys from their community, which eventually result in marriage.

Not all lower-class communities have the same patterns of sexual activity, however. Among Italian and Spanish groups, virginity is highly valued, and the community is organized to protect unmarried girls through such mechanisms as chaperones. In these communities, young men go elsewhere for sexual activity before marriage and return to the neighborhoods when they wish to settle down and marry. Black communities, on the other hand, view sexual activity as natural for unmarried males and females, and there are no negative sanctions applied to unmarried girls for sexual activity (Cavan, 1962:107). Thus, sexual activity for girls varies depending on differential community and ethnic values in the lower class. While some of the values might be considered much looser than middle-class values, others are much stricter.

Cavan also assessed the sexual activity of juvenile females in terms of problem solving. Young lower-class girls who run away from home have few survival resources, but they can survive by picking up men, as well as by petty larceny. Girls who find themselves in this situation are likely to be apprehended by juvenile authorities since they must actively seek partners. Therefore, girls who come into contact with the juvenile authorities are likely to have engaged in other crimes besides sexual offenses. It is understandable, then, how the juvenile authorities come to suspect that girls who are picked up for delinquent activity unrelated to sex are guilty of sexual offenses as well.

Another form of juvenile sexual activity among lower-class youth involves homosexual relationships between juvenile boys and male adults. Reiss (1961) found that these relationships were organized in such a way that the boys did not develop conceptions of themselves as homosexuals, and their homosexual encounters were transitory. Essentially, the boys hustled adult homosexuals, who paid the boys to allow them to act as fellators. The boys did not consider themselves to be hustlers but instead saw their homosexual activity as merely one of many things they did in what was often a pattern of delinquency. "Getting a queer" was a way to make money; theft and burglary were other illegal activities to the same end. In their collective definition of their activities, the boys did not see themselves as engaging in homosexual activity, and "getting a queer" did not imply anything other than that the boy earned some money, not unlike a waiter getting a tip. As one boy explained,

> "No matter how many queers a guy goes with, if he goes for money, that don't make him queer. You're still straight. It's when you start going for free, with other young guys, that you start growing wings." [Rechy, 1961:118]

Furthermore, boys who use homosexual adult males to earn money typically do not enter the gay life but instead, when they are able to hold a job or decide to settle down, they give up "getting queers" (Reiss, 1961), enter into conventional adult roles, and raise a family. No stigma is attached to them for their activity with homosexuals when they were juveniles.

However, even though the boys do not define their activities as homosexual, the juvenile authorities do. Moreover, the authorities are likely to see their intervention in a boy's life as "saving" him from the advances of adult homosexuals instead of denying the boy his freedom. Heterosexual relations for boys, as we noted above, are considered a sign of normal adolescent development, but homosexual activity is viewed as damaging. It is of little interest to the juvenile authorities that the boys do not define their activities as homosexual and consider "queers" as a world apart.

Perhaps the best way to understand the relationship between lower-class boys and adult homosexuals is to view it as part-time or occasional male prostitution. From the boys' point of view it is clearly not homosexual activity on their part, and if the juvenile justice system is interested in protecting boys from becoming homosexuals, they are not doing so by incarcerating boys who hustle adult male homosexuals. Ironically, the juvenile justice system is more likely to encourage homosexuality by putting boys together in detention centers. In these so-called training schools, boys may form homosexual relationships with boys their own age without any financial exchange, and that's when they "start growing wings." It would seem that the juvenile justice system could better meet its goal by providing lower-class boys with legitimate opportunities to earn money rather than incarcerating them. However, since the juvenile authorities see the boys as homosexuals and the problem as sexual rather than as an illegitimate means employed by certain cohorts of lower-class boys to earn money, it is unlikely that the system will contribute to meaningful change.

Changing morals and values among the young and their parents, especially in the middle class, point to less concern with sexual chastity, and the more this "new morality" permeates society, the more likely it is that adolescents will engage in sexual activity. As this occurs, more boys and girls will come to the attention of the juvenile courts; but at the same time, we suspect that sexual offenses will not be officially adjudicated— not so much because the juvenile justice system will become less interested in "protecting" the young as because many of the girls who come to their attention will be middle class and will be more likely to question the system's right to be the guardian of their private activities. Boys will probably be left alone for sexual offenses except for homosexual activities, including those of self-defined nonhomosexuals who hustle. The homosexual laws in several states are changing, and homosexual activity may soon no longer be considered a crime: this may lead to less interest in adult and juvenile homosexual activity. If "hustling"—i.e., making money from "suckers"—is redefined as male prostitution, it is likely that different approaches to the problem will be initiated. Thus, we can expect to see fewer boys incarcerated for sexual offenses and more programs developed to offset the need to raise money by hustling.

GOTTA GET OUT OF HERE: THE RUNAWAYS

One of the most common forms of juvenile-status offenses is running away from home, but unfortunately this has been one of the most neglected areas in the study of juvenile delinquency. Those included in the runaway statistics range from the Huckleberry Finns who leave home for a few days to the young who have been placed in foster homes and are attempting to escape "home" permanently. Some are attracted to the freedom once promised in youthful hangouts such as San Francisco's Haight Ashbury district and New York's East Village; others are squeezed out by family problems; still others simply want to exercise their autonomy. Like other juvenile-status offenses, running away from home is not a crime for which an adult would be committed, but since it is typically reported by parents to the police, it is the most visible juvenile-status offense.

For the police, runaway juveniles present both problems and opportunities. On the one hand, juvenile detectives can establish a relatively high "clearance rate" (the proportion of cases solved to those reported) since runaway juveniles typically frequent certain specific locations and the police generally have a description and a photograph of the juvenile. On the other hand, police would rather concentrate on more serious crimes and not have to bother with runaways (Sanders, 1974). The dilemma for the police is now to handle the runaway problem without devoting too much time to it. In the first eight months of 1973, the Los Angeles police received 4,360 runaway reports; the previous year the total was 7,601, representing a great deal of investigative time (Stumbo, 1973). A single juvenile investigator in Los Angeles during a single day in 1973 had seventy-one runaways to locate, and this caseload left him no time for any other work.

The significance of the runaway in the context of juvenile delinquency and the juvenile justice system is that parents typically initiate the characterization of the act as a problem to be handled officially by the police. Although many parents do not report their children for other juvenile-status offenses, the parents of runaway children usually do, regarding the children as in need of protection. This was dramatically illustrated in 1973 when twenty-seven young boys in Houston, Texas, were found to have been sexually assaulted and murdered (Stumbo, 1973). It was later learned that a number of the dead boys had been reported as runaways, and the police were blamed for not having done anything to find them before the wholesale slaughter. This led to a greater concern to locate runaways not only by the police but also by parents. Those who had reported their children missing began to apply increased pressure on the police to find them, and parents who normally would not report their children missing started calling the police and demanding that the children be found. However, the panic caused by the Houston murders was transitory; although such spectacular cases may result in policy changes in police departments, they do not linger long in the public's mind as new dramas draw attention elsewhere. Nevertheless, the police will use the killings to justify their work, including policies that reward them for seeking out juveniles who are not in the control of their parents.

As the juvenile justice system ponders new policies to "protect" runaway juveniles, parents need not initiate the process whereby a juvenile comes to be arrested for runaway. Originally, the police waited until a worried parent called to report that his child had left home. When the pressure increased to locate missing youths, police departments initiated the policy of arresting any juvenile who was not in his parent's control, using as the criterion the fact that the youth was in a city or county where the parents did not reside. Many young people who were not considered runaways by their parents came to be defined as such by the police. Thus, we have come full circle from the parents' being the initiators of runaway reports to the police's taking an increasingly active role in defining which juveniles are within the sanctioned control of parents. Considering the scope of the problem, there are relatively few studies of juvenile runaways. However, by looking at what findings there are, we can begin to get a picture of why youths leave home.

According to Homer (1973), most people believe that all runaways have experienced conflict at home and that by intervening in the home social workers can solve the runaway problem. It is true that a number of youths leave home because of family conflict, but many leave to seek adventure, and many of those who leave home because of conflict do so only long enough for things to cool off. Moreover, it has not been shown that the problem can be resolved by intervening in the home situation. Another myth explains runaways as a "cry for help" by the juvenile. The explanation that runaways "want attention" is unfounded, and even though some youths may want to *call attention to a family crisis*, it is not true that they leave home so that attention will be heaped on them. Finally, it is believed that runaways are children of the wealthy who are repudiating middle- and upper-middle-class values. Homer (1973:474) found in her study of runaway girls that they were from predominantly lower- and lower-middle-class backgrounds, with 70 percent from families on welfare.

Most of these girls were either "pushed" or "pulled" out of the house. Some 35 percent who left home were running *from* an unpleasant family situation, but most were running *to* something. Many girls were attracted by sex, drugs, liquor, and other "pleasures" forbidden in the home. Additionally, there was peer-group support for running away and engaging in numerous adventuresome activities, usually including crime.

The runaway girls' explanations of their own activities fell into four categories: (1) could not tolerate home situation; (2) don't know; (3) want to be with boyfriend; and (4) like running, as well as what happens on the run. The last two were the most frequently offered explanations. As we noted in discussing Goffman's explanation of juvenile delinquency, some juveniles are structurally denied character-building situations and therefore create their own. By running away from home, a youth is not only able to show that he or she has the strength of character to make it without parental support but can also locate and manufacture "action." Moreover, since many runaways leave home in a group of two or more, differential association theory is applicable here as well; by thinking of runaways as a peer-oriented, action-seeking group, we can better understand why juveniles leave home. Instead of placing all the emphasis on the runaway's home life, we should look to his other associations and the possible adventures in self-realization available outside home and school. Today's runaways leave home with friends in search of adventure, the same reason that drew Tom Sawyer and Huckleberry Finn.

In another study, English (1973) found that there is more than one type of runaway and that, depending on the type, running away is either a transitory or a permanent state. English differentiates four types of runaways depending on the circumstances under which their departure occurred and the extent of their commitment to staying away from home.

Floaters

Those who leave home to release tensions caused by the home-school milieu are called floaters. They have no intention of staying away from home and leave only "until things cool off." A call to parents or a little prodding from just about anyone is enough to encourage the floaters to return home. However, if there is no encouragement to return home and if they find shelter along with someone to teach them how to exist on the streets, floaters may become full-fledged runaways.

Runaways

The difference between floaters and runaways is in the length of time they stay away from home. While floaters stay away for only a few days, runaways will be away from home for weeks or even months. The reasons for leaving vary. Unlike Homer, English found that the initial homeleaving was more a case of running *from* something than *to* something. One common reason was to get out of a destructive family situation. Another, more complex reason was to call attention to the problems that existed at home. One runaway girl explained:

> "My old man's got a girlfriend and my mother refuses to believe it. Instead she's starting to hit the bottle real hard and all kinds of bad stuff is coming down so I split.
>
> "I don't want to go back unless things are going to get better. Like, I figured if I split they might see how bad things are. . . . I think I better stay away for a few days so that they really get worried—that way they may be ready to talk." [English, 1973:23]

The girl did not want attention for herself but left home so that her parents would realize the state the family was in. She hoped her absence would bring her parents to the realization that they should try to resolve family problems.

A third reason juveniles leave home is the presence of a difficult and unsharable problem (cf. Cressey, 1971). They believe that if their problem became known others would be hurt as well as themselves. The following interview by English (1973:23–24) with a fifteen-year-old boy and his fourteen-year-old girlfriend illustrates one kind of secret unsharable problem:

> ERIC: Hey, can we talk to you? Like we are really hung up.
> ENGLISH: Sure, what's wrong?
> ERIC: Like me and Mary have been on the run for a couple of months.
> ENGLISH: Yeah, I knew that and I've wondered how you been makin' it.
> ERIC: Well, that's our problem 'cause Mary's knocked up and that's why we split in the first place.
> ENGLISH: How far is she?

ERIC: A little over four months.

ENGLISH: Well, that's a little late for an abortion. Is that what you want to do?

ERIC: Well, man, it's a little more complicated than that. Like someone told us that if she did some speed she would drop the kid.

ENGLISH: So you tried some speed. What happened?

MARY: I ran some speed a few times and I think I got hepatitis.

ENGLISH: Have you seen a doctor?

ERIC: Not yet, and that's not all. You see when we first hit town we didn't know anyone and didn't have a place to crash so we stayed with Tim and those dudes for a while.

ENGLISH: So what happened?

ERIC: Well, they threatened to throw us out unless Mary put out for them all and well, like we were real up tight and it was really cold out and well, she screwed for them a couple of times.

ENGLISH: That's pretty bad.

ERIC: I know, but now it looks like Mary has the syph.

Not only did these young people feel that they had no one they could trust for help in the adult world, but when they sought help on the streets, they were hurt and exploited. It was learned later that Mary did have syphilis, and she eventually aborted the baby and was placed in a detention home. Had the couple turned to the adult authorities in the beginning, Mary would probably have been sent to a detention home anyway and judged to be delinquent. Had the juvenile authorities provided some real help, it would have been unnecessary for Mary and Eric to resort to the course of action they took. Thus, in a very real sense, because of the structure of the juvenile justice apparatus, they were left with running away as the only solution for their problem.

Splitters

The splitters, a third type of runaway, are very similar to the pleasure-seekers described by Homer. Having run away from home and returned, the runaway juvenile acquires a new status. The youth's peers see the runaway as a "bad boy" or "bad girl," and depending on the milieu, this is a high- or a low-status ranking. Additionally, the parents may begin asking themselves, "What did we do wrong?" and the runaway will be made to feel significantly more important than before. Moreover, a juvenile probation officer will fuss over the youngster in an attempt to find out why he or she ran away from home. In short, much is made of the returning runaway.

However, as is true in all homecomings, the fanfare soon dies down, although by the time it does, the runaway has firmly established a new self-conception as an adventurer. He begins to find home and school boring as compared with his exciting and independent life among his friends on the streets. As things "get old" at home, the appeal of the adventures on the run lures the youth away from home again and he packs up and leaves.

Returning to the streets, the runaway is greeted by his "old friends," and this time the splitter is street-wise. The initial trauma of being alone away from home is not present, and soon the splitter is back in the swing of things. As the street life "gets old," the youth again returns home to relax and recuperate until that "gets old," when he returns to the streets. This cycle represents a continual search for something new and exciting. By alternating between home and the streets, youths attempt to keep their life fresh until they are prepared to leave both home and the streets as they enter adulthood.

Hard-Road Freaks

The final type of runaway has left home for good, having rejected the straight world for life in the streets. Hard-road freaks are older, generally between seventeen and twenty, and many would not be considered juveniles. They make up the stable (if that word can be used) core of the transient young. Being completely independent, they make a living by various legal and illegal means. They generally have at least one legitimate skill, such as carpentry or painting, and also have extensive hustling experience. They have the highest status among the transient youth population, and the younger runaways and splitters look to them for guidance. In turn, the hard-road freaks exploit their young admirers in the guise of providing street experience.

A high percentage of hard-road freaks are from working-class backgrounds and, unlike middle-class runaways, do not rely on verbal skills but instead tend to aggressive physical action. This feature gives them a considerable edge over the middle-class runaway, for they are likely to use physical aggressiveness to exploit and intimidate middle-class juveniles.

It is unlikely that any single floater will become a hard-road freak. In fact, relatively few floaters become runaways. Similarly, few runaways become splitters, and even fewer splitters become hard-road freaks. What is important for our analysis is the existence of these various delinquent patterns and the possibility that juveniles will be exposed to them. The extent to which the juvenile's home and school milieu lacks opportunities for youthful fulfillment provides a structural "push" into the street life of the runaway. Additionally, the lack of support by the juvenile justice structure and process limits the avenues available to youth for resolving their problems legitimately. The "pull" is provided by the adventure of life on the run; while the "fun" may be greatly exaggerated, it is seen as better than life at home and in school. Furthermore, the returning runaway is labeled as somehow deviant, whether or not this is a hero's label. This serves to separate the juvenile from the standard life style expected of youth. Thus the process intended to correct runaways operates to push them out and away from the desired path.

YOU'RE TOO YOUNG: WAITING TO BE AN ADULT

The adult American male and female as portrayed in the mass media are fantasies. Men are pictured on television and in magazine advertisements as hard-drinking, virile, athletic adventurers. Women are economy-minded housewives, sexual Amazons, or examples of the "new woman," liberated and independent. Young men and women may see these stereotypes for what they are—caricatures dreamed up by advertising copywriters. Nevertheless, the images are generally more appealing than the more mundane picture of the organization man and woman, the factory worker, or the unfulfilled housewife in the workaday world. But whatever image of an adult self the young take on, they are expected to sit and wait on the sidelines until they become of age. Very little practical experience is provided in either the forbidden aspects of adult life, such as sex and drinking, or in the routine activities of everyday life. Those who experiment with sex, drinking, or the "real" world (e.g., the world of experience) are labeled delinquent; yet they are expected somehow to know about adult activities and responsibilities when they reach the age of eighteen, twenty-one, or whenever their particular state happens to say adulthood begins. In this sense, as Paul Goodman (1956) has implied, growing up in America is absurd.

Perhaps the greatest absurdity is the belief that the juvenile laws protect youth from the abuses of the adult court as well as from becoming involved in the evil excesses of adults. Until 1967 the adult courts afforded more protection of citizens' rights than the juvenile courts did. In that year, in the case *In re Gault*, it was brought out that juveniles were commonly denied the following rights: (1) Notice of charges, (2) Right to counsel, (3) Right to confrontation and cross-examination, (4) Privilege against self-incrimination, (5) Right to a transcript of the proceedings; and (6) Right to appellate review. In a sense, it was assumed that anyone brought before the juvenile court was guilty and that since the court existed to "help" and "protect" youth, nothing bad could come from anything the court did. Even the false conviction of an occasional youth would not cause harm since the juvenile justice system did not punish youths but only "helped" them.

Anyone who believes that juveniles are not familiar with sex and liquor because they are prohibited by law from being so is unaware of adolescent life styles. In self-report surveys of adolescents, Short and Nye (1958) found that more than half had tried liquor; in a similar survey twelve years later, Sanders (1970) found that about two-thirds had tried liquor. Likewise, sexual experimentation is widespread, and even the juvenile justice system, which expresses concern about rampant venereal disease, acknowledges that it has hardly been successful in preventing adolescent sexual activity.

What does the juvenile justice system hope to accomplish by trying vigorously to enforce the laws against juvenile-status offenses? The system's action does not "protect" the young's innocence for they are exposed to sex, drinking, and life on the road through legitimate channels, such as television. Moreover, parents maintain a baffling double standard in regard to these activities—especially to sex—that pushes daughters in one direction and sons in the opposite. As Chesney-Lind (1974:43) notes:

> The traditional American family exerts close control over its daughters to protect their virginity. A "good" girl is never sexual, although she must be sexually appealing, while a healthy boy must prove his masculinity by experimenting sexually.

Moreover, the juvenile court has served to lessen parents' control of children, although, ironically, a lack of parental control is the cause to which the court often attributes delinquency. If parents would rather have their children learn how to drink responsibly instead of sneaking out and endangering themselves by getting drunk, or if parents would rather have their daughters learn about birth control and sexual hygiene instead of sexual guilt and the fear of contracting venereal diseases, the juvenile court would be an anachronism. While officialdom carefully guards an outdated morality, many families have changed their attitudes toward childrearing. For these families, the court serves to undermine parental authority.

This is not to say that a "new morality" is sweeping the country or that the morality apparently held by the incumbents of the juvenile justice system is not shared by many parents. Rather, in a pluralistic society, where there is no consensus on what constitutes a "proper" upbringing, the juvenile justice system has taken it upon itself to be the "parents" (if not the Big Brother) of society's young. As a result, many young people are held accountable for behavior that is not offensive to their parents, their peers, or even the community at large. By criminalizing such behavior, the juvenile justice system is responsible for creating delinquency where there is no deviance.

CONCLUSION

In trying to answer the question of why juveniles engage in various juvenile-status offenses, we have seen that running away, sexual experiences, and experimentation with assorted vices are peer-supported adventures among the young and that they are supported by the larger culture as adult activities. "Acting like an adult" often involves delinquent behavior. Yet the juvenile courts judge these activities, which are not considered bad by the population at large, to be evidence of delinquency. To explain why juvenile-status offenders make up a good part of the delinquent population, then, we must point to the juvenile justice process. Without the strenuous efforts of the juvenile justice system to declare runaways, youthful drinkers, and girls who experiment with sex to be delinquent, there would be far less delinquency. Finally, since the detention facilities provided by the juvenile justice system throw together juvenile-status offenders with "hard-core" delinquents such as burglars, rapists, and robbers and thereby provide the associations and opportunities for learning some of the skills and attitudes necessary for more serious delinquency, the juvenile justice structure encourages and makes possible the very alternatives it is designed to prevent.

4 Ripoff
Juvenile Property Crimes

Property crimes, including various forms of larceny, burglary, and vandalism, are committed by juveniles more frequently than by adults. In 1965 the eleven- to seventeen-year-old age group, representing 13.2 percent of the American population, accounted for over 50 percent of the arrests for property offenses involving burglary, larceny, or motor vehicle theft (President's Commission, 1967:56). More than 60 percent of the motor vehicle thefts were committed by juveniles, and even though many cars are stolen merely for joy rides and then abandoned, felony theft is involved. The fact that a relatively small proportion of the population is held responsible for so large a percentage of property crimes suggests that these crimes have a juvenile "character." Even though property crimes are committed by adults as well, we need to understand why juveniles are far more likely than adults to engage in these crimes.

One characteristic of juvenile property offenses is that they tend to be committed by groups (Short, 1968:79). The group tradition among juveniles has frequently been noted. Clifford Shaw (1933) pointed out several examples in his pioneering works on delinquency. More recently, Irving Spergel (1964) found that juveniles belonging to "theft subcultures" typically engage in group stealing. Moreover, he found that groups of juveniles who engage in property crimes are likely to "specialize" in stealing as opposed to drug use or fighting, and that where there are strong subcultures centered around stealing, proportionately more larceny takes place than where such subcultures do not exist.

Furthermore, as we noted in chapter 2, juvenile thievery is not always utilitarian in terms of the value of the property taken but is often seen as an occasion for juveniles to show one another that they have the courage and composure to steal or as a kick, undertaken for the thrill of flirting with danger. Adults, on the other hand, are more likely to steal property for money. However, stealing for fun by juveniles is often regarded in retrospect as training for those who later become adult thieves and burglars. This pattern was explained by an older thief as follows:

> Pete said that when he was a kid the guys used to go around from car to car and see if they could break into glove compartments. They did this mainly to see who was the best "stealer." Pete recalled that he was "busted" when he was fifteen years old for stealing hubcaps. Actually, he didn't get much money out of it. Much of it was a matter of who could steal the most hubcaps. Richie said that you couldn't help learning while you were doing these things . . . and when you got older you didn't rob for "kicks" but for money. That's what most of the guys who were in trouble did now. [Spergel, 1964: 51]

Thus, even though these juveniles did not steal for profit, the skills they developed in stealing for kicks could be and were utilized later in stealing for money.

Rosenberg and Silverstein (1969) report that most youths begin tapering off their group stealing activities at around sixteen years old. Group support for shoplifting and other forms of stealing lessens, and instead of being defined as a kick or a demonstration of character, these pursuits come to be seen as "kid stuff." The same group pressures that lead juveniles to go along with stealing also lead them away from stealing a few years later.

The exception to this pattern is the alienated hard-drug addict who operates on his own (Rosenberg and Silverstein, 1969:103). He steals only to supply his drug habit, and he gets his kick from the use of heroin, not from the stealing. Drug addicts will steal anything they think will bring them money to buy drugs, and they will steal from anyone. It is not at all unusual for youthful addicts to steal from their parents, for example, although most other juvenile thieves and burglars have some limits, perhaps parents or blind people or church collection boxes.

BOOSTING

Although it is probably inaccurate to say that all juveniles steal, it is true that a good deal of stealing is committed by juveniles. Juveniles themselves have been heard to say that "everyone" steals, meaning "everyone our age" or "everyone in our group" (Rosenberg and Silverstein, 1969:97). In the Short and Nye (1958) study, more than 60 percent of the high school boys and more than 90 percent of the training school boys admitted to having taken things that didn't belong to them. Similarly, more than 30 percent of the high school girls and almost 80 percent of the training school girls reported that they had stolen something. Most of these confessions probably involved some form of shoplifting—stealing from stores during regular operating hours.

In considering shoplifting, we must first consider the opportunity structure for taking things from stores—how simple it is, or appears to be, for someone to take something without paying for it. Most stores display merchandise so that shoppers can pick it up and examine it or take it to a cashier and pay for it. Providing easy access to the merchandise for shoppers minimizes the number of clerks necessary and permits the shoppers to get a close look at the articles they are considering purchasing. But this arrangement not only allows legitimate shoppers access to merchandise; it also provides shoplifters with access. Small items can be placed in a pocket or purse or held in the hand, concealed from the clerks. It is very simple to pick up a lipstick case, for example, and leave the store without paying for it. In large stores this appears to be even easier, for there are more places in the store where one can carry on illicit activities unobserved.

At the same time that shoplifters are aware of the opportunities for shoplifting, so too are store owners and managers. In small stores, clerks are alerted to watch for shoplifters, and in larger establishments, special security teams are hired to apprehend them. However, the stores must be careful in accusing people of shoplifting, for they don't want to offend their customers or be charged with false arrest. Therefore, they usually wait until the suspected shoplifter is outside the store before stopping him or her. (It is commonly believed that a person must leave a store with the merchandise in order to be stopped, but that requirement exists in only a few states.) Even if the merchandise is in the subject's possession, he or she may claim that failure to pay for it was a case of forgetfulness. Often a store manager will accept such an account, especially from a regular customer.

With juveniles, on the other hand, store owners are less concerned about the possibility of giving offense to a customer, because juveniles don't spend much money anyway, and the status of juveniles is such that they are often offended by adults. If there is the slightest suspicion of juvenile involvement in shoplifting, store detectives will take the subject "to the office." Even if the youth is innocent, it is less consequential to stop him or her than to pick up an innocent adult (Robin, 1963:171). Juveniles can almost always be accused of "disorderly conduct" or some similar disturbance; if an adult is falsely accused, there is more likely to be a lawsuit or, at the very least, an offended adult shopper who may boycott the store.

In a study in Philadelphia, Gerald Robin (1963) found that the majority of those caught shoplifting were juveniles. In part this was because juveniles are more likely to be accused than adults, but this fact alone does not explain the overrepresentation of persons under eighteen among those apprehended for shoplifting.

Like other forms of juvenile stealing, shoplifting is a group activity. In 75.3 percent of the cases Robin studied, juveniles apprehended for shoplifting were in the company of other juveniles at the time. This compares with only 23.3 percent of the adult shoplifters caught in groups. Typically, juvenile shoplifters divide the labor, with one acting as the lifter and the other as the lookout or distractor (Cressey, 1972). However, it is questionable that this division of labor is employed as an efficiency measure; most juvenile shoplifters like to have someone along to "keep them company" and fortify their nerve. As one girl who reluctantly went along on shoplifting activities explained:

> I was always invited. I never went on my own. I didn't care for it. I never stole anything. I just used to be the lookout. I'm too nervous.

Or, more directly, one boy admitted:

> When I go stealing, I got to be with somebody because I get scared being by myself. [Rosenberg and Silverstein, 1969:104]

Thus, juveniles who shoplift in a group are able to "go along" with the others, and supply peer support for the activity.

Once apprehended for shoplifting, it is unlikely that a juvenile will be prosecuted, even if he is caught red-handed. Store detectives have three options in handling juveniles. They can (1) release them, (2) turn them over to the juvenile authorities for court action (i.e., arrest), or (3) turn them over to the juvenile authorities for remedial (i.e., unofficial) action (Robin, 1963:167). With adult shoplifters, the detectives can either release them or have them arrested.

It would appear at first that juveniles have a marked advantage, since there is the option of informal handling by the juvenile authorities. For example, in one of the stores Robin studied, all juveniles apprehended for shoplifting were turned over to the juvenile authorities, and in only 5.5 percent of the cases did the official recommend prosecution. Of the adults who were apprehended, 25.8 percent were turned over to the police for arrest. But *all* of the juveniles received some kind of official record of law violation, even though only a small percentage were prosecuted; by contrast, only about a quarter of all adult shoplifters apprehended received a criminal record. The fact that most juveniles were not prosecuted does not mean that they received no record, for it has been found that some official record is made for all juvenile arrests, whether or not there is any prosecution (Sanders, 1974). Thus, we find that juveniles apprehended for breaking the law are four times more likely than adults to have an official record.

It should be noted here that unlike juvenile-status offenses, in which no victim is involved, shoplifting does have a "victim"— the store detective or manager who reports the crime. Many stores have a policy of leniency toward first-time offenders, reflecting the management's desire not to be seen as harsh. Since store owners generally believe that handing juvenile offenders over to the juvenile authorities is an "informal" process that may not involve official sanctions or prosecution, they think this is being lenient. They do not understand the impact of a juvenile record, whether "informal" or "formal." This is not to criticize store owners or even to say that juvenile shoplifters should not have records, but merely to point out that if store owners desire leniency for juvenile shoplifters, they should not expect to achieve it through the juvenile justice system. A previous record of shoplifting will be used in interpreting a juvenile's subsequent behavior even if that behavior has nothing to do with shoplifting. For example, suppose a boy is found to be drinking beer with some friends and is picked up. If he has a record of shoplifting, his biography will be interpreted as that of a delinquent. The record, no matter how informal, will be used to document his "delinquent" character (Cicourel, 1968; Garfinkel, 1967:77–79). In deciding how to handle cases involving juveniles, judges and probation officers are more likely to be harsh with youths who have records than with those who do not. Thus, any official handling of shoplifting, whether or not prosecution is involved, leads to some form of sanctioning.

The implications of shoplifting, then, go far beyond a single occasion when a juvenile is caught and "warned." It is known by those in the juvenile justice system and by security people in department stores that a delinquent record has detrimental consequences. Otherwise the system would not go to such great lengths to keep the records secret from the public, nor would store managers insist on lenient treatment of juvenile shoplifters. However, *within* the juvenile justice system, a juvenile's record is no more secret than the time of day. Even though the record-keeping activities are designed to protect them, the juveniles are not protected from the "protectors."

The dilemma for the juvenile justice authorities is to keep track of shoplifters but at the same time not to criminalize juveniles for a single offense. To meet this goal they issue a warning for a first offense. However, they must keep some record of those whom they have warned so that if the same juvenile is apprehended on subsequent occasions, his or her recidivism will be known to them. If no records were kept, they would have no way of differentiating first-time offenders and recidivists. Nevertheless, the records do serve as "criminalizing" devices since the juvenile's moral character is evaluated in terms of his record. No matter how lenient the juvenile authorities are with first-time offenders, the record remains as a stigma.

An important feature of shoplifting is the number of females who are caught. Robin (1963:167) found that 60 percent of the suspected shoplifters he studied were women. The large number of women suspects may be due in part to the fact that a significant number of store detectives are women, who are more likely to watch women than men and more likely to stop females, especially juveniles, than males. However, independent of arrest patterns, a good many female juveniles are involved in shoplifting.

In a study of middle-class delinquency, Norman Weiner (1970) found not only that a large number of adolescent girls were involved in shoplifting but also that they were fairly sophisticated in their methods. They would choose a downtown department store rather than a suburban one because they believed that store detectives in the downtown stores are more likely to keep an eye on the lower-class juveniles who shop there than on well-dressed middle- and upper-middle-class youths. Likewise, they reasoned, the store detectives would be less likely to offend a middle-class youth than a lower-class one. Therefore, even if a detective suspected a middle-class youth of shoplifting, he would be unlikely to stop such a suspect.

The actual shoplifting activity also demonstrated some forethought and method. For example, one girl described by Weiner took along a stapler and a staple-remover as tools of the trade. She would buy something that would be bagged and stapled with the sales slip on the outside of the bag. Then she would take a number of dresses into the dressing room along with the bag of goods she had purchased. Inside the dressing room she would unstaple the bag, put one of the dresses inside, then restaple the bag and leave without paying for the dress. Thus, rather than being haphazard, shoplifting among middle-class adolescent girls is systematic and, if we can generalize from Weiner's findings, sanctioned by associates.

Shoplifting among middle-class youth does not appear to bring on pangs of guilt or self-condemnation. Instead they "neutralize" (Sykes and Matza, 1957) their delinquency by establishing and maintaining a vocabulary of motives (Hartung, 1965) that justifies their activities. Weiner [1970:216] explains how they viewed thier own shoplifting activities:

> Karen is not unusual. Her whole crowd steals. The same reasons are always heard. "I needed it; I only take from big stores." They only take what they "need," or, more precisely, what they claim they need. They never use the word "steal." It is always "get." They set up a vast web of rationalizations and excuses: "The large stores are impersonal and coldly efficient; they can stand the loss." This is merely an extension of the attitude that most people feel toward vending machines. To whom does one complain when a soda machine proffers a cup but no Coke? Thus, when a person gets back too much change from such a machine, he believes he is justified in keeping it. When these middle-class adolescents steal, they feel the same elation that most of us feel when we get something for nothing, especially if they think they have beaten the system.

The patterns of shoplifting and the vocabulary of motives rationalizing the illegal activity are available to adolescents whether they are lower class or middle class. Without the justifications for shoplifting, it is unlikely that there would be so much shoplifting (Sutherland and Cressey, 1974:75). Furthermore, this vocabulary enables us to account for the high incidence of female involvement in shoplifting, for "shopping" is a normal role performance for women, and shoplifting is typically couched in terms of the normal role of shopping.

To summarize, juvenile shoplifting is a group-oriented activity among both boys and girls. The official reaction to shoplifting, while ostensibly lenient, results in an official record more often for juveniles than for adults. Thus, the consequence for juveniles of being caught shoplifting is often to become involved in the criminal justice system of records.

JOY RIDING

More than half the cars stolen annually in the United States are taken by persons under the age of eighteen (Hughes, 1970:113). Most juvenile car thieves have no intention of keeping the cars or selling them (Schepses, 1961). The cars are not used as getaway vehicles, nor do juveniles typically belong to car theft rings. Instead, they take the cars for a "joy ride," and the thrill of riding in a stolen car serves as the end. The stolen cars are driven a few blocks and then abandoned. This is why the police are relatively successful in recovering stolen automobiles.

The laws pertaining to auto theft usually do not differentiate between "joy riding" and "grand theft auto." Stealing a car is a felony. However, juveniles are not subject to adult penalties, and most law enforcement agencies and the courts make de facto distinctions between "joy riding" and "auto theft" (Daudistel and Sanders, 1974). Nevertheless, taking someone's automobile without permission is considered a serious offense (Wattenberg and Balistrieri, 1952) and, unlike a number of juvenile-status offenses and shoplifting, it is not something "everybody does."

Although adults also commit car theft, juvenile car theft has certain "juvenile characteristics." Like a number of other forms of delinquency, it usually involves groups rather than individuals (Schepses, 1961). Further, as we have noted, juveniles take cars for the thrill of the joy ride whereas adults are more likely to steal cars for use in the commission of a crime (Conklin, 1972) or for the money (Cavan, 1962:145). When adults choose to steal cars in groups, it is in order to make the car theft more efficient by dividing the labor. One felon will act as lookout and the other will break into and start the car. Juveniles accompany one another in car thefts for the shared thrill of stealing the car and taking it for a joy ride.

Given these differences between juvenile and adult car theft, what we see are actually two different events, although the law (on the books at least) makes no distinction. Since the law forbids stealing cars by anyone, juvenile or adult, we are dealing in both cases with criminal activities. Nevertheless, there are enough qualitative differences in the ways in which the crimes are committed and the goals of the activity to warrant regarding the typical juvenile car theft as a phenomenon of juvenile crime. Those juveniles who steal cars to use in a holdup or for sale can be treated analytically as "acting like adults": conversely, adults who take cars for a joy ride are exhibiting "juvenile characteristics" in their crime. In this context we can see that "stealing cars" is an inappropriate classification by itself. We need to examine the occasion of a car theft in order to form an accurate picture of the event. Merely pointing out that stealing cars is against the law does not help us to understand delinquency.

Who are the juveniles who steal cars? The few studies that have been done find that juvenile car theft is generally a middle-class male activity (Gibbons, 1970:152). As compared with the general population of delinquents, the typical juvenile car thief is older, brighter, a better reader, from a higher socioeconomic status and a more secure home, and more likely to be white (Schepses, 1961). Wattenberg and Balistrieri (1952) found the same pattern in their study of juvenile car thieves shortly after World War II, and the persistence of this pattern, which is contrary to other forms of delinquency, needs to be examined.

Perhaps the best explanation of middle-class car theft is the car consciousness that developed in the suburban middle class. Youths in the suburbs are more likely to learn how to operate an automobile and to be aware of its value than are youthful urban dwellers, who can use public transportation or walk to the highly concentrated center of an urban setting. Since the suburban youths are also more likely to be well educated and white and to hold the other characteristics of youthful car thieves, it is not surprising that those juveniles who are arrested also hold these attributes. Conversely, urban youths, especially the poor, may not learn how to drive a car until they are older, if ever. It is true that these youths admire those who can afford big cars, and Harlem pimps are famous for their sleek, expensive automobiles, but the cars are merely status symbols, not practical modes of transportation in the congested city. The automobiles owned by the pimps are symbols of what their money can buy, and a pimp would never consider stealing a car, for this would be a sign of his failure as a pimp. Similarly, youths who are aware of automobiles as status symbols are concerned mainly with the money that can be used to buy such a symbol. If an automobile is stolen for the purpose of making money from the sale of the car or its parts, such a theft is a means of obtaining cash. However, since juvenile car theft typically consists of joy rides for kicks, it is not surprising that patterns of car theft are heavier in the middle-class suburbs than in the inner city ghetto, where stealing a car is a means to an end and not an end in itself.

In conclusion, automobile theft is generally committed by white middle-class youths in groups of two or more, largely for "kicks." Analytically, we might refer to juvenile car theft as "group action," using Goffman's (1967) specific meaning of "action," discussed in chapter 2. However, since the available studies of juvenile car theft have been based on police data of arrests and incarceration, it would be risky to suggest that the findings are conclusive. Further studies are necessary, especially for learning more about the "juvenile" character of car thefts, how youths become exposed to joy riding patterns, and why certain groups that make up the bulk of the identified delinquent population do not become exposed to these patterns to the same extent as relatively affluent youth. Since juveniles account for the overwhelming majority of car thefts, more research is necessary for a complete understanding of this aspect of delinquency.

TRASHING

Vandalism, an enormously expensive and widespread form of delinquency, has been stereotyped as largely the doing of bored middle-class youth. In the 1960s in California, high-school surfers were identified as responsible for vandalism around the beaches. Similarly, high school and college students during protest demonstrations or at wild parties have been accused of massive destruction on and off campus.

A number of theories citing "alienation" or "overpermissiveness" have been wheeled out to explain the rash of vandalism. These theories reflect a reaction to the sensationalism of popular journalistic accounts rather than any systematic examination of vandalism. One case of "vandalism" that was quickly explained will serve to caution students of juvenile delinquency against hasty conclusions and at the same time exemplify an activity that is typically included under the general category of "vandalism."

Some years ago in a West Coast city, a number of schools were broken into. The school offices were ransacked, set afire, and generally vandalized. Reporters covering the story decided to locate some experts on this kind of behavior and question them about the cause. Several explanations were proffered, the most popular being that youth were reacting to the impersonality and aloofness of the educational system, which had failed to respond to their identities and needs. The newspapers carried these stories along with the experts' collective and individual explanations of why the schools were being vandalized. Eventually the culprit was caught. He was not a juvenile and in fact was not a vandal but a burglar. He stole typewriters, adding machines, and other office equipment, and to make it look as though the theft was the work of juvenile vandals, tore up the offices before he left.* The moral of this story, of course, is that one should move cautiously before making pronouncements.

Vandalism can be defined as the destruction of property, and it is usually treated by the police as an instance of malicious mischief (Martin, 1961). This definition covers activities ranging from environmental pollution to carving one's initials on park benches. Strip mining in West Virginia and Montana probably causes greater and more permanent damage than all of the juvenile vandalism in the country combined, but it is unlikely that the mining companies will be accused of malicious mischief. Likewise, it is unlikely that we would consider the colonists who threw British tea into Boston Bay to be vandals, even though they intentionally destroyed someone else's property. Similarly, the thousands of tourists who visit national monuments and take chips and pieces as souvenirs wreak havoc in the same way as do vandals who intentionally disfigure a schoolroom.

In examining juvenile vandalism, it is necessary to limit our discussion to those types of activity that the courts view as malicious mischief, for delinquency is always tied to legal definitions and actions. Admittedly, what the police see as malicious mischief is not a well-rounded picture of actual vandalism according to our definition, but it serves to illustrate some aspects of this type of delinquency.

Residual Vandalism

When vandalism is the result of some criminal activity, the "residue" is property destruction, known as *residual vandalism.* For example, if a house is torn apart so that the copper wiring can be taken out and sold, the damage to the house is residual vandalism. The economic payoff, rather than the de-

---

*I am grateful to Donald R. Cressey for this example.

struction, is the objective of the act. John Martin (1961), who refers to this activity as "predatory vandalism," points out the utilitarian nature of the activity, whereas most theorists assume that vandalism is nonutilitarian in nature (cf. Cohen, 1955). Residual vandalism is a consequence of another crime, which is itself utilitarian in the conventional sense.

A number of types of residual vandalism are typically committed by juveniles. Old houses contain much material that can be sold to junk dealers—for example, lead from pipes, copper wiring, and other fixtures. The money this material yields can be worth the effort to remove it, but the damage caused to the structure is extensive and expensive. For example, Thrasher (1936:150) reports that two boys got three dollars from a junk dealer for some lead pipe they tore out of a house, but they did two hundred dollars' worth of damage to the house. Rubinstein (1973) says that in Philadelphia abandoned houses are commonly vandalized by young boys who tear out anything they think they can sell, but the police rarely consider this vandalism serious enough to write a report about, even if the house is not intended for demolition. Residents of neighborhoods where this kind of vandalism is common report it, usually as burglary, but since they know that the police rarely do anything about vandalism reports, they attempt to keep houses occupied until new residents move in, for once a house is believed to be unoccupied, the kids destroy it.

Residual vandalism is also committed on cars by juveniles in search of parts they can sell. This may be done on an "orders taken" basis or simply in terms of opportunity. One juvenile who stole car parts explained how he took specific orders:

> You go around and hear them talking that they need a wheel, they need a battery, and they only got so much money to give you. So you take a guy aside and tell him you could get it. If you don't know the guy you tell him, "Give me the dough, and I'll bring you the wheel." You keep the dough and don't bring him no wheel. . . . If I know you and you need a wheel, you tell me the size and stuff, I go around walking normal like, and I look at all the wheels and I figure out which one you need. Then I go

get the rest of the guys, and they haul up the car while I pick up the wheel, and we take that one wheel. [Rosenberg and Silverstein, 1969:100]

Juveniles also take car parts for use on their own cars or for some other purpose of their own. Car radio antennae, for example, are often broken off for use as weapons in gang fights or for making more sophisticated weapons. In describing how to make a zip gun, one boy explained:

Ya get a car antenna and a piece of wood and a can opener. Ya cut out a piece of wood in the design of a gun. Then ya drill a hole [lengthwise] right through the middle on the top and stick ya antenna in there and then ya take ya can opener and take the top off—what ya turn with—then ya file a point on it. Then ya have a hole in the gun and ya stick the can opener in it. Then ya tie rubber bands on it and pull it back ta fire ya gun.

When asked why the boys never considered buying an antenna he explained:

Why should ya buy one when they're out on the street to take? They cost a coupla dollars. [Martin, 1961:51]

Parking meters, vending machines, public telephones, and any other device that yields money when destroyed are also targets of residual vandalism. For example, store windows are broken not merely for the fun of it but to permit "smash-and-grab" thefts by juveniles and others. A bottle of liquor, a piece of jewelry or clothing, or anything else displayed through a window, not the window itself, accounts for the shattered glass.

It appears, then, that residual vandalism, is "done for the money," since the vandalism is a means and not an end. However, the correct question to ask in studying this type of vandalism is, Why did the culprit choose this particular means? Residual vandalism is certainly not a "nonutilitarian" reaction, as Cohen (1955) would have us believe, but instead involves learning an available pattern of delinquent behavior. In his study of vandalism, Martin (1961:48) found that residual vandalism was a form of delinquent activity that was passed on as a community tradition. Referred to as "junking," the vandalism was seen to be merely one of many forms of delinquent activity.

It was learned in association with other delinquents, and it was usually committed with other delinquents.

We can account for the patterns of residual vandalism in terms of differential association. For example, consider the formula for making a zip gun. The formula is relatively complex, and it is unlikely that anyone who had not learned that technique of making a zip gun would consider using a car antenna for doing so. In a similar way, the boys learned that it was "stupid" to pay money for a car antenna. It was best to rip it off someone's car. In other words, residual vandalism is a delinquent technique that is learned as anything else is learned.

Vandalism for Kicks

A second form of vandalism identified in the studies of juvenile property destruction has been labeled "wanton vandalism" (Martin, 1961), but we will refer to it as "vandalism for kicks" (Madison, 1970) because, from the point of view of those who commit it, they were "just having fun." There is a wide range of activities that constitute this type of vandalism, from breaking windows to destroying whole towns. For example, a boy described some of his activities:

> We did all kinds of dirty tricks for fun. We'd see a sign, "Please keep the street clean," but we'd tear it down and say, "We don't feel like keeping it clean." One day we put a can of glue in the engine of a man's car. We would tear things down. That would make us laugh and feel good, to have so many jokes. [Martin, 1961:95]

Easter-week school vacations often result in large-scale destruction in such places as Fort Lauderdale, Florida, and Balboa, California. Once a town called Zap, North Dakota, decided to try to attract vacationing students; by the end of the first night the National Guard had to be called in to save the town from total destruction. As it turned out, Zap lost more in property damage from the rampaging students than it received in revenues. Every store in town suffered serious damage (*Time*, 1969).

Numerous additional examples could be provided. Many readers can probably remember their own juvenile high jinks that resulted in some form of property damage. The problem, however, is to explain why this activity occurs. At first we might dismiss differential association as an explanation, since most people learn at an early age that property has value and since this form of vandalism is not a residue of some other activity; therefore we cannot explain it in terms of learning illegitimate means for obtaining learned and desired ends.

However, there are a number of actions people learn that might lead them to see property destruction as "fun." For example, consider Halloween. The kids in the neighborhood extort "treats" from people by the threat of pulling some "trick," like breaking a window or burning the house down. Of course the literal sense of "trick or treat" is probably employed only rarely, and the folks in the neighborhood who don't come up with something for their nocturnal visitors are rarely vandalized on Halloween. But the point is that we do have institutions that teach the fun of vandalism even while they are apparently designed to contain· it. Similarly, children hear stories from their parents of stunts they pulled in college, or the father returning from a convention in some distant city relates as a joke the petty vandalism he and his pals pulled (Madison, 1970).

Just about everyone learns that some fun can be had from vandalism. He also learns that a large part of the fun derives from the victim's reaction of helpless rage and frustration. The adventure of being chased by a vandalism victim is a thrill, a kick (Madison, 1970:38). In Goffman's (1967) term, it provides "action," something out of the mundane, routine life juveniles must lead at home and at school. In that this form of vandalism provides action, it fits into Goffman's framework of activities that provide adventure for the young.

Here we should note that pointing out the motives underlying any form of vandalism is not meant to provide a justification for the activity; nor does it matter in terms of the consequences whether the vandalism was caused by thieves or pranksters. What is important is that the acts resulting in vandalized property may differ from the point of view of the actor and also in terms of the judgment others make regarding whether these acts are delinquent or not. The qualitative results may be identical, but since the understandings of the acts as well as the ends of the acts are qualitatively dissimilar, we need to understand the various forms. In fact, we should treat different types of vandalism as distinct types of activity, just as we differentiate burglary and running away from home. The legal pronouncement may be the same for the record—"malicious mischief"— but the police, courts, and probation officers understand the culprits not merely in terms of the consequences but also in terms of what they consider to be the motives (Cicourel, 1968).

Malevolent Vandalism

Malevolent vandalism, also called "angry vandalism" (Madison, 1970) and "vindictive vandlism" (Martin, 1961), is activity in which property is destroyed out of malevolent motives on the part of the perpetrators. Schools, the most common target of juvenile vandalism, are often wrecked because of juveniles' distaste for these institutions. For example, Cavan (1962:147) describes the extent of damage committed by juvenile vandals on schools:

> Over the Memorial Day weekend, 1960, 25 Chicago schools received an estimated $50,000 worth of damage. Classrooms and offices were ransacked, a fire was set in the principal's office, windows were broken and ink was splashed on walls and used to make crude drawings or write obscene phrases; in one school a radio, phonograph and records were damaged. In some schools lunchroom iceboxes were broken into and food was thrown against walls and ceilings. Many schools not entered had windows broken from the outside.

A more troubling and equally prevalent form of malevolent vandalism expresses the deep-seated racial and ethnic divisions of the general population. Children pick up the stereotypes and hatreds of their parents. For example, synagogues are often the target of anti-Semitic acts of vandalism. During World War II, when the United States fought the Nazis and a popular distaste for anti-Semitism was widely expressed, the following episode occurred:

> Temple Ohabed Zedek, 954 ——— Avenue, is part of a two-family house. The rabbi and his family lived upstairs. Windows were broken in the synagogue on the nights of March 9, 10, 11 and 16, 1943. Vandalism stopped when a policeman was stationed outside. Five members of a gang were arrested. . . .
>
> [One of them,] K.D., eighteen, testified that he had broken windows "to try to get the Jews off the block." In 1941 he had broken into a store owned by Jews and stolen money, cigarettes and shoes. Caught and held delinquent, he blames Jews because the store was "Jewish." He said his gang believed Jews were no good in the war, they were "yellow." K.D. had transferred to high school from parochial school. He left school at sixteen. . . . [Tenenbaum:1947:104]

Like residual vandalism, vindictive vandalism is probably learned in association with others. However, instead of being a phenomenon of peer relationships, it is more likely to be passed on to youth by adults.

A Little at a Time: Erosive Vandalism

When vandalism is the result of a long procession of "little vandalisms," it is called "erosive vandalism" (Madison, 1970:25). The most common example can be seen on the nation's highways and public parks, which have been turned into junkyards by litterbugs whose collective carelessness results in damage that no single rampage could produce. However, even though erosive vandalism is certainly as destructive as any other type, it usually is not seen as an instance of malicious mischief or as a peculiarly juvenile activity.

One form of erosive vandalism that *is* peculiarly juvenile has emerged recently and is worth consideration. This is the use of aerosol spray paint to deface public and private property. In New York City it is difficult to find a subway car or station that is not liberally covered with spray paint. In addition to the names and street numbers of the perpetrators, such as "Taki

168," abstract designs are to be found as well. Gangs in various other parts of the country paint their gang names and slogans on walls and fences. For example, in the Watts district of Los Angeles one can find "Denver Lanes" and "Bounty Hunters" sprayed on fences, while in the Hyde Park area of Chicago one finds "Black P. Stone Nation" or "Stone Rules."

One group of youths in New York City who were especially active with spray paint redefined their activities as "art" and organized themselves into the "Graffiti Artists United." They were commissioned to paint a mural at one of New York City's public colleges in their unique style and received others' recognition for it. A spokesman for the graffiti artists explained:

> A lot of people don't like it, man, but like it or not, we've made the biggest art movement ever to hit New York City. [Shirey, 1972:49]

Apparently the state of New York sees the activity in the traditional frame of reference and has passed laws stipulating 1,000-dollar fines and a year in jail for convicted graffiti writers. The New York City Transit Authority estimates the costs of removing graffiti at 1.3 million dollars per year, and it is unlikely that it will ever considering selling a transit car as a work of art (Shirley, 1972:49).

Numerous explanations have been offered for this activity. Some writers have pointed out that the impersonal character of public buildings offends the spray paint vandals, who make these alien monoliths the targets of violence (Haskell and Yablonsky, 1974:274). When Columbia University in New York City instituted a program to open its facilities to neighborhood youth, the incidents of vandalism diminished as the youths came to define the university as part of their community. However, since many of the spray paint vandals decorate their own communities with their names and slogans, it is not necessarily true that a feeling of community reduces this form of vandalism. It may well be that the spray painting is regarded as a decoration or even as a celebration of their identity with the community. Or it could be a way of "claiming" territory or immortality. All we know for certain is that the introduction of aerosol spray paint was a prerequisite for the activity and that its use is widespread. The last feature suggests that this is not an idiosyncratic form of vandalism but one that is probably picked up by kids from one another. That is, like so many other forms of delinquency, spraying the walls with anything from obscenities to name and street number is learned in association with other spray paint vandals.

Characteristics of Vandals

In examining the characteristics of vandals, we are actually looking at a subset—namely, juveniles who are arrested for vandalism. Without data on all juvenile vandals, we cannot generalize with confidence. Martin (1961) found that juvenile vandals were typically male and that there was a higher proportion of males among the vandals than in the general delinquent population. Of the delinquent vandal population, 96.9 percent were male compared to 87.6 percent of the general delinquent population. Similarly, Martin found that the average age of delinquents was slightly higher than that of the vandal population. The average vandal was 13 years old; the average delinquent was 14.5 years old. There seemed to be no other differences between vandals and delinquents except for a slightly (but insignificantly) higher proportion of whites and Puerto Ricans in the vandal population and the fact that the vandals were generally from a lower socioeconomic stratum.

Martin (1961:28–71) identified three types of vandals: (1) disturbed, (2) essentially law-abiding, and (3) subcultural. The "disturbed" group included those who committed vandalism because of some psychological disturbance; the "essentially law-abiding" kids had somehow been talked into or had stumbled into the opportunity to commit vandalism; and the "subcultural" group committed vandalism as one of several delinquent activities. Two-thirds of the incarcerated juvenile vandals were part of this last group. Generally the vandalism committed by the subcultural group was the residual type, where the boys would steal something of value. It appears that this type of vandal comes into contact with patterns of vandalism and those who commit vandalism, thereby learning the patterns. For example, one boy explained that

> he and his brother were never "in trouble" before moving to Third Avenue, although there had been ample opportunity for breaking into places where they had previously lived. Frankie continued by saying, "But when ya live here ya see a lotta guys —big guys—doin' that and doin' this and then ya get the habit of it."

Since the subcultural vandal is the most common type, we can account for the bulk of vandalism through differential association. To the extent that a group employs vandalism as a group activity, we find varying incidence of property destruction.

CONCLUSION

In reviewing juvenile property crimes, we find that one feature stands out: they are typically committed by groups. Rarely do juveniles shoplift, steal cars, or commit vandalism alone. This points to shared techniques and normative patterns and suggests that, instead of being idiosyncratic delinquencies, stealing and vandalism are learned. Thus, we can account for this form of delinquency in terms of differential association theory.

Secondly, when we look at the intended ends of these activities, we find that a good deal of it is done "for fun" or kicks." Many of the shoplifters can afford to buy what they steal, and most juvenile car thieves have no intention of keeping the automobile. The excitement generated by the activity, not the money to be realized from the stolen or destroyed property, is the prime motivating element. The performance, moreover, is done not merely for themselves but also for the others who go along on these escapades. They find intrinsic excitement in breaking the law and also the opportunity to show others that they have the strength of character to carry it off.

The group interaction provides a generating force not available from any single member. Methods, justifications, challenges, and solidarity are all made available through group interaction; only the methods exist for the lone delinquent. The structure of the interaction makes delinquent property offenses possible and even, in some instances, obligatory in the same way that different interaction structures make other people feel obliged to mow their yards, wash their cars, and generally "keep up with the Joneses."

5 Dope
Drug Use by Juveniles

Discussions of drugs are rarely objective, and if we examine the literature on drugs and drug use, we will find enough contradictory findings to confuse even the most detached analyst. One problem, paradoxically, is that many researchers, especially medical researchers, have tried to be objective. Thus they describe the physiological effects of drugs in a way that bears little relation to the subjective experience of drug users. For example, one doctor has described the effects of marijuana use as follows:

> Physiologically, dilation of the pupils frequently occurs. . . . Presumably, increased secretion of adrenalin produces a rise and then a sudden fall in blood sugar, which calls forth an increased appetite, especially for sweets. Hunger is observed more often in the beginner than in the chronic user. . . . Another difference is the drowsiness that many mention toward the end of a marijuana session, whereas wakefulness is the rule with strong psychedelics. . . . It is when [the marijuana user] is under stress that difficulties in judgment and coordination may arise. [Cohen, 1969:52]

The physiological effects of using other drugs have similarly been described in a matter-of-fact fashion.

However, drug users characterize drug use quite differently; they speak of "getting high," "having a rush," or "getting a buzz on." In order to understand why juveniles take drugs, we must understand their subjective formulations of what it means to take drugs as well as the physiological effects. If we can understand the drug users' experience in addition to the medical facts, we will be less likely to accept the official mythology without question.

Polsky (1969:170) noted that the official position may be less than candid.

> Although the better-educated segment of the public is now aware of the myths for what they are—knows, for example, that the myriad college students who currently smoke marijuana are not thereby "led to" heroin addiction—this has in no wise lessened the efforts of the Federal Narcotics Bureau to perpetuate the myths and otherwise suppress the scientific evidence of marijuana's harmlessness. The Bureau's undiminished efforts have led a number of sociologists, including myself, to come round to the view long maintained in heroic isolation by Alfred Lindesmith of Indiana University (1947), that some Bureau officials are not dedicated truth-seekers having honest differences of opinion with the academic investigators but, on the contrary, dedicate themselves first and last to extending the power of the Federal Narcotics Bureau—to the extent of deliberate falsification of evidence.

Ironically, this mythology, some investigators believe, is responsible for some of the drug experimentation by juveniles. When a youth tries the "killer weed" and finds that he does *not* turn into a heroin addict, he is likely to dismiss as a lie *anything* he hears from the officials. A nineteen-year-old user of and dealer in narcotics explained:

> A person . . . can't have helped but hear that grass is, you know, when you're growing up that grass is, you know—marijuana and juvenile delinquency and all that. And . . . I think a person who tries it, having had all this knowledge about it before, suddenly he realizes something he has been told is all wrong, that this can't help but lead him to think the same way about other things. [Carey, 1968]

Our focus in this chapter is on how and why juveniles become involved with drugs. Where appropriate, we will discuss some of the consequences of drug use, both physical and social, but we will not take sides in the debate on drug use, either attempting to establish that it is inherently evil or—equally wrong and foolish—that it is harmless. Instead, we will delve into the subjective meanings of drugs and drug use, the understandings that juvenile drug users have of this activity, and the general milieu of drug use. In this way, we hope to add light rather than heat to this complex issue.

TRENDS IN DRUG USE BY JUVENILES

Officially, we can see that there has been an increase in juvenile drug use by examining the FBI's *Uniform Crime Reports* (1972). In 1960 there were only 1,583 drug arrests of urban youth aged eighteen years and under. In 1972 there were 79,449 arrests. Thus, in only twelve years, there was a 5,000-percent increase in drug-related juvenile arrests. The police did beef up their narcotics squads during this period, and in part this may account for the increase in the number of arrests, but data from self-report surveys also show massive increases in juvenile drug use. In a study in 1958, Short and Nye found that fewer than 2 percent of their high school subjects had used narcotics of any kind; in a study of suburban high school students in the Midwest twelve years later, this author found that about 20 percent had used some narcotic—a 1,000-percent increase (Sanders, 1970). Since the 1970 study was conducted in an area where there was generally less crime than in the urban centers, the overall increase in juvenile narcotic use was probably even greater. These figures show that something happened between the late 1950s and the early 1970s that led to a surge in juvenile narcotic use.

Lumping all drugs in a single category results in inaccurate medical and social understandings, and later we will examine patterns of drug use in terms of different drugs. However, because the surge in overall drug use occurred in a relatively short span of time and because drugs are legally grouped together, we can discuss the recent trend in illegal narcotic use by juveniles in general terms.

During the late fifties and early sixties, there was relatively little drug use. This period in the United States saw the short-lived but well-publicized "beat movement" (Polsky, 1969:144–82). The mass media churned out articles on the beats, usually emphasizing their bizarre and "exhibitionist" activities, but according to Polsky the beats preferred solitude to publicity. Many of them were runaway teenagers, but the majority were in their twenties and thirties. Most were middle class. The beat activities included drug use, but, significantly, the mass media generally did not pick up on this ubiquitous feature of beat life. Although some articles written about beats did note that drug use occurred, it was never widely publicized, either by the beats or by the press. According to Polsky, there were few beats who did not use some drug, usually marijuana but also heroin, peyote, hashish, and synthetic mescaline. However, unlike their spiritual decendants, the hippies, the beats kept their drug use as private as possible.

There are two significant consequences of the beats' furtive drug use. First, it did not draw the attention of the police, even though there were a few undercover agents spying on various beat groups. Secondly, imitators who adopted the outward appearance and expressed the generally known sentiments of the beats but were not full-fledged members of the beat movement did not know their drug-use patterns. These factors explain why the beat movement never initiated a widespread drug culture, as did the hippie movement later in the sixties.

The connection between the beats and the hippies is indirect, but they did to some extent share the same life style and world view. Unlike the beats, however, the hippies emerged at a time when youth was becoming increasingly vocal in its demands for change. The beats were antipolitical, whereas the hippies were at first apolitical and then, later, as yippies, were actively political. Both groups were anti-Establishment, rejecting the existing social institutions and life styles. The hippies, though, were far less secretive about their activities, including drug use. For example, Timothy Leary, a onetime university professor, publicly urged others to use drugs and drop out of the Establishment. His slogan, "Turn on, tune in, and drop out," had all the pithy eloquence of a television commercial, but it served to summarize much of the hippie philosophy and it was easily communicated. This was in 1965.

When the mass media began examining the hippie phenomenon, it was impossible for them to overlook the use of drugs. Hippies smoked marijuana openly, discussed psychedelic drugs in terms of their "magical" properties, and attacked the drug laws as unjust and stupid. The large number of nonhippies who sympathized with the hippie attitude toward drugs and who smoked marijuana with no ill effects made it difficult for the Federal Bureau of Narcotics to continue to portray every drug from marijuana to heroin as addictive and damaging, and discredited the old myths generated by the Bureau. At first, LSD was looked upon as another drug the Bureau had lied about, but after a number of disconcerting experiences the hippies developed their own sense of caution about its use. Similarly, Methedrine ("speed") was at first used widely but proved to be dangerous and even fatal to many users. Marijuana, however, remained a staple drug in the hippie scene, and its use became commonplace.

The hippie phenomenon did not spread independent of the larger social context. There was general disillusionment among the nation's youth, especially with the Vietnam war. A series of lies regarding the war and national policy in general were uncovered, and the credibility of the entire authority structure was crumbling on several fronts. It was discovered that marijuana was not the killer weed it had been described to be. Material wealth did not bring happiness as had been promised, and many other things youth had been told were found to be doubtful or simply untrue. The distrust of adults—"anyone over thirty"—became a rationale for experimentation with activities that the young had been warned not to try. The number of youths actively involved in the hippie life style was relatively small, but the ideas and images faithfully carried by the mass media provided rapid dissemination of their message. Part of that message was that drugs were a necessary component of being "hip."

For years television had been plugging various drugs as essential for the "good life." A "bad mother" was shown yelling at her children and husband; then she took a tablet or pill and was transformed into a loving, caring person. However, these were "good drugs," "wonder drugs," "miracle drugs," and the stuff sold on the streets was "dope," the road to perdition and damnation. According to the ads put out by the drug companies, wonder drugs made you happy, popular, and healthy; dope made you dependent, nauseous, and wicked. But since there had been a tendency for the lawmaking bodies to group drugs, it was only a small step to collapse the "good drug" category with the "bad drug" category. Indeed, some of the "good drugs," such as a number of legally produced barbiturates, found their way into "bad hands" and became part of the street market for drugs.

The impact of pharmaceutical advertising on the American view of drugs cannot be precisely determined, but clearly the sponsors, at least, believe that advertising does something to promote the use of products. Four of the five top spenders for television commercials are drug companies. One researcher points out:

> Drug advertising is not the *only* cause of drug abuse, but I do believe it is an important contributory cause. Advertising, in general, has a great deal of power to affect behavior. The over-the-counter drug industry is absolutely convinced of the ability of advertising to sell drugs. Advertising agencies argue that they can affect behavior. This means that advertising has social consequences, for if large numbers of people do something—whether it be purchasing a car or a cold remedy—that is a social consequence, with implications as far as social actions are concerned. [Berger, 1974:208]

Clearly drug advertising has only an indirect affect on drug abuse, but it provides a model for coping with problems of living. Berger (1974:209) has characterized this model as the "Pain-Pill-Pleasure" sequence. Some kind of discomfort is presented, a drug is taken, and the person is free of pain and feels pleasure. A specific drug is claimed to have the best results for a certain type of ill—whether nervous tension or a condition invented by the drug companies, such as "the blahs." However, there are so many drug companies saying the same thing and presenting the same model that not only do the specific drugs become glossed into drugs-in-general but the ills are meshed into problems-in-general. The result is the general belief that "drugs can make you happy."

Turning to illegal drugs, the same model can be applied. If aspirin can reduce pain and bring pleasure, so can marijuana, LSD, and heroin. Simon and Gagnon (1968) found that children whose parents had tolerant views regarding the ingestion of drugs as a general problem solver were more likely to use drugs, especially marijuana, than those whose parents relied less on drugs, whether "good or bad." Simply by substituting marijuana for, say, Vanquish, juveniles engage in the same patterns of drug taking for pleasure as do their parents. The widespread use of alcohol, which is, of course, a drug, also points to parental patterns picked up by children.

In view of the conditions that existed in the mid-sixties we can understand how the dam broke on juvenile drug abuse. First, there was a general movement of youth dissatisfied with the Establishment; secondly, there was a drug-oriented society fed by the mass media and drug companies; thirdly, there was an articulate group, the hippies, that proselytized the use of drugs. In the late fifties and early sixties, the televised drug commercials were well established, but there was no general youth movement, and the beats were not openly advocating the use of drugs. There was a clear differentiation between "good drugs" and "bad drugs" at that time. How did the definition of drug use come to change so that there was a massive increase in the use of drugs in the mid-sixties? To understand this phenomenon, we must appreciate how the hippies were able to redefine narcotic drugs.

We must remember that such a "redefinition" of what drugs are and what they do must be in terms of some established definition. The definition of drugs fostered by the Federal Bureau of Narcotics was a "redefinition" of what the general understanding of narcotics was before the Bureau's campaign to warn the public of the dangers of narcotics. Similarly, the drug companies not only define and redefine the therapeutic value of their products but formulate an ever-increasing number of situations in which their products may be properly used. In the context of their subculture, the hippies do nothing more or less than what these so-called legitimate definers do in the context of the media subculture.

Becker (1967) points out that the drug-using cultures are continually defining the effects of drugs for novices. If novice users are uncertain of how to evaluate their experiences, they are assured by other users that the effects must be properly interpreted for pleasure or that the unpleasantness is only transitory and a pleasant sensation will follow. There is a culturally shared definition of the situation of drug use in that the drug's effects come to be verbalized in patterned formulations. As Becker (1967:168) notes:

> They [experienced users] redefine the experience he [the novice] is having as desirable rather than frightening, as the end for which the drug is taken (Becker, 1963:66–72). What they tell him carries conviction, because he can see that it is not some idiosyncratic belief but is instead culturally shared. It is what "everyone" who uses the drug knows. In all these ways, experienced users prevent the episode from having lasting effects and reassure the novice that whatever he feels will come to a timely and harmless end.

This implies, of course, that the effects of drugs are not solely, or even predominantly, physiological. Lower-class blacks and Puerto Ricans used marijuana before engaging in gang fights, and if it was defined as making them better fighters, it probably had that effect. And some couples use marijuana before making love, expecting and perhaps experiencing similar improvements. However, it is doubtful that the subjective experiences of the gang youths and lovers were similar even though the marijuana may have had similar physiological effects on both groups. That is, the definition of the situation, which depends on expectations and the occasioned activities (i.e., what takes place in the context of a given occasion), is of more actual consequence than whatever physiological rearrangement may occur.

We have just seen how the sense of a drug experience is dependent on linguistic formulations. Similarly, there are verbalizations that induce juveniles to attempt drugs in the first place. As we pointed out, the slogans and jingles used by drug manufacturers are believed to be effective in attracting consumers to try one kind of drug or another. Those advertisements promote the use of so-called legitimate drugs and constitute a vocabulary of motives for drug use. We also noted that the official position against the use of illegal drugs provides slogans for *not* taking drugs. For example, in one television antidrug commercial the audience is asked, "Why do you think they call it dope?" This is part of a vocabulary of motives for not taking illegal drugs. What we must now determine is how the argument for *not* taking illegal drugs was replaced by the rationalizations *for* taking illegal drugs.

First we must understand the group context of drug use. Typically, juveniles with no drug-using associates do not take up drugs. One study found that 99 percent of those juveniles who took drugs had at least one friend who used drugs (Sanders, 1970:15). Experienced drug users provided the novice with a vocabulary of motives for trying the drugs and also, as noted above, with the definition of the situation.

The structure of the drug-using occasion also creates pressure on nonusers to try various drugs. For example, when marijuana is smoked, the smokers typically hand the cigarette from one person to the next. Each person in the group draws on the "joint" and passes it on. This pattern forces some amount of conformity, and nonusers are obliged to "at least try it." During these initial experiences, novices are provided with the necessary vocabulary of motives and learn how to use dope (Becker, 1963).

In explaining the belief system that fosters drug use, Sherri Cavan (1970) likened the "hippie ethic" and the "spirit of drug use" to Max Weber's classic formulation of the Protestant ethic and the spirit of capitalism. Like the early Calvinists, the hippies had a vision of life—a transcendental vision. Drugs, especially LSD and other psychedelics, helped them to realize this vision, and in this way drug use had a central place in their belief system and life style in the same way that work has a predominant position in the Protestant ethic and capitalist production.

The "pure" vision of the hippies, like the "pure" vision of the Protestants, is not a necessary condition for drug use, and the large numbers of drug users who imitated the actions of the hippies probably did not hold this "pure vision." The Protestant work ethic took on a life of its own. While it had its historic taproots in Calvinistic visions, it was subject to changes in interpretation and to the materialistic demands of capitalist production. Similarly, the imitators of the hippies learned enough to establish a vocabulary of motives allowing drug use, but instead of being immersed in the substance of the hippies' belief, they could only mouth the slogans.

However, the important thing about the hippie beliefs was that they constituted the beginning of a new type of drug-using culture in America, which at the time was acceptable to and received by a large number of youth from many areas of society. As the drug-use pattern grew, drug use became more and more a social activity, without the visionary ends sought by the hippies. Like the work ethic, which lingers in American society, residues of the hippie ethic linger in the drug-using groups. However, as the once pure Protestant vision of Calvin became diluted, the transcendental vision of the hippies survives as only a vague remnant of an articulate past.

"EVERYONE SMOKES POT"

We have noted that there was a notable jump in juvenile drug consumption in the early sixties. Most of this increase was due to marijuana use, although other drugs, especially LSD, also contributed. In a 1970 study, the author found that roughly 20 percent of a group of suburban Midwestern high school students had used marijuana at least once, but about 50 percent of the students in the same study said they had a *close* friend who had tried marijuana. When asked to estimate the percentage of the student body who used drugs, the students replied as shown in table 5.

Table 5: Student Estimates of Marijuana Use among Peers

Less than 5 percent	16 percent
Between 5 percent and 20 percent	41 percent
Between 20 percent and 50 percent	33 percent
Over 50 percent	10 percent

The modal estimate (between 5 and 20 percent) was an accurate guess of the amount of marijuana use, according to self-reports. However, 43 percent of the students estimated a good deal more marijuana use than was reported. This perception of the popularity of marijuana use strengthened the notion that a "drug culture" exists among the student population in general.

When we examine the groups of students involved in marijuana use, we find the reverse of what is normally found in studies of juvenile delinquency: those from the *highest* socioeconomic class are the most likely to use marijuana (table 6).

Table 6: Marijuana Use and Socioeconomic Status

SES*	Percent Who Had Tried Marijuana
Professional	43
Semiprofessional and Business	20
Clerical and Sales	11
Farmer	0†
Factory and Other Blue-collar Worker	18

*Socioeconomic status of student's father, or mother in father's absence.

†Only 3 cases out of 583 sample total; cannot be considered significant.

If a marijuana culture did exist, it was located predominantly in the upper socioeconomic strata and not, as is typical with other forms of delinquent behavior, in the lower classes (Schub, 1973; Blum, 1970). Since members of the same socioeconomic grouping share one another's company, those in the upper strata of the group studied are more likely to come into intimate contact with marijuana users than are those in other classes. We now need to examine the nature of the marijuana-smoking group and culture and to explain why relatively few juveniles from the higher social classes get in trouble with the police.

First of all, when we discuss a "culture" we imply that a distinctive way of life and world view exist. The extent to which a whole way of life revolves around the use of marijuana and other drugs points to a distinct culture, and the hippie way of life and beliefs, as described by Cavan (1970), would certainly stand as a distinct culture. However, if a group of students use marijuana while not significantly altering their other behaviors and beliefs from those of the dominant culture, we are discussing a partial culture or part-time culture. The beliefs and values that foster the use of marijuana may be the only vestiges of the full-blown hippie culture of the late 1960s. Marijuana use has been added onto otherwise normal juvenile activities for some users, while for others it is an ongoing part of life. For example, a college freshman explained his use of marijuana:

> I have been smoking in the evening a lot, but usually I am straight during the day. On the weekend, if it is sunny, it is really nice to smoke in the morning and just spend a completely stoned day.
>
> *So when you smoke dope* what happens, what does it do to you?*
> Well, it depends largely on the dope.
>
> *There's different kinds of dope? Different potencies?*
> Definitely, but more than different potencies, I have been getting into a thing lately where I think of dope as being wired dope or good dope.

---

*"Dope" in this context refers to marijuana, although the term is often used for all illegal drugs.

How is "good" different from "wired"?

Well, when I smoke, if I smoke a joint after dinner of supposedly good dope, ah, I get physically tight sometimes and I get speedy. And I am getting to the point where I can control that now by consciously saying, you know, relax, take it easy. But I still have a feeling, like I know that my heart speeds up when I smoke dope, period, but, ah, cause, like I have been lying in bed sometimes after I have smoked and I just feel my heart beating. So there is the wired thing and then there is good dope, which is, I can relax my body without a hassle and, ah, it is a head thing, you know?

No, tell me.

All right, with good dope I can either concentrate very heavily on one thing, such as playing guitar, and just be completely into the music; all my senses are listening and feeling the music. I find in a conversation I can be really in depth into one thing and just carry it, carry the conversation to its ultimate conclusion you know, or, ah, if not its ultimate conclusion, really, it's whatever happens to it, it just goes on and on, like I could take just one thing and continue about it. Or take a starter, talking about my school thing and getting into friends of mine, just getting completely off the thing, but not hassling about it. It's fun, things don't have to be connected. On the other hand I find, well, now I might be getting off the beaten track.

I am interested in knowing what you think the effects of smoking are, and you have been covering that. Can you think of anything else to say about that?

I get more divorced from that, ah, as I smoke more, ah, I can just sit and get into something I haven't gotten into before, like silence maybe, like something visual, like looking at a picture in a different way, ah, yeah. It is in a different way cause I am, my perception is changed, and I can talk fairly easily about music, like when I am playing guitar, the more loaded I get, I'll be more willing to try something completely experimental on the guitar, like if I am playing a lead, to hit a bunch of notes I don't know, you know, are going to come out in a specified pattern that I have played lots of times before. [Wallace, 1972: 17–18]

Some sense of "cultural" belonging can be inferred from this articulation of what smoking marijuana has to do with the speaker's life, and more might be inferred about the youth's world view. Whatever the inferences, it is clear that smoking marijuana is a significant part of his life.

As compared to this heavily involved young man, there are other juveniles who use marijuana instead of some other form of "high," such as beer or whiskey. It may be conceived of as a fad that has become popular among a certain set of youth (cf. Simmel, 1950). Such youth may employ the jargon and even affect some of the styles of the group that initiated the popularity of marijuana, whether it be the hippies or any other group, but since the use of marijuana is not a central feature of their life style, they cannot be considered to be a "drug culture." In the 1950s "hot rods" were the fad, and many of those who were part of the era but not "into" what might be called the "car culture" nonetheless paid attention to their automobiles in terms of certain aspects of the car culture. Similarly, when surfing was popular on the West Coast in the early sixties, many juveniles took it up, along with the language and general surfing style, but were never dominated by it in the same way a hard-core few were.

Compared to the college freshman quoted above, for whom marijuana use was a daily affair, there is a substantial group which is in no way an integral part of a "drug culture." Even though these youths use marijuana, they have only a "piece of the culture" around which drug use revolves. They may experiment with marijuana a few times or use it occasionally, but they do not smoke pot all the time. Only 25 percent of the college-aged smokers used marijuana more than once a week (Knocke, 1973:35), and only 22 percent of the high school students who smoked marijuana used it regularly (Sanders, 1970:13).

We can see from these data that juveniles who use marijuana need not adopt a "drug culture." The existence of a drug culture, along with beliefs, attitudes, and language revolving around drug use, appears to be a prerequisite for large-scale change in the patterns of use, but the total adoption of that culture is unnecessary for the use of marijuana. One can adopt a piece of the culture with no great alteration in other patterns.

That marijuana smoking or other drug use necessarily leads to a change in basic behavior patterns appears to be true only of youth who adopt the entire culture: when only the activity of marijuana smoking is adopted, a small part of the culture is integrated into otherwise normal juvenile activities.

We might compare the majority of marijuana smoking with the majority of liquor consumption. While the skid row inhabitant's life may revolve around the bottle, one need not adopt the entire life style of skid row (Spradley, 1970; Wiseman, 1970) to become either an alcoholic or a social drinker. Most drinking is situational; unless an occasion arises when alcohol is appropriate, most people do not drink. Similarly, among most juvenile marijuana users, the use of marijuana appears to be not ubiquitous or constant but situational—in preparation for a rock concert (Wallace, 1972), at a party, and on similar occasions when marijuana smoking is sanctioned. For those who are caught up in the drug culture, almost any time is appropriate, just as for skid row bottle gangs any time is appropriate for drinking. For the typical marijuana smoker, there are only a limited number of specified occasions on which marijuana is used.

The importance of the fact that most juveniles who smoke marijuana are not involved in a drug culture is that those who are "into" drugs and a way of life revolving around drugs are not likely to limit their drug use to marijuana. The available data indicate that there is a rapid falloff in the percentage of juvenile marijuana smokers who admit the use of stronger drugs. We infer that those who use all sorts of drugs are truly "into" drugs and a drug culture, and those who only smoke marijuana are not. It might be noted, further, that the erroneous belief that smoking marijuana leads to the use of other drugs is typical of the kind of distorted logic that so often characterizes officialdom. Getting into a drug culture may lead someone to use all kinds of drugs, and the first illegal drug used is likely to be marijuana. However, if one does go on to use other drugs, it is not because of some inherent property of marijuana that "leads" to the use of other drugs but because of involvement in a drug culture.

HIGHER AND HIGHER

The single drug most popularized by the hippie movement was LSD (lysergic acid diethylamide), commonly called acid. Regardless of its medical and pharmacological properties, LSD came to be defined by the hippies as having "mind-expanding" or "mind-blowing" properties. It served as an initiation into the hippie world. LSD was provided to the novice in a setting controlled by users. The music, lights, and other props used by the initiators were arranged to provide a specific definition of the drug experience, and herein lie the important social conditions that lead to the unique acid trip.

At the time of the initial acid trip, the novice is introduced not only to the physiological effects of the drug but also to the culture. Various backstage activities (cf. Goffman, 1959) are brought to the fore to be seen in the light of the altered perception brought on by the drug. The user may confuse the actions of the initiators with the effects of the drug, and he is unable to distinguish between what is happening and the drug's effects. If the user is unprepared and unaware of what to expect, he may react violently or with terror, or he may accept and adopt the activities and world view of drug users. The more the novice knows about what to expect, the better equipped he is to choose whether or not to try the drug and the accompanying experience. Like the backstage behavior of most groups, however, the activities on a drug trip are kept secret until the novice's acceptance of the action or his discretion is assured. A person who has self-administered LSD is hardly in a position to call the cops or anyone else for help. By accepting the activities and the culture, he becomes a co-conspirator; if he rejects them, he becomes an informed, but silent, outsider.

From the literature on drug use, it appears that many writers are unaware of the initiation ritual, but some have noted the significance of the social situation in which people are introduced to LSD. Simmons and Winograd (1966) noted that some initiates to the underlife of the drug scene are shocked by what these researchers describe as a "cultural" phenomenon. The initiate may be revolted or fascinated by the explosive confrontation with what he sees at first as an alien culture. If he has any idea of what to expect, he is more likely to accept it, but the uninformed may have what psychiatrists call a psychotic reaction. What is important, as Simmons and Winograd make clear, is that the physiological effect of the drug is not the only, or even the most significant, aspect of the acid trip. Further, the initiation to LSD is often an initiation into a world view.

As we pointed out in the general discussion of drugs and drug cultures, the language of a group provides a unique reality. The medical community has a language with which to discuss drugs, and the drug-using subcultures also have a language. The medical talk is no more objective or accurate than the talk employed by the drug users; it is merely another way of formulating a sense of what happens when people use drugs. In fact, if everyone talked about drugs the way medical experts do, it is unlikely that many people would take them. For example, Sidney Cohen (1969:14), a physician, describes the effects of LSD as follows:

> The single most notable physical sign of LSD action is dilated pupils which do not contract completely when illuminated. Nausea, more rarely vomiting, and chilliness and tremulousness are sometimes seen. Aside from a rare convulsion, the serious physical side effects are minimal.

If LSD users described the experience in this way to a nonuser, he would wonder what is appealing about an activity that produces dilated pupils, nausea, vomiting, and chilliness. However, LSD users speak about "insight," "mind expansion," and other effects attributed to the drug. This kind of talk provides an interpretive scheme for enjoyment and excitement, and the LSD user elaborates any LSD experience in terms of such schemes and talk (cf. Garfinkel, 1967).

Thus physicians and users have competing interpretive frameworks for LSD use, and each group believes its position is the more valid. As one LSD user explained:

> Just taking LSD doesn't insure that you get any insight out of it. There are a lot of people whom I have met who have taken LSD who are just as nutty as they can be. I have seen people blow

their minds from LSD. People whom I was very close to and living with. The experience of stepping out of the social structure is a very liberating experience, especially if the structure has been oppressive and has made them distrustful of their own inner nature or uncomfortable with their own inner nature. To step out of that is a pleasant experience. For some people getting out is an end in itself. That's all they are interested in doing. They keep stepping out, and stepping out, and stepping out.

Each time they do, they give up their personality, or ego, or whatever you want to call it. They see shedding their ego as a virtue because it feels good. They have set up a structureless personality for themselves. That leads them to become relatively passive people, who don't have the perimeters of a personality. They have what might be referred to as "blown minds."

They have to restructure themselves if they want to come out of this. Most of them convince themselves that there is nothing they can do. They don't believe in anything. I met a guy who had taken two hundred acid trips and he didn't believe anything. That's what he told me, but actually, what he did believe in was that there is nothing to believe in. Do you follow me? And that was something that he had imposed upon himself and then conditioned into himself.

Now he was on a closed circuit where there was nothing to believe in. "There is nothing to believe in." And he just keeps taking acid and believing in nothing. And he tends to be cynical and unhappy.

On the other hand, if you take acid with the proper preparation and in the proper setting, in order to go inward and with specific goals to accomplish, it's fantastically effective. It can assist you in making any changes that you want to make. If your body is not well, it can place you in harmony with your body, so that your body can heal itself. If you are locked in very heavy ego games you don't understand, you can step out of those games and look at them and see what's happening, and then step back into them and act in a different way.

What's your opinion of Dr. Sidney Cohen's opinion on hippie patterns of LSD use?

Cohen is on a Sidney Cohen trip. He is out to be *the* expert on LSD. He's going to be the Establishmentarian expert. No matter what happens or what is determined, he is able to channel it into the Establishment's viewpoint on LSD.

The mass society would like to hear that LSD is the answer to all their dreams, which it is. But there are a lot of people in political power who want people to keep coming to work every day at nine o'clock and stay there until six. Then they can go home and watch TV until they fall asleep. And then come back the next morning at nine and work there the whole day. They should also wear white shirts and neckties. If these people started taking acid, they wouldn't do that any more. LSD could liberate these people but they won't let it happen. Many professionals are rewarded by the Establishment with grants, professorships, and awards to say what they want to hear, that LSD is not good and it will kill you. LSD could liberate many more people than hippies, but the Establishment won't let it happen. [Yablonsky, 1968:255–57]*

As can be seen from this description, LSD users have a linguistic reality that differs from that of the medical experts. They do not describe the experience in terms of possible physiological damage. This is not to say that the hippies are "right" and the medical experts "wrong," or vice versa. Rather, each group is operating in terms of its own linguistic reality. It is something like a debate between a Chinese and an Italian, each speaking in his own language.

As the LSD advocate claims, the purpose of the drug use was to "get out of ego games," "find oneself," and the like. In general, there is support for these ends in the larger society. Thus, the values of the hippies have at least something in common with the larger culture. The *means* by which these ends are achieved are the point of difference. The Girl Scouts and the Army, for example, advertise that members have a chance to "find themselves" by joining the group; in a sense, the hippies are doing the same thing. They back up their claim by pointing out that the Establishment has failed to provide opportunities for self-discovery and that drug use is a much faster route than the conventional modes.

*From *The Hippie Trip* by Lewis Yablonsky, copyright © 1968 by Western Publishing Company, Inc., reprinted by permission of the publisher, The Bobbs-Merrill Company, Inc.

Other illegal drugs that became part of the drug scene also came to be interpreted in terms of the drug culture's linguistic format and interpretive schemes. Amphetamines, such as Methedrine, were ingested or injected for a "high" or "trip," and the influence of "speed" was discussed in terms of its special assumed properties. When certain devastating effects of amphetamine use came to light, the hippies developed negative linguistic terms to interpret the dangers (e.g., "bummer") and warn others ("speed kills"). This and other drugs that were found to produce physical deterioration came to be used less frequently (Haskell and Yablonsky, 1974:309–10).

The acknowledgment of the existence of a drug culture undermined the myth that drug use is "antisocial." While the call to "drop out" of society appeared to some as antisocial, it was actually an invitation to join another social group and partake in a different life style. In addition to a new language, initiates to drug use learned new types of relationships with one another and with the rest of society. Drug users had their own norms and sanctions. For example, it was a cardinal norm among drug users not to "fink" on their supplier or on fellow drug users. To say that such behavior is antisocial not only is inaccurate but it puts the focus of drug studies in the wrong place. If we recognize the very social nature of drug use, we are in a better position to come to terms with it and understand that causes juveniles to turn to drugs.

What followed the early drug movement was what we might call the "war of glosses." The antinarcotic forces put all illegal drugs in the same boat and claimed that all were dangerous or at least led to the use of dangerous drugs. On the other hand, members of the new drug-using culture developed glosses for "getting high" on almost anything, and it was not until later that they particularized their talk and actions concerning drug use. Research from the scientific community did little to confirm or refute the allegations regarding drug use. However, a dialogue of sorts did develop between those who preferred formal terminology in their talk about drugs and the hippies, who spoke their own language. In an effort to communicate with youthful drug users, some physicians began to explain drug-related problems in the terminology of the young. "Getting high" and "coming under the influence" mean pretty much the same thing even though the connotations are different. Being "strung out" is close to being "addicted." More importantly, some physicians honestly began to differentiate among types of illegal drugs and came to learn how to relate to someone on a "bad trip." Marijuana was less and less seen to be a "bad drug" that inevitably led to heroin use, and became something kids "experimented" with. One police department, which screened recruits with a lie detector test, was unable to find a single applicant who had not smoked marijuana; so it began asking potential recruits whether they had used marijuana in the previous six months.* After all, "a little pot" was not seen to be harmful.

The transformation in the talk about drugs, especially marijuana, led to a reconsideration of what was delinquent. Since for the police and others the term "getting high" did not carry the same connotations as "killer weed," kids who used marijuana were not seen to be necessarily hard-core delinquents. This is not to say that the police did not arrest them for breaking the law, but, for the most part, the police did not believe that a juvenile who "just smoked a little pot" was necessarily bad. As one juvenile detective put it, "Yeah, sure she smokes grass, but she's a good kid" (Sanders, 1974). Thus, as the drug-culture language permeated society, social understandings of drug use changed, and as that happened, the conception of delinquency changed as well.

JUVENILE JUNKIES

Many heroin users, or junkies, say that they "began" with marijuana and went on to the heavier drugs, eventually becoming hooked on heroin. However, as we have noted earlier, it is inaccurate to say that marijuana use necessarily leads to the use of heroin. First of all, most marijuana users do not go on to

*This practice was related to me by a member of the department, in the southeastern United States. The officer and the police department will remain anonymous for obvious reasons.

heroin or, in fact, any other drug (Sanders, 1970). Conversely, although almost all heroin users did use marijuana before starting with heroin, they also did a lot of other things before using heroin, such as drink alcohol. However, most drinkers do not go on to use marijuana (or to become alcoholics); in the same way, most marijuana smokers do not go on to heroin.

Heroin use is a serious problem because it may be physically addictive, as may alcohol use. Once a person starts using heroin, he is likely, but not certain, to become physically dependent on the drug and the life surrounding its use. If we can identify the social situation in which one begins to use heroin, we can account for the initial cause of heroin use. Once started, the heroin user is pulled along not only by his physical dependency on the drug but also by the life style that goes along with it.

To see how juveniles begin taking heroin, consider the following two cases (*Time*:1970):

> *Sheera is 14, red-haired and wholesome-looking, the teenage girl next door. Her father manages a restaurant in New York City; her mother works in the records department of a city hospital.*
>
> I didn't start using heroin until I was 13. I guess I started using drugs to be like everyone else. There were older kids that I looked up to, but there were kids my age, they were also using drugs. I wanted to try it too. I messed around with pills and pot. Then I went to Israel for a summer and came back, and all my friends were on heroin. I snorted [ingested through the nose] a couple of times, skinned [injected in the skin] a lot, and after that I mained [injected in vein] it. I was sent to a school for emotionally disturbed children. Getting drugs there was easier for me than on the streets. Except for heroin. There wasn't much of that.
>
> I don't know if I would have been accepted by my friends if I hadn't used drugs. My feelings are that I wouldn't have been. I wanted to be like them. They were all using drugs because they got bored with things. My parents never spoke to me once about drugs before I got involved. After I got involved, I used to see my father, but my father wouldn't say anything. My mother used to lay down a few rules. I talked to them about it. I used to go and tell my mother, kind of hoping that she'd say to me, "Stop and that's final." But she never did.

Bill is 16, and a bit withdrawn; his father is a New York City librarian.

There were no big problems with my family. The main thing is that the friends I was with—there was so much drugs that everybody was using them. My friends would say let's get high. I didn't want to say no, so I got high with them. I'd just say all right. I got started through drinking and then smoking reefers. I started heroin when I was 14. I wasn't really strung out. I wouldn't get sick and upset. I used to take money from my father's drawer and ask for money on the street, some change sometimes. I used to get heroin from anywhere. I'd get it in my building, the next building, on the street corners. I got arrested with my friends. We were shooting up in the hallway, and a cop came along and busted us.*

From these two accounts, it can be seen that involvement with heroin had its roots in the association with friends who used heroin, not with some shadowy figure who hung around the school grounds and lured juveniles into the habit; nor was it the case that these juveniles were reacting to intolerable home situations or conditions of poverty. Quite simply, their friends were users and got them involved.

Heroin is a killer, but this medical fact has a sociolegal context. In 1969 in New York City 224 teenagers died from heroin overdoses or heroin-related infections (*Time*, 1970). Overdoses are due to the user's inability to determine the strength and purity of the drug that is available to him in the street, and most infections are due to the filthy conditions under which heroin users shoot the drug into their veins. Because the use of heroin is illegal, users are forced to take a chance on the unregulated heroin available on the street; because unprescribed possession of hypodermic needles and syringes is also illegal, they often share a set of works or fashion makeshift outfits to inject the drugs. Infection, especially hepatitis, is caused by using unsterilized paraphernalia.

Not all heroin addicts, however, are subject to the dangers of poor quality and uncontrolled doses of heroin or unsafe needles.

*Reprinted by permission from *Time*, The Weekly Newsmagazine; Copyright Time Inc.

In a study of physicians who were narcotic addicts, Winick (1961) rarely found an overdose problem or infection from the use of heroin or morphine. Since the physicians had access to controlled dosages of drugs and also to sterilized needles for injecting drugs, they rarely overdosed or contracted diseases associated with drug abuse. However, most juvenile users have neither the knowledge nor the equipment available to physicians.

In Great Britain, heroin use is illegal as in the United States, but heroin addicts are registered and can get the drug legally if necessary, without turning to illegal outlets. For as little as fifty-two cents, a registered addict in Britain can buy enough heroin to prevent withdrawal symptoms, but not enough to get "high." In this way, the British have been able to regulate the flow of heroin without legalizing it. Moreover, registered addicts rarely die from overdose, impurities in the heroin, or diseases contracted from the paraphernalia (Whitten and Robertson, 1972:143).

Under the British system we would expect heroin use to be widespread since the drug is cheap and does not involve the stigma attached to drug use here. However, we find the opposite to be true. The rate of addiction in Great Britain was 5.1 per 100,000 in 1968 and 4.7 in 1970. In the United States the rate was 157 per 100,000 in 1969 and 335 in 1971. Assuming that the 1970 rate in Britain remained the same for 1971, we see that the United States has seventy times the amount of heroin addiction of Great Britain—and, as we have mentioned, the dangers of heroin, to both the user and society, are a great deal more severe here than in Britain, where it is regulated.

The use of heroin, like the use of other drugs and other kicks, will be seen as "something to do" as long as there is some group sponsorship and support for it. Juveniles who get into heroin use do so in much the same way as they come to use other drugs. If they conceived of their drug use as dangerous, they probably would not begin in the first place or encourage others to use drugs. Massive warnings of drug dangers have been distributed through every media by the government, and these warnings may have had some effect, but until there are changes in the drug groups that provide the justifications and vocabulary of motives that make it "all right" to use drugs, it is unlikely that juvenile drug use will decline. When juveniles are no longer supported by an intimate group of fellow drug users, not only will numerous users drop the habit but fewer juveniles will take up with drugs.

DRUG USE AS A SOCIAL, MEDICAL, AND LEGAL PROBLEM

As the use of drugs increased among the young, especially in the middle and upper-middle class, new methods other than incarceration came to be employed to "cure" the problem. The legal sanctions seemed to have little effect, and many people were beginning to see drug use as a medical and/or social problem. "Free clinics" began to spring up to help kids on bad trips and to treat drug-related diseases. Methadone programs were introduced to get users off their heroin habit, and organizations such as Synanon (Yablonsky, 1965) began to work on reforming addicts' personalities. Some localities even changed their laws to make marijuana use a misdemeanor. Ann Arbor, Michigan, for example, reduced the penalty for possession of marijuana to a small fine, which was treated very much like a traffic ticket.

The success of these programs varied, and some, such as halfway houses, were outright failures (Wieder, 1973). However, they were no more failures than the legal sanctions, and a few of them, notably Synanon, appeared to work. What is important is that they were tried at all. For years before drug use became a popular activity among more affluent youth, it had been a massive problem among the poor. When Synanon began, in Santa Monica, California, there was a great deal of opposition in the community to the idea of having a bunch of "dope fiends" in the area who were not under lock and key (Yablonsky, 1965). As each new program was introduced, it had to deal with suspicion by the community. However, as the members of the community, especially the influential members, saw *their* kids using dope, the act came to be seen as a "sickness" to be treated instead of a crime to be punished. "Help" for these juveniles became increasingly respectable and viewed as the right thing to do.

The reaction of law enforcement agencies also changed. Instead of concentrating on the kids who were using drugs, they began to go after the "pushers" or "dealers." Police task forces were organized; governmental pressure was put on countries where opium was legally grown, especially Turkey, to curtail production; and users came to be seen as victims rather than offenders. This reaction, of course, solved the problem of how to handle the drug-using children of the affluent while at the same time continuing to condemn the traffic in illegal drugs. Now juveniles who used dope could be sent to some kind of treatment center, and the real villains, the dealers, could be sent to jail.

A final development in the drug scene that should be noted is the establishment of an illicit market structure (Knocke, 1973). Many youths who got into the drug scene also got into the drug business. The profits to be realized from selling marijuana and other drugs were considerable, and a youth who began dealing generally found them too attractive to give up. A former student of the author's who came from an upper-middle-class background explained the operation of dealing cocaine. There was no feeling on his part that the activity was wrong; his only concern was to avoid being caught. Moreover, as a dealer, he enjoyed high status in the youthful community. When he became involved in dealing, he found that the money to be derived from selling cocaine on the wholesale level was astronomical. Like any other going economic concern, such a market structure, once established, is difficult to shut down, and because there is always someone to profit from the high "criminal tariff" (Packer, 1968) imposed on illegal goods and services, it is unusually lucrative.

CONCLUSION

In this chapter we have attempted to explain why juveniles use drugs. Much has been written on the horrors and the glories of drug use from the medical, psychological, and sociological points of view, but the effects of drugs and the causes of drug use often become blurred. Here we have concentrated on the processes whereby juveniles come to be attracted to various illicit drugs.

Since drugs have been around for quite a while, we cannot simply say that the greater availability of drugs is the cause of increased use. In fact, the supply increased to meet the increased demand. Therefore, we have sought to explain why the demand became so great, especially since the middle of the 1960s. We found that the "hippie ethic" provided a new way to look at and mold the drug experience. Additionally, we saw that the mass media have encouraged Americans to take drugs as problem solvers. The main difference between the illegal and legal drugs, besides the interpretation of the effects, is that it is against the law to use the former but not the latter.

By redefining illegal drugs, it was possible for juveniles and others to establish a general drug-using subculture. As "bad drugs" were reformulated as "good dope" and backed by a drug-using subculture to provide new understandings, juvenile use of illicit drugs multiplied. This new conception of drugs has permeated many other segments of society as well; in some states, for example, certain formerly illegal drugs have been decriminalized. Thus, we see the power of interpretation, not only to explain why juveniles changed their ideas about drug use but to account for changes in the rest of society as well.

6 Hanging Together
Juvenile Gangs

Many people think of juvenile gangs as composed of characters from *West Side Story* and *Lords of Flatbush*—romantic stereotypes from the 1950s. In fact juvenile gangs existed long before the 1950s and in places other than the United States. Henry Mayhew in 1861 described juvenile groups in England that closely resembled American gangs today, and Gilbert Geis (1965) has found evidence of juvenile gangs all over the world, from the *Vandervogel* in pre–World War II Germany to the postwar Japanese gangs known as the *shintaro*.

Gangs in the United States also have a long history. Walter Miller (1969:11) cites the report of an observer in Brooklyn in 1856:

> At any and all hours there are multitudes of boys . . . congregated on the corners of the streets, idle in their habits, dissolute in their conduct, profane and obscene in their conversation, gross and vulgar in their manners. If a female passes one of the groups she is shocked by what she sees and hears.

Descendants of the gangs that shocked the residents of Brooklyn more than a century ago can be found in Brooklyn today, still hanging around street corners and still making shocking comments to female passersby. A gang called the Red Raiders has hung out on the same corner in Boston since at least the 1930s, and a war between the "Tops" and the "Bottoms," which started in the 1930s in West Philadelphia, was still going on in 1969 (Miller, 1969:11–12).

How many gangs there are depends on what one considers to be a gang. Miller (1969:25) defines a gang as "a group of urban adolescents who congregate recurrently at one or more nonresidential locales, with continued affiliation based on self-defined criteria of inclusion and exclusion." Note, first of all, that Miller defines gangs in terms of "urban" residence, which excludes groups of suburban, or mainly middle-class, youth. Secondly, this definition, as we will see later, points to a flexibly structured type of group. This type has a high survival potential, and their flexible structure accounts for the transgenerational survival of gangs.

There is a problem in placing all gangs in urban areas and thus implicitly excluding suburban middle-class youth from ganglike behavior. It is true that gangs are typically viewed as a lower- and working-class phenomenon (Gibbons, 1970:126–41), but the implicit characterization of the activities of lower-class youth as "ganglike" and those of middle-class youth as "clublike" may express nothing more than class bias. In a comparison of a middle-class group and a working-class group of boys both of which engaged in numerous delinquent acts, it was found that only the lower-class group was considered delinquent by the community (Chambliss, 1973). The middle-class boys routinely indulged in truancy, drinking, wild driving, petty theft, and vandalism, but instead of being defined by the authorities as a delinquent gang, they were characterized as young men "sowing wild oats." On the other hand, the working-class boys who engaged in delinquent activities were seen by the community, the school, and the police as young hoodlums and criminals. The middle-class gang actually committed *more* delinquent acts than the working-class gang, but they were accorded the status of good, upstanding youths with promising futures. The working-class gang's style of delinquency probably accounted for their being labeled delinquents since they were less likely to act contrite when apprehended and more likely to fight; however, since under the law a delinquent act is a delinquent act, demeanor and social class should have nothing to do with whether a group is accorded the status of a delinquent gang.

If we keep in mind that the social definitions of delinquency are the ones that matter, it would be socially accurate to deal with working-class gangs and other groups defined by the community, schools, and police as delinquent gangs. This does not mean that middle-class youth do not engage in ganglike delinquent activities, but since their activities are treated by the community as mere youthful high jinks, the consequences of their actions are not *in fact* delinquent. That is, if the agencies that label youths delinquent do not define middle- and upper-middle-class youths as delinquent, *socially* they are not delinquent. Even though it is possible to demonstrate class bias in the social labeling practices, a redefinition of delinquent gangs would not change these practices. We are dealing with delinquent gangs as defined by the community and not in terms of what can be shown to be their involvement in ganglike delinquency.

With this understanding, we can now begin to assess the prevalence of juvenile delinquent gangs. By various criteria we can come to an approximation of the number of delinquent gangs. In Philadelphia the police estimated that there were about 80 gangs comprised of some 5,000 members, and of the 80 gangs, 20 were at war. At the same time, however, social agencies in Philadelphia believed that there were 200 gangs, 80 of which they described as "most hostile." The social workers' "most hostile" gangs were *all* the gangs the police identified; the 120 gangs enumerated by the social agencies were considered nonexistent by the police (Miller, 1969:25). Thus even among the agencies responsible for the labeling process there is no agreement as to what constitutes a gang. Nevertheless, they do agree that gangs exist and that some configuration of juveniles constitutes a "gang." Even the low police estimates for Philadelphia suggest that numerous juveniles are involved in some kind of gang activity.

THE STRUCTURE OF JUVENILE GANGS

A youngster's identification with a juvenile gang depends to a large extent on the makeup of the gang and the gang activity. If a gang is loosely structured and membership is casual, then members' identification with the gang is likely to be casual and weak. Also, we can differentiate between a core membership, whose identity is tied up in the gang, and peripheral members, who have little of their identity tied into the gang.

Gangs can be divided along sex and age dimensions, and even though there is an identity with the entire gang, each member sees his or her place in the gang in terms of these subdivisions. For example, Miller (1969) identified six subdivisions in a gang he referred to as the Bandits. There were four male groups. (1) the Brigands, aged eighteen to twenty-one; (2) the Senior Bandits, sixteen to eighteen; (3) the Junior Bandits, fourteen to sixteen; and (4) the Midget Bandits, twelve to fourteen. The two female subdivisions were the Bandettes, aged fourteen to sixteen, and the Little Bandettes, aged twelve to fourteen.

Yablonsky (1962) characterized gangs as having "diffuse role definitions, limited cohesion, impermanence, minimal consensus on norms, shifting membership, disturbed leadership, and limited definitions of membership expectations." This characterization, in contrast to most popular notions of fierce gang loyalty and cohesion, was confirmed by Short (1968). However, other observers have found a good deal of loyalty and cohesion among gang members over time. For example, in a study of female gang members, Quicker (1974) notes: "Perhaps the most impressive quality of these groups is the overwhelming emphasis on group loyalty. Its closest analogue on this dimension is the family." Quicker quotes the following assertions by female gang members attesting to this loyalty:

> To us, we're like one big family, if they do wrong to my homegirl or homeboy [fellow gang member], it's like they're doing wrong to me and it hurts me.

... They are like our sisters, you know, and how would you feel about them if they came home and told you somebody did this and this to you or one of your relatives, someone you're really close to? You'd get mad.

Similarly, Miller (1969:25) summarized his findings about juvenile gangs in terms of strong ties and gang structure:

The experiences of Midcity gang members show that the gang serves the lower-class adolescent as a flexible and adaptable training instrument imparting vital knowledge concerning the value of individual competence, the appropriate limits of law-violating behavior, the uses and abuses of authority, and the skills of interpersonal relations. From this perspective, the street gang appears not as a casual or transient manifestation that emerges intermittently in response to unique and passing social conditions but rather as a stable associational form, coordinate with and complementary to the family, and as an intrinsic part of the way of life of the urban low-status community.

The disagreement among sociologists as to the makeup of and identification with juvenile gangs indicates a need for more information. However, since Yablonsky and many other sociologists spent most of their time studying fighting gangs whereas Miller (1969), Quicker (1974), Cloward and Ohlin (1960), Cohen (1955), and others studied less violent gangs, it may be that different types of gangs vary in the group identification and loyalty of members. Gangs differ not only in the type of their activities but also in the structure and type of their community relationships. Thus, the strength of gang loyalty may vary with the makeup of the gang.

The differences among the findings on gang loyalty may also be rooted in different understandings of gang structure and leadership. Haskell and Yablonsky (1974) characterize the gang as a "pseudocommunity" which develops out of defective socialization, alienation, dissociation, and paranoid reactions. In this view, the gang members are seen as sociopathic personalities, and the highly unstable structure of the violent gang constitutes a pseudocommunity. This same structure, however, can have an entirely different interpretation. Miller (1969) contends, as we have noted, that the structure of gang membership and leadership is highly flexible, and this loose, flexible structure may be misinterpreted as "unstable." Instead of having a single, well-defined leader, gangs have several leaders, but this is far from being a sign of weak structure; on the contrary, it is a highly resilient form of leadership. If one leader is arrested, another leader can hold the gang together. Thus, the gang's leadership structure provides for the contingency of a gang leader's absence. Furthermore, in that the gang members are willing to follow more than a single leader, those studied by Miller show a great deal more identity with the gang as a whole than with a single charismatic leader. This attests to very strong group identification and loyalty.

Determining the members' identification with the loyalty to a gang has more than merely academic importance. The extent to which members identify with a gang determines the extent to which they will participate in the gang's activities. If there is strong identification and loyalty, there is greater likelihood that members will engage in the activities, delinquent and non-delinquent, that are typical of the gang. For example, if a gang is involved in stealing and the gang members are going out on some caper, a member who strongly identifies with the gang is more likely to go with them than one who does not. Conversely, if the gang is one with little member identification, none of the members feels pressured or obliged to do what the other gang members do.

Furthermore, if a gang member has strong identity ties with the gang, it is less likely that he or she will be exposed to nondelinquent behavior patterns and belief systems. A member can become somewhat isolated from delinquent patterns if there is only a casual identification with the gang, but in delin-quent gangs in which there is total identity and association, it would be very difficult for gang members to have the intimate association with nondelinquent others that is necessary if they are to take on nondelinquent values. In questioning members of a Chicana (female Mexican-American) gang, Quicker (1974:10) found that there was little association outside the gang.

> All the girls that go down to my house are from M [name of gang]. All the guys that I know that I am close to are from M.
> *Don't you have any friends that aren't from M?*
> Ya, from school, you know, there are always people who aren't from the gang. But they are the ones that are my friends, my real friends, the ones I consider my friends, they are all from M.

The isolation from others is not a physical matter, for, as this gang member indicated, there were girls in school she knew. However, they were not considered "real" friends. In further questioning, Quicker found why this gang member drew all her friends from the gang.

> I don't trust anybody else, that's why. They're the only ones I can depend on, cause I know if I get into hassles they'll help me, and the other girls like one time we went to B———, we used to go to hang around there, and some girls were going to jump me, and all the girls I was with took off and they left me there alone. . . . That's when I said I was only going to hang around with my homegirls. [Quicker, 1974:10]

This finding is consistent with the findings of Haskell and Yablonsky (1974:179–80), who point out that a violent gang has its origins in part in paranoid reactions to the social milieu. According to Haskell and Yablonsky, members develop "delusions of persecution," the feeling that others are out to get them, and they seek out the gang's protection. However, it is questionable whether the fear of others is always a delusion. The Chicana gang member we have quoted was attacked by girls from another gang, and such beating by other gang members is not uncommon. Fear of others, then, may not be a delusion of persecution; there is actual danger (cf. Lemert, 1962) in the slums, barrios, and ghettos, where violent gangs are most common. While it may be the case, as Haskell and Yablonsky argue, that gang members greatly exaggerate the danger of their situation, it is nevertheless true that they define it as very dangerous and act in terms of that definition (cf. Thomas, 1923; McHugh, 1968).

In conclusion, while not all gang members have the fierce loyalty described by Quicker (1974), it does *not* appear that gangs are so transient in their makeup as to have the minimal loyalty and identification described by Yablonsky (1962). Rather, it seems that gang members do identify with their gangs to the extent that a great deal of their delinquent activity can be explained in terms of going along with gang expectations. Later, when we discuss gang violence, we will explain the structure of identity involvement that leads to delinquency. Here we merely wish to note that gang members define themselves to a significant extent in terms of their gang membership.

TYPES OF GANGS

Delinquent gangs have been characterized on a continuum from primarily social to extremely delinquent and in terms of various types of modal delinquent activities. Our discussion will focus on modes of delinquent activity and will exclude so-called social gangs (Haskell and Yablonsky, 1974:172), which are only rarely involved in delinquency. Instead, following Short's (1968) typology, we will look at conflict, criminal, and drug-using gangs.

Conflict Gangs

Gang conflict is not restricted to conflict gangs. Other types of gangs also engage in violence, including some "social gangs," which engage in very little delinquency. By "conflict gangs," we mean gangs whose major reason for existence is to fight and maintain a reputation for toughness. Haskell and Yablonsky (1974:175) describe these gangs as follows:

> In contrast with the other gang types, the violent gang is primarily organized for emotional gratification, and violence is the theme around which all activities center. Sports, social, even delinquent activities are side issues to its primary assaultive pattern. The violent gang's organization and membership are constantly shifting in accord with the emotional needs of its members. Membership size is exaggerated as a psychological weapon for influencing other gangs and for self-aggrandizement. Small arsenals of weapons are discussed and whenever possible accumu-

lated. These caches include switchblades and hunting knives, homemade zip guns, standard guns, pipes, blackjacks, and discarded World War II bayonets and machetes. The violent gang is thus essentially organized around gang-war activities, although occasionally certain youths will form delinquent cliques or subgroups within the overall violent gang.

The structure of conflict gangs reflects their focus on battle activity. For example, such positions as "war counselor" and "armorer" exist in conflict gangs but not in other types of gangs (Short, 1968:20). These roles are high in status, and the incumbents jealously guard their positions. The war counselor serves to identify enemy gangs and prepare for fights with other gangs or assaults on isolated enemy gang members, and the armorer sees that the necessary arsenal is maintained. The very existence of these roles in the gang structure makes it probable that the gangs will engage in some form of conflict.

The number of actual gang fights is relatively small; most gang conflict is a combination of "cold" and "guerilla" warfare rather than major battles. Generally violence is visited on single members of a gang by members of another gang. However, sometimes the beating of a lone gang member will lead to a full-scale war between gangs. For example, a journalist reports a telephone call from a street gang worker:

> "I thought you might be interested," he said. "The Cherubs are rumbling. They just put Jerry Larkin, from the Stompers, in the hospital. Caught him out of his neighborhood and left him for dead. He'll be all right, but they beat him up pretty bad. I think they worked him over with one of those iron tire chains." He said that there was now a full-scale war between the Cherubs and the Stompers, and that he had been talking with members of both groups, trying to get them to call it off. [Bernstein, 1957]

Spergel (1964) contends that different types of subculture spawn different forms of delinquent activity. In comparing neighborhoods with high delinquency rates, he found four times as many gang fights in Slumtown, an essentially conflict-oriented subculture, as in Racketville, a neighborhood characterized by a highly organized criminal subculture. Table 7

Table 7: Major Gang Fights, Actual and Threatened, in Two Communities*

Neighborhood and Group	Threats of Gang Fights	Gang Fights	Total
Racketville			
Vultures	2	4	6
Stompers	3	5	8
Slumtown			
Regals	10	17	27
Noble Lords	8	19	27

* Calculated from answering-service messages and street club worker estimates, Big City Youth Board, for a twelve-month period, with age of group members and size of groups held approximately constant. A major gang fight threat was any threat important enough to be telephoned in to the answering service.

Differences between Racketville and Slumtown groups are statistically significant, using a *t* test, *p*(*s*) .05.

Source: Irving Spergel, *Racketville, Slumtown, and Haulburg* (Chicago: University of Chicago Press, 1964).

shows the differences between the two neighborhoods in this respect.

As can be seen from this table, there is a greater trend toward violence observable in Slumtown as compared to Racketville. A major gang fight took place or was threatened on the average of every two weeks for each gang in Slumtown, while in Racketville there was a threat or fight on the average of every two months for each gang. Spergle explains this difference on the basis of the different subculture and neighborhood which gave rise to the gangs.

Criminal Gangs

Haskell and Yablonsky (1974:174), using the term "delinquent gang," describe the kind of group we call "criminal gang":

> The delinquent gang is primarily organized to carry out various illegal acts. The social interaction of the members is a secondary factor. Prominent among the delinquent gang's activities are burglary, petty thievery, mugging, assault for profit—not simply kicks—and other illegal acts directed at "raising bread." It is

generally a tight clique, a small, mobile gang that can steal and escape with minimum risk. It would lose its cohesive quality and the intimate cooperation required for success in illegal ventures if it became too large. Membership is not easily achieved and must generally be approved by all gang members.

This definition points to the utilitarian nature of delinquent activities; however, a good deal of delinquency in the criminal gang is performed for "kicks"—for example, stealing cars—or for building a "rep" as a competent thief or burglar (Short, 1968:81). The gang's expectation that its members are worthy of gang membership is realized through daring thefts, burglaries, and robberies. Although many of these crimes are certainly profitable, many are committed primarily to build a reputation. Members of criminal gangs strive for recognition through their crimes and collect any newspaper items that recount their exploits. Miller (1969:17) notes:

> Newspaper citations functioned for the Senior Bandits somewhat as do press notices for actors; gang members who made the papers were elated and granted prestige; those who did not were often disappointed; participants and nonparticipants who failed to see the stories felt cheated.

Because the crimes committed by criminal gangs are so frequent, arrests are numerous. Because of the high frequency of arrests for law violation among criminal gangs, flexible leadership is a necessity for the gang's survival. At any one time a gang is likely to have several members in the reformatory. Miller documents the trouble one gang had with authorities:

> The frequency of the Senior Bandits' crimes, along with the relative seriousness of their offenses, resulted in a high rate of arrest and confinement. During the contact period somewhat over 40 percent of the gang members were confined to correctional institutions, with terms averaging 11 months per boy. The average Senior Bandit spends approximately one month out of four in a correctional facility. This circumstance prompted one of the Bandettes to remark, "Ya know, them guys got a new place to hang—the reformatory. That bunch is never together—one halfa them don't even know the other half." [Miller, 1969:17]

Like the conflict gang, the criminal gang is more likely to be found in a certain type of community and neighborhood than in another. Spergel differentiated between the Racketville and Slumtown gangs not only in their patterns of violence but also in the types of criminal gangs they represented. In Racketville, criminal activities were highly organized, involving a large number of people in a bureaucratic structure (Spergel, 1964:30). The gang boys hoped to "get a piece of the action" when they grew up, and they acted in apprenticeship roles in the rackets during their youth. Their orientation was in terms of gaining access to the illegitimate opportunity structure, which was best accomplished through connections with those in the rackets. However, in the theft subculture of Haulburg, where no organized rackets existed, the delinquent boys were oriented to more conventional beliefs about getting ahead in life, even though they engaged in a great many delinquent activities. Boys from Racketville were more likely to be involved in the policy racket ("numbers") or loan sharking, while the Haulburg boys were more likely to commit car thefts, apartment burglaries, and other types of stealing. For example, Spergel (1964:51) provides the following illustrations of Haulburg thefts:

> Patrolman K. showed me a list of names of boys from ——— Street who constituted a serious problem during the last three years. These boys, seven or eight of them, were repeatedly picked up for breaking into the coin boxes of public washing and drying machines in the building basements. They also broke into parking meters. They were constantly appearing in court but the judges were reluctant to send them to the training school at so early an age. Patrolman K. said that he had been able to persuade the local settlement house to assign a street-club worker, half-time, to this group.

Thus, even though the boys from both Racketville and Haulburg formed criminal gangs, the gangs differed because the communities in which they lived differed. Whereas conflict gangs typically formed in disorganized communities, criminal gangs were more commonly found in more organized neighborhoods.

Drug Use and Gangs

The drug-using gang today would probably be characterized as a group of young hippies who hung around together. If the group was using marijuana, it would likely be upper middle class; if it was using amphetamines, it would probably be a lower class.

The problem in characterizing a cohort that uses drugs as a "gang" is that the members' identification with the cohort does not have ganglike qualities. A drug-using group and another kind of gang may have similar grouping qualities and even a similar territory pattern (e.g., hanging around certain corners); however, the members of the former may see one another as a bunch of guys or a clique instead of as a gang that will persist over time with a different set of members. Modern drug-using groups appear to lack the durability of the gangs we have described.

Members of other types of gangs often view drug users as unreliable, and drug-using members of either violent gangs or criminal gangs have low status or are ostracized. For example, in talking about other gang members who used drugs, one respondent said:

> "Man, that Jo-Jo!" Benny said. "He's stoned *all* the time."
> "What's he on—horse?" Ricco asked, meaning heroin.
> "Who knows with that creep?" Benny said.
> I asked Benny if any special kind of boy went in for dope.
> "The creeps," he said. "You know, the goofballs," He searched for a word. "The *weak* kinds. Like Jo-Jo. There ain't nothing the guys can't do to him. Last week, we took his pants off and make him run right in the middle of the street without them."
> "You wouldn't do that to Dutch," Ricco said.
> "Man, Dutch *kicked* the habit," Benny said. "We told the guy he didn't kick the habit, he was out of the crew. We were *through* with him. So he kicked it. Cold turkey." [Bernstein, 1957:28]

This exchange occurred in the 1950s. Since then there may have been some alteration in attitudes toward drugs, especially marijuana, but there is still a good deal of negative feeling about drugs among gang members. Discussing new gangs, a *Newsweek* (1972) reporter found:

> Their rules on drugs are notably strict. Most gang members have no aversion to dropping acid or blowing grass, but sticking a needle in their arms is seldom tolerated. In the Javelins, for instance, the penalty for messing with heroin is twenty lashes if you're a girl and a thrashing if you're a boy. Like the gangs of old, however, the chief object is still achieving a "bad rep."

Thus, while some gang members use drugs, there has been little change in gang attitudes toward addictive drugs, which threaten a gang's reputation. For the gang members, there is a simple rationale for their stand on drugs. If they are attempting to achieve a reputation as a tough gang, they have to fight. Members who are junkies or strung out on an addictive drug cannot be relied on in a fight. Therefore, the gangs use their own means to control drug use among members. It is not moralism but practicality that guides their attitudes.

In terms of Merton's subcultural scheme (1957:153), drug use is seen to be a retreatist adaptation. That is, those who turn to drugs have given up not only legitimate means to achieve success goals but also the culturally prescribed goals themselves. In more contemporary parlance, they have "dropped out."

It was found that many drug users had been engaged in other forms of delinquency before they turned to drugs; it appears, therefore, that instead of drug use leading to delinquency, it may be the failure to achieve success through delinquent means that leads to drug use. Cloward and Ohlin (1960:177) sum up their position on drug use and retreatist adaptations as follows:

> Generally speaking, it has been found that most drug addicts have a history of delinquent activity prior to becoming addicted. In Korbin's research, conducted in Chicago, "Persons who became heroin users were found to have engaged in delinquency *in a group-supported and habitual form* either prior to their use of drugs or simultaneously with their developing interest in drugs" (Korbin, 1953:6). And from a study of drug addicts in California, "A very significant tentative conclusion [was

reached]: namely, that the use of drugs follows criminal activity and criminal association rather than the other way around, which is often thought to be the case" (California, Board of Corrections, 1959). In other words, adolescents who are engaged in group-supported delinquency of the criminal or conflict type may eventually turn to drug use. Indeed, entire gangs sometimes shift from either criminal or conflict to retreatist adaptations.

Individuals who take on the retreatist mode include boys who have low status in criminal or conflict gangs, which indicates failure through illegitimate means. As we saw, the gang's treatment of retreatist drug users lowers their status in the gang even further. Group adaptations of retreatism through drug use point to gangs that have lost their rep and are no longer considered "reputable" by other gangs. Moreover, when a gang loses its rep, it also loses its ability to attract new members, and this spells the end of the gang. Thus, when the gang turns to hard, addictive drugs, it begins its disintegration.

GANG VIOLENCE

As we have noted, violence is a major identifying feature of conflict gangs but gang violence is not peculiar to such gangs. For example, in Chicago during the first six months of 1969 there were 33 killings and 252 injuries attributed to gang violence (Miller, 1969:12). In New York City between October 1962 and December 1968, there were 257 shootings, 250 stabbings, and 205 fights involving juvenile gangs (Miller, 1969:12). Therefore, we need to examine violence as it relates to gang membership. Although juvenile violence need not be gang-linked in any way, here we will deal only with violence that is somehow related to gang membership.

The best definition of gang violence is provided by Horowitz and Schwartz (1974:238–39), who conceptualize it as follows:

> As we define it, a clash between peers must satisfy three conditions to be classified as an instance of gang violence. First, at least one party to a face-to-face encounter must feel that the presence of the other party in this setting or his behavior on this occasion

endangers his safety and impugns his dignity. In light of the actor's definition of the situation as threatening and provocative, he must make a decision on the spot. If he does not assume the role of an aggressor, he may play the part of a victim.

Second, the actor must respond to this emotionally charged situation in a way that visibly reveals his resolve (i.e., he feels his words, gestures, or actions express a definite intention) to inflict physical injury on his antagonist or by actually doing so.

Third, the actor must account for his conduct on this occasion in terms of his status as a member of a gang.

According to this definition, for gang violence to occur there must be (1) perceived danger and/or on attack of one's honor and (2) physical assault or a commitment to it, and (3) all this must be in terms of one's gang membership.

We have already discussed the aspect of real or imagined danger among lower-class gang members. If there is some actual danger, then there is likely to be a good deal of imagined danger in a gang milieu. However, it is probable that far fewer gang fights arise from threats to safety than from the desire to build or protect the gang's honor and reputation.

To fight over "honor" may seem quaint in this modern age. However, not so long ago a President of the United States declared that this country would not pull American troops out of Vietnam until we could have "peace with honor." Delinquent gangs are also willing to fight, maim, and even kill over honor. As we have noted, reputation is the measure of a gang's or gang member's standing in the community. If a gang's rep is questioned and the members do nothing to rebuke the questioner, then others also will cast aspersions on the resolve and character of the gang. When this happens, the gang's status falls, and much of the point in having a gang at all is lost.

To understand the place of honor among lower-class boys and the relationship between honor and violence, we need to understand what resources for obtaining status are available to males in the lower-class community. Lower-class boys have little opportunity to accumulate material wealth legitimately, and athletic honors are limited to a highly skilled few. At the same time that legitimate status resources are limited, illegitimate resources abound. One such resource is violence, and it is used to maintain self-respect. However, in no way does this imply that the boys see violence as legitimate or good. Miller (1969:23) paraphrases what he considers to be the typical gang boy's attitude toward violence:

> "We know perfectly well that what we are doing is regarded as wrong, legally and morally; we also know that it violates the wishes and standards of many whose good opinion we value; yet, if we are to sustain our self-respect and our honor as males, we *must*, at this stage of our lives, engage in criminal behavior."

In our earlier discussion of Erving Goffman's theory of delinquency (chap. 2), we noted that character was built around risk. Since engaging in violence involves both the risk of one's physical well-being and the possibility of an encounter with the law, it has a double capacity to show the world that one is to be treated, if not honorably, at least seriously. A new gang trying to establish a "bad rep" is forced to commit some kind of violence to show everyone that it "means business." Once having established its rep, it can ease off (*Newsweek,* 1972). However, to maintain a reputation, both within the community or neighborhood as a gang and within the gang as a member in good standing, one must deal forcefully with any threat to one's individual or collective honor. Otherwise, the gang or the gang member will lose status.

At the same time that one attempts to raise his own status and that of his gang, he also shows, or attempts to show, that other gangs have less status. To do this involves making statements to the effect that the other gang or its members somehow lack character. These insults in turn provoke the other gang to retaliate, and the result is further violence. Thus, we can see a cycle of defending one's honor and attacking another's. The cycle ends only when one gang becomes so strong so as to be able to coerce others to its ranks. Given the territorial parochialism of gangs and their lack of large-scale organizational skills, this is unlikely.

Middle-class youth, whose status is built on their parents' ability to provide them with material symbols, rarely display physical violence. In middle-class adolescent groups, a show of coercive force demonstrates a lack of control as well as of the intelligence to manipulate the situation to advantage without resorting to violence. Thus, lower-class youths in a middle-class setting find themselves in much the same situation as police in lower-class settings. They can bully the population into grudging compliance, but they cannot gain the respect and honor they seek. Therefore, since there is little payoff for being tough and engaging in violence (other than the organized fights on the gridiron), we find relatively little violence among middle-class youth or in suburban settings as compared to the slums, ghettos, and barrios.

Given the system of provocation and defense of honor, it would seem that there should always be a rash of violence, but according to Miller (1966:111), violence is usually a matter of simple assault (a fistfight), and the severity is low. There is evidence, however, that the severity of violence has increased since Miller's work. Horowitz and Schwartz (1974) attribute this to the use of guns by gang members. The zip gun, a relatively harmless homemade weapon, has been replaced by the more deadly commercially produced handgun, and the number of gang shootings has increased.

> In June 1973 the initiator of a partly successful area-wide peace movement was shot while standing in the corner in the park on the western section of the community, talking about peace to a group who was having problems with another gang. At a memorial ceremony, it was estimated that fifty gang members had been killed in gang conflicts over the past five years. This did not stop the shooting even though all the gangs in the area, except the gang that shot him, were present for the service. [Horowitz and Schwartz, 1974:239–40n]

Once one gang begins using guns to maintain or establish its reputation, other gangs are forced to do the same thing, and considering the relative ease with which guns can be obtained, it is not too difficult for gangs to be well armed. The gangs' behavior is analogous to the international arms race, in which each country attempts to outarm all others. Of course, the logic of an arms race is based on the assumption that the other side or sides will do anything to gain the upper hand, and the fact that gang members are typically in a paranoid or a nondelusional state of fear suggests that the severity of violence will escalate in the future.

Perhaps the most widely popularized form of gang violence is the "rumble," in which two opposing gangs meet in full strength to do battle. As we have noted, such battles are comparatively rare, but they do occur from time to time, and they constitute a unique form of juvenile delinquency. In his study of gangs, Miller (1966) found only one fight involving two gangs, but there were several threats of gang fights that never reached the stage of full-scale battle. A fully developed gang fight was conceptualized by Miller as involving four stages: initial provocation; the initial attack; strategy, planning, and mobilization; and finally counterattack. The provocation was typically a question of honor, and the initial attack was an isolated fight. To defend its honor against further assault, the gang would then prepare for full-scale battle, and subsequently, unless there was some interference, the gangs would clash.

However, Miller found that even though the beginning stages of the gang fight were not uncommon, it was rare that the gangs would let it go to a full-scale battle. Sometimes each gang would send a representative to engage in a "fair one"— that is, to fight each other. Sometimes they would call the police and have them break up the fight before it could occur, or they would allow themselves to be "convinced" by a street worker to mediate their differences.

By preparing for an all-out fight, the gangs were able to maintain the impression of toughness and keep an honorable posture. At the same time, they were able to avoid the very real dangers of the fight. In this way, they could have their cake and eat it too. They would fight like devils if they were the subject of humiliation or if provoked, but the situation of provocation rarely resulted in anything more than an isolated beating, for during the time between the provocation and scheduled fight, they could usually rely on a face- and limb-saving solution.

TURF

Gang territory, or "turf," is especially important in understanding gangs. On the one hand, turf defines the gang and the perimeters of gang activity; on the other hand, it serves as a boundary between gangs and therefore as a possible point of honor and conflict (cf. Cavan, 1963).

As a general sociological concept, we can take Lyman and Scott's definition (1970:92) of "home territories" as "areas where the regular participants have relative freedom of behavior and a sense of intimacy and control over the area." These authors paraphrase Zorbaugh (1929) and Jacobs (1961) as follows:

> Among the most interesting examples of colonizing on the public lands are attempts by youths to stake out streets as home territories open only to members of their own clique and defended against invasion by rival groups. Subject always to official harassment by police and interference by other adults who claim the streets as public territories, youths resolve the dilemma by redefining adults as non-persons whose seemingly violative presence on the youths' "turf" does not challenge the latters' proprietorship.
>
> Streets are the most vulnerable to colonizing in this manner and indeed, as the early studies of the Chicago sociologists illustrated so well, streets and knots of juxtaposed streets become unofficial home areas to all those groups who require relatively secluded yet open space in which to pursue their interests or maintain their identities. [Lyman and Scott, 1970:94–95]

The transformation of a public thoroughfare into a home territory is accomplished in part with the cooperation of those who live in or near the place where the gang hangs out. In his discussion of white gangs, Miller (1969:15) describes how a store owner watched over a gang of boys who hung around the corner where his store was located:

> Ben was a bachelor, and while he had adopted the whole of the Bandit neighborhood as his extended family, he had taken on the 200 adolescents who hung out on the Bandit corner as his most

immediate sons and daughters. Ben knew the background and present circumstances of every Bandit and followed their lives with intense interest and concern. Ben's corner-gang progeny were a fast-moving and mercurial lot, and he watched over their adventures and misadventures with a curious mixture of indignation, solicitude, disgust and sympathy.

There was some reciprocity in the gang's recognition of home territory. Gang members would not allow members to shoplift in "their" corner store, nor would they allow boys from other neighborhoods or gangs to steal or cause trouble on their corner. Miller goes on to describe how members of the Bandits protected their corner store:

> At least three times during the observation period corner boys from outside neighborhoods entered the store obviously bent on stealing or creating a disturbance. On each occasion these outsiders were efficiently and forcefully removed by nearby Bandits, who then waxed indignant at the temerity of "outside" kids daring to consider Ben's a target of illegal activity. One consequence, then, of Ben's seigneurial relationship to the Bandits was that his store was unusually well protected against theft, armed and otherwise, which presented a constant hazard to the small-store owner in Midcity. [Miller, 1969:15]

The extent to which gang members consider their corner to be home territory was documented by Werthman and Piliavin (1967:58–59) in their study of a West Coast gang:

> Since all routine life functions are at one time or another performed on the streets, the conventional standards of public decorum are considerably relaxed. Entrance into the private space or hangout occasions a noticeable relaxation of physical posture. Shoulders slump, shirttails appear, and greetings are exchanged with an abandon that is only achieved by people who usually receive houseguests in the kitchen. A good deal of time is also spent combing hair in front of store windows and dancing to rock and roll (often without a partner and without music) as if completely absorbed in the privacy of a bedroom.
> Yet as soon as the boys leave the street corner, they become self-consciously absorbed in the demands of a public role. They pay careful attention to uniform—either casually immaculate

("looking sharp") or meticulously disheveled ("looking bad")—and cover the territory in the characteristic hiking style ("walking pimp"). Most of the boys would no sooner start a poker game two blocks away from the privacy of the hangout than more respectable citizens would think of making love in their front yards. Of course there are many notable exceptions to this rule, and on an irregular basis most boys do both.

The patterns of carving out home territories in public places can be understood, in part at least, in terms of the limited availability of private space to most gang members. Private space can be defined in terms of *continuous discretionary* control over who crosses one's boundaries (Stinchcombe, 1963). By this definition, the home territories of the gangs are to them at least private places. However, the police, among others, do not recognize the gang's right of possession of their territory even though they may well understand that a certain gang considers a certain corner to be its own. Now, since the police have restricted access to private places, homeowners, apartment renters, and the like are relatively free from police intervention. Middle-class youths typically have access to large yards or their own rooms as well as other places, such as rooms in their schools, where they can congregate without fear of disturbance or invasion. Lower-class youths, on the other hand, have limited access to private space, and the space that has been made available to them by public agencies is either uncongenial to their desired activities (i.e., subject to restrictions as to time and form of activity) or in short supply (e.g., school playgrounds). Therefore, the youths make private space out of public space, and therein lies their conflict with the law. And as Stinchcombe has noted, the less access one has to private space, the more likely one is to come to the attention of the police.

CONCLUSION

Juvenile gangs are not a new or recent phenomenon, nor are they found only in the United States. Certain areas have had and will continue to have groups of young men and women congregating in a little niche of public space, which they claim as home territory. Gang violence, while less frequent than some believe, is nevertheless a part of most delinquent gangs. Most of the violence can be traced to the members' identification with a gang and their continual effort to build and maintain a reputation in terms of the gang. Different types of gangs will be more or less violent depending on the type of neighborhood where they are found, but all gangs engage in some violence, with the sole exception of drug-using gangs, which in effect are not gangs.

Of all the forms of juvenile delinquency, gang delinquency is perhaps the most widely studied and the most noticeable. Given the flexible character of gang structure, plus the fact that gangs have existed all over the world for centuries, we can expect this form of delinquency to persist for years to come.

7 Busted
Juveniles and the Police

A youth's transformation from a juvenile who has broken the law into a juvenile delinquent begins with the police. As we noted in chapter 6, being noticeable increases the likelihood that one will come to the attention of the police, and those with limited access to private space are more likely to be subjected to police scrutiny. However, it is not merely the inability to go unnoticed that causes a person to be questioned or arrested by the police. Nor, as we have suggested elsewhere, does the likelihood of being arrested depend solely on one's involvement in delinquent acts. Once an arrest has been made, however, a juvenile has been officially designated a probable delinquent and may be well on the way to being stigmatized as delinquent by the community. We are not suggesting that it is the police who cause a juvenile to be labeled a delinquent; rather, we are attempting to show the importance of understanding the situations in which juveniles and police encounter one another.

The police have much more latitude in dealing with delinquent youth than with adult criminals. When we examine how the police select juveniles for arrest, we can see how the discretionary process operates. In their 1964 study, Piliavin and Briar outline five alternatives for police handling of juveniles in situations where it is the police who decide whether or not to make an arrest: (1) outright release; (2) release and submission of a "field interrogation report" briefly describing the circumstances that led to the police-juvenile confrontation; (3) "official reprimand" and release to parents or guardian; (4) citation to juvenile court; (5) arrest and confinement in juvenile hall. It is the last two alternatives that are involved in a juvenile's coming to be seen and treated as a delinquent.

In this chapter we will examine the process carefully to see how the criminalization process takes place and how juveniles' encounters with the police influence their later fate.

ENCOUNTERS WITH THE MAN

In cases involving serious crime, such as robbery, homicide, or rape, the police exercise very little discretion with juveniles or adults; however, in about 90 percent of the cases studied by Piliavin and Briar (1964), the actual violation played only a minor role in the police decision of whether to be lenient or harsh in dealing with the juvenile actor. Piliavin and Briar found that some juveniles were released and others were arrested for similar offenses. The question they posed was, "What is it in the discretion situation that leads the police to choose a more lenient or more harsh disposition?"

Next to the seriousness of the offense, they found that the juvenile's prior record was the most important influence. If the police knew that the juvenile had a delinquent record, they were more likely to make an arrest than if the juvenile had no record, but police in the field rarely have access to records. However, sometimes an officer would know the juvenile personally and whether or not there was a police record, and in such situations this information could be used as a resource in making a decision.

Since the police usually had no knowledge of a juvenile's record, Piliavin and Briar sought to learn whether or not a juvenile's demeanor in the discretion situation had any effect on the officer's decision. They found that the more cooperative a youth was with the police, the more likely he was to receive a mild disposition. Those juveniles who were polite and appeared to be apologetic for their actions were most often given an informal reprimand or "admonished and released."* On the other hand, juveniles who were uncooperative and generally showed lack of respect for the police were most likely to be arrested or given a citation or official reprimand.

Table 8: Severity of Police Disposition by Youth's Demeanor

Severity of Police Disposition	Youth's Demeanor		Total
	Cooperative	Uncooperative	
Arrest (most severe)	2	14	16
Citation or official reprimand	4	5	9
Informal reprimand	15	1	16
Admonish and release (least severe)	24	1	25
Total	45	21	66

Source: Irving Piliavin and Scott Briar, "Police Encounters with Juveniles," *American Journal of Sociology* 70 (Sept. 1964), p. 210.

Table 8 shows the disposition of sixty-six cases observed by Piliavin and Briar. As table 8 clearly indicates, juveniles who were uncooperative were far more likely to be arrested than those who were cooperative (14:2). Those who were cooperative were far more likely to receive the least severe disposition (24:1). In fact, it was extremely unlikely that uncooperative youths would receive a lenient disposition. We can conclude that, given the same crime, a youth's demeanor, not his delinquent involvement, is the chief determinant of his being arrested.

In the Piliavin and Briar study, cues in the interaction situation were used to determine whether or not the youth under

*When there is an "informal reprimand," the police write up a "field interrogation report" describing their contact with the juvenile. No record of any sort is made when they merely "admonish and release" a juvenile.

suspicion was a "good kid." Included in these cues were the "youth's group affiliations, age, race, grooming, dress, and demeanor." Those who were most likely *not* to present the necessary cues to be considered a "good" or "decent" boy were

> older juveniles, members of known delinquent gangs, Negroes, youths with well-oiled hair, black jackets, and soiled denims or jeans (the presumed uniform of "tough boys"), and boys who in their interactions with officers did not manifest what were considered to be appropriate signs of respect. [Piliavin and Briar, 1964:210]

The fact that the chief criterion for arrest was a lack of manifest respect toward the police and the situation did not escape the notice of the boys who most frequently encountered the police. When asked how best to avoid arrest, one gang member responded:

> If you kiss their ass and say, "Yes Sir, No Sir," and all that jazz, then they'll let you go. If you don't say that, then they gonna take you in. And if you say it funny they gonna take you in. Like, "Yes *Sir, No Sir!*" But if you stand up and say it straight, like "Yes Sir" and "No Sir" and all that, you cool. [Werthman and Piliavin, 1967:87]

Since the boys were aware of what the police expected of them, one might wonder why they did not always display this demeanor. That is, why did some of the boys act in a way that they knew would anger the police in a situation where the police were deciding whether or not to send them to jail?

Among the gang boys, the reason was bound up in their notion of honor and respect. "Kissing ass" would enable them to maintain their freedom. However, it would cost them the respect of their peers and themselves. Through artful displays of insolence, the boys can maintain their dignity while not giving the police enough rope to hang them on demeanor; however, if the police demand more than civility, the boys will often respond with acts of blatant disrespect. Thus, by demanding more respect than they expect to receive, the police can set up situations in which both their own authority and the honor of those they confront are at stake. As long as the situation is framed in such a manner, there can be no winners. Similarly, if the gang boys refuse to give the police the minimal respect they accord to others, they set up threats to the policeman's authority, and the same cycle is started all over again.

From these studies, it would seem that police prejudice and character cues play more important roles in an arrest situation than does the nature of the law violation. We certainly cannot deny the importance of prejudice; however, in an extensive study of policy encounters with juveniles, Black and Reiss found that the most important factor in the police disposition decision was the complainant's desire that an arrest be made. In no case where the complainant lobbied for leniency did the police arrest a juvenile; and in cases where the complainant demanded an arrest, the police were more likely to arrest the suspect than in any other type of situation. In the cases studied, 21 percent of the black victims and 15 percent of the whites demanded that an arrest be made. Moreover, white complainants were more likely to request an informal disposition (58 percent of the cases), while only 31 percent of the blacks showed a preference for an informal disposition (Black and Reiss, 1970:71).

Given the relative preference for leniency in situations with white complainants, we could expect more white offenders to receive informal dispositions instead of an arrest. In encounters with blacks, we find that there is a 21-percent arrest rate, and in police encounters with whites there is only an 8-percent arrest rate (Black and Reiss, 1970:68). That is, the arrest rate for blacks is well over twice that for whites. In situations where *only* the police and the suspect are present (i.e., no complainant is present), a white youth is only slightly less likely to be arrested than a black youth—10 percent versus 14 percent, respectively. Thus, even though black youths in general are more likely to be arrested than whites, it appears that the police act to minimize the inequity in arrests. The citizens who make the calls and are present when police must decide whether or not to make an arrest play an extremely important role in the determination of the disposition. The racial difference in arrests can be attributed largely to citizen preferences and not solely or even necessarily to police prejudice.

Black and Reiss also examined suspects' demeanor. Unlike Piliavin and Briar, they did not find a direct relationship between demeanor and the likelihood of arrest. Black and Reiss distinguished degrees of deference from "very deferential" to "civil" to "antagonistic." We would expect the most arrests in situations where juveniles behaved antagonistically and the least where juveniles acted in a very deferential manner. However, this was not the case. Those who were antagonistic were the most likely to be arrested, those who were very deferential were next most likely to be arrested, and those who were merely civil were the least likely to be arrested (Black and Reiss, 1970:75).

In accounting for this pattern, Black and Reiss suggest that juveniles who know that they are liable to arrest and serious sanctions may attempt to behave in an especially deferential way in an effort to stave off going to jail. Realizing that those who are overly polite may be hiding something, the police may be more likely to arrest them than youths who are simply civil in their manner. In the cases examined by Black and Reiss, the majority of juveniles (57%) were civil in encounters with police. Juveniles were antagonistic in 16 percent of the cases and very deferential in 11 percent. The relationship between the juvenile suspect's degree of deference and the likelihood of his being arrested suggests that most juveniles took the course of action that was least likely to draw suspicion to themselves.

Perhaps the most important thing to note in the Black and Reiss study is the overall leniency of the police. In fully 76 percent of the situations where the police encountered antagonistic black juveniles, no arrests were made, and this group had the highest likelihood of arrest. In only 12 percent of their encounters with juveniles where the police either suspected or were certain that a crime had been committed did they make an arrest. In part this low percentage is due to the need for situational evidence. It is rare for the police to make an arrest without strong evidence that a crime has been committed by the person who is taken into custody. Even though arrests can be made on the basis of "suspicion" of almost anything, the police do not appear to be abusing their power to make arrests.

What the police do appear to be doing is following an informal processing or harassment model of controlling juveniles instead of the formal processing model (Black and Reiss, 1970:74). That is, instead of sending juveniles into the formal mechanisms of the juvenile justice system by invoking the law, they tend to "keep them in line" by harassing them. The police view the juvenile justice system as at once too harsh and too lenient. For those whom they consider "hard-core" delinquents, the police see the juvenile justice system as too soft; for those who merely need a "good spanking" or a firm hand, they see the imposition of a delinquent record as far too harsh a punishment. Using their own informal techniques, they can mete out the appropriate amount of sanctioning to juveniles and at the same time maintain some semblance of law and order.

This kind of "curbside justice," as it is often called by the police, is for the most part a breach of police duty, if not actually against the law. However, informal handling of juveniles is by no means necessarily a bad or corrupt practice. Of course, it can lead to excesses and brutality. Typically, though, the police see their activities in terms of their mandate of enforcing the law and maintaining order. By harassing juveniles, they are able to maintain order and enforce the law, yet at the same time control all aspects of the situation. If they merely make arrests, they lose control of the fate of the juveniles. A juvenile who is freed without sanction by the juvenile authorities for what the police regard as serious misconduct no longer sees the police as a threat, and the police feel that they have lost respect and authority in his eyes. More importantly, though, the police believe they are better able than the juvenile authorities to individualize sanctions and work through complex situations. In their view, they can differentiate between kids who are "really bad" and those who are not, since they are the only ones in the criminal justice system who see the kids in the streets.

In a study comparing two cities, Wilson (1968) attempted to determine whether police professionalism had any effect on police handling of delinquents. The "Western City" police department was characterized as a modern department with a high degree of professionalism; "Eastern City" was one with low professionalism. The police officers of Eastern City had a punitive and restrictive attitude toward juveniles and interpreted problems in terms of personal and familial morality. In contrast, Western City police were more likely to interpret problems in terms of psychosocial complexities and saw the solution in terms of rehabilitation instead of punishment.

It was expected that the officers of Western City would be less likely to make arrests or engage in actions that would lead to formal legal sanction. However, the opposite results were found. The department in Western City, which was considered more likely to restrict the freedom of juveniles, processed a larger proportion of suspected offenders and arrested a larger proportion of those processed. This finding can be accounted for in part by the stricter regulations in a "professionalized" police department. Officers are more likely to "go by the book" in such a department, and, instead of giving a juvenile a "second chance," are more likely to arrest him, sincerely believing that the rehabilitation promised by the correctional facility will in fact come about.

The far less professionalized Eastern City police operated with what would appear to be much greater leniency. They had a "pass system" whereby a juvenile would be given a reprimand the first few times he was caught. Even though this is clearly "unprofessional," it cannot be considered inhumane. One officer explained it as follows:

> Most of the kids around here get two or three chances. Let me give you an example. There was this fellow around here who is not vicious, not, I think, what you'd call bad; he's really sort of a good kid. He just can't move without getting into trouble. I don't know what there is about him. . . . I'll read you his record.
> 1958—he's picked up for shoplifting, given a warning. 1958— again a few months later was picked up for illegal possession [of dangerous weapons]. He had some dynamite caps and railroad flares. Gave him another warning. 1959—he stole a bike. Got a warning. 1960—he broke into some freight cars. [He was taken to court and] continued without a finding [that is, no court action] on the understanding that he would pay restitution. Later the same year he was a runaway from home. No complaint was

brought against him. Then in 1960 he started getting into serious stuff. There was larceny and committing an unnatural act with a retarded boy. So he went up on that one and was committed to [the reformatory] for nine months. Got out. In 1962 he was shot while attempting a larceny in a junkyard at night. . . . Went to court, continued without a finding. Now that's typical of a kid who just sort of can't stay out of trouble. He only went up once out of, let me see . . . eight offences. I wouldn't call him a bad kid despite the record. . . . The bad kids: we don't have a lot of those. [Wilson, 1968:10]

As can be seen from this account, the boy was given a number of chances before the police took any action, and after his arrest he was given several breaks by the courts. Most interesting, however, is the officer's conception of the boy. One would think, given his extensive delinquent record, that the police would characterize someone like this as "bad"; however, as we noted when discussing the Piliavin and Briar study, a juvenile's being seen as basically good or bad depends not so much on what he does in terms of breaking the law but on whether the juvenile shows the proper deference to the police officer. Furthermore, although the police will arrest some of those who do show the proper demeanor, this does not mean that the police consider them "bad." When they "have to" arrest someone they consider to be a "basically good" kid, they tend to think of the juvenile as "falling into" or being "unable to avoid" trouble instead of as one who *causes* the trouble. The "bad" kids create trouble and the "good" kids somehow stumble into it. By focusing most of their attention on the "bad" kids (i.e., those who do not show the proper respect for police authority), the police believe they are making efforts in the right direction.

Given this conception of delinquency by the police, we find that lower-class and upper-middle-class groups of boys who come to the attention of the police receive different treatment by the police. In a study by William Chambliss (1973), the "Saints," who consisted of upper-middle-class boys, were seen as "basically good" boys by the police, and the "Roughnecks," a lower-class group, were seen as "basically bad." Chambliss describes the differential treatment of the boys as follows:

The local police saw the Saints as good boys who were among leaders of the youth in the community. Rarely, the boys might be stopped in town for speeding or for running a stop sign. When this happened the boys were always polite, contrite and pleaded for mercy. They received the mercy they asked for. None ever received a ticket or was taken into the precinct by the local police; [however,] over the period that the [Roughnecks were] under observation, each member was arrested a number of times and spent at least one night in jail. While most were never taken to court, two of the boys were sentenced to six months' incarceration in boys' schools. [Chambliss, 1973:26]

As can be seen, one group presented themselves to the community and the police as "good boys" and were accepted as such, but their activities belied this image, for even though the Saints did what was necessary when confronted by authority, they were by no means nondelinquent. In fact, Chambliss points out,

In sheer number of illegal acts, the Saints were the more delinquent. They were truant from school for at least part of the day almost every day of the week. In addition, their drinking and vandalism occurred with surprising regularity. The Roughnecks, in contrast, engaged sporadically in delinquent episodes. While these episodes were frequent, they certainly did not occur on a daily or even a weekly basis. [Chambliss, 1973:28]

Why were the Saints treated with leniency while the Roughnecks were not? First of all, the Saints were not so likely to fight. In fact, they never fought either among themselves or with others outside their group. This is not to say that they did not endanger others' physical well-being, for their driving was at best risky and at worst nearly fatal. The Roughnecks, on the other hand, did engage in physical conflict, and this behavior was viewed as indicative of delinquency. It was not difficult for the police and others to formulate activities such as drinking and truancy as "high jinks" or "youthful pranks," but fighting was more difficult for them to regard as anything other than outright delinquency.

The Roughnecks were also more visible than the Saints in their delinquent activities. As Chambliss explains:

This differential visibility was a direct function of the economic standing of the families. The Saints had access to automobiles and were able to remove themselves from the sight of the community. In as routine a decision as where to go to have a milkshake after school, the Saints stayed away from the mainstream of community life. Lacking transportation, the Roughnecks could not make it to the edge of town. The center of town was the only practical place for them to meet since their homes were scattered throughout the town and any noncentral meeting place put an undue hardship on some members. Through necessity the Roughnecks congregated in a crowded area where everyone in the community passed frequently, including teachers and law-enforcement officers. They could easily see the Roughnecks hanging around the drugstore. [Chambliss, 1973:29]

As we noted earlier, the Saints were more likely to act contrite when approached by the police. The Roughnecks sometimes tried to act pleasant, but their general disdain for the police and other authorities usually showed through any facade of deference. In part the nature of the interaction between each group and the authorities reflected the reciprocal expectations of the boys and the police. The Saints were virtually certain to receive leniency in response to their deferential demeanor, and they were generally approached by the police, teachers, and other authorities in a civil manner. Being treated politely, it was easier for them to reciprocate in kind. The Roughnecks, who were assumed to be "bad," were approached with less civility and reacted with less civility.

A final consideration is how the police and the community came to see one group as "good" and the other as "bad," although both committed delinquent acts. As we have noted, the Saints' activities were characterized as "sowing wild oats" or by some similarly disarming idiom. Delinquent activities that are discussed and regarded as nondelinquent are for all intents and purposes nondelinquent. When an interpretive scheme is provided for particular acts, the acts are *made to be* whatever the scheme elaborates them to be. An underlying pattern is assumed to go with a given linguistic formulation, and the particulars are elaborated in terms of the formulation (cf. Garfinkel, 1967). More simply, there is a reflexive relationship between talk about the activities and the activities themselves. The talk elaborates the specific sense of the action, and the action warrants the particular talk. Thus, when people talked about the Saints' vandalism as "pranks," the authorities were dealing with mere pranks instead of with vandalism. Conversely, when the Roughnecks' "goofing off" was formulated as "delinquency" by the authorities, then the social reality of the situation was delinquency. What is important is not the content of the act, for the content of acts is always subject to an infinite number of linguistic formulations given an unlimited number of possible underlying assumptions. Rather, it is the interpretive practices that lead to one sense or another that must be understood. Delinquency is inexorably tied to the interaction between events and the formulations that interpret the events in one sense or another.

THE KIDDIE KOPS

In most modern police departments, special assignments and positions exist for handling juveniles who have broken some law. For the most part this is not considered a choice position. Juvenile officers are called "Kiddie Kops" by other police officers, and much of the work they do involves minor crimes which go unheralded in the department (Sanders, 1974:206). In fact, however, juvenile officers often have the most demanding and difficult task in police work. They must be familiar not only with adult violations but also with the intricacies of juvenile statutes.

In a study of juvenile detectives (Sanders, 1974), the author found a relationship between the policy of the juvenile detail and the official labeling of certain juveniles. In all police departments, crimes are ranked on a hierarchy from those that will receive the most investigative attention to those that will receive the least. In the juvenile detail, reports of runaway juveniles received the highest priority and therefore the most investigative efforts, while more common cases, such as petty theft, received less investigative time. Table 9 (Sanders,

1974:211–12), a log of the reports received over a three-month period by two juvenile detectives, provides an idea of the frequency with which various different types of crime are reported in the juvenile detail.

Table 9 is a fair representation of the kinds of activities that lead to contact between juveniles and the police. However, the detectives, as we have noted, spent most of their time on cases involving runaways, and it is this group of juveniles who had the greatest probability of coming into contact with them.

Table 9:   Reports Received by Juvenile Detectives

Crime	Number of Reports	Percent of Total Cases
Theft	81	47.4
Malicious mischief	40	23.4
Runaway	17	10.0
Mailbox tampering	12	7.0
*Burglary	4	2.3
Wife/child beating	3	1.8
Assault	3	1.8
Possession of stolen property	4	2.3
Loitering around schoolyard	1	0.6
Mental case	1	0.6
Child stealing	1	0.6
Forgery	1	0.6
Oral copulation	1	0.6
Annoying children	1	0.6
Prowler	1	0.6
Total	171	

*Since in most burglary cases it was unknown whether the suspect was juvenile or adult, these cases were typically worked by burglary detectives.

Source: William B. Sanders, "Detective Story: A Study of Criminal Investigations," Ph.D. diss., University of California, Santa Barbara, 1974 , pp. 211–12.

In a study of the distribution of serious crimes, however, runaways were ranked 137th out of 140 (Rossi et al., 1974:229) while petty theft and malicious mischief, the two most commonly reported juvenile offenses, were ranked higher in seriousness. Since the police usually devote most investigative resources to those crimes considered socially and legally the most serious, it is worth noting that so much police time is spent hunting down juveniles who ran away from home. In order to understand the intensity of police efforts to find runaways, it is necessary to understand the interaction between parents of runaways and the police.

Those who report that their children have run away from home are generally very concerned and distraught. They demand action. In contrast, those who report thefts rarely expect to see their missing goods again. Moreover, detectives often tell victims of theft that there is little chance of recovering their goods, since typically there are no leads in such cases. Failure to recover missing juveniles, however, is cause for alarm among parents, who put increased pressure on the department. Even though the act of running away is in itself not considered to be socially serious, it is extremely serious to the parents; juvenile detectives therefore give these cases the highest priority.

The result is that juveniles are more likely to be labeled delinquent for running away from home than for any other delinquent acts. This is not because the juvenile officers believe that runaways are the most dangerous delinquents; they do not consider them to be delinquents at all. Rather, the department gives highest priority to runaway cases as a result of parental pressure, and it is for this reason that runaways are the most likely to be officially judged and recorded as delinquents.

Because juvenile detectives in most cases, work mainly if not exclusively with juveniles, they have greater discretion than other detectives. With runaways, of course, there is virtually no discretion; if a juvenile detective finds a runaway, he has no choice but to take the youth into custody. In cases where the detectives do have discretion, they assess the juvenile's character in terms of appearance, demeanor, and past record. Unlike most other officers, who are regular patrol officers or detectives in other details, the juvenile detective who contacts a runaway usually has an accurate idea of the youth's previous record. Juveniles with a record are assessed not merely in terms of what the record reports but also in terms of how those detectives who were involved in the case characterize the record. If a juvenile has been in trouble before, the record reflects just those items which could be officially put down on paper. Subjective assessments of the juvenile's moral character are not in the police records, and in order to find out what the juvenile is "really" like, the detectives often ask the officers who were actually involved in the case. Thus, a long record of contact with the authorities is not automatically taken to be indicative of a juvenile's moral decline by the detectives. Conversely, a short record of apparently trivial offenses does not necessarily indicate a "good kid." Sometimes a detective who has been involved in a case dealing with a juvenile explains that the juvenile is not so bad but got into trouble because of circumstances beyond his control.

If a juvenile has no record at all or an equivocal record, the juvenile detectives rely on their encounter with the juvenile to make an assessment. In one observed case, a juvenile detective was sent to investigate a theft by a boy who had a record involving a minor incident in the past. The detective explained before the visit that he had no intention of arresting the boy, especially if he admitted the crime and returned the money that he was reported to have taken. When the detective went to the boy's house, he was not at home, and the mother asked him to return later. When the detective returned, he found that the house had been cleaned by the boy's mother and a Bible placed in full view, along with the boy's athletic trophies. The boy appeared in athletic shorts, explaining that he had been practicing track at the high school when the detective came by earlier. In the observer's opinion, the boy was arrogant, uncooperative, and unwilling to accept responsibility. Nothing the detective could do elicited a confession from the boy, and he finally decided to drop the case. Later, he told the observer that he was unsure of the boy's guilt. He explained that the youth's interest in athletics indicated that he was a "basically good kid," and the detective saw no reason to disbelieve him. The boy's demeanor in the encounter was of the kind typically taken to indicate questionable character; however, his athletic activities were taken to be a stronger clue to his true identity. Therefore, demeanor in the encounter was not sufficient by itself to be taken as indicative of "badness" in the boy.

Often detectives make a tentative decision as to their disposition of a case before encountering the suspect. In these cases, an exemplary performance by the suspect, for better or worse, sometimes changes the detective's mind. In one case, for example, a group of boys had knocked another boy off his bicycle and sprayed him with paint. When the detective interviewed the boys, they reported that their victim had been defacing a wall with the spray paint when he was caught and attacked by the group. Since all the boys eventually admitted their participation in the attack and the boy who was attacked had been committing a delinquent act himself, the detective decided only to give them a warning and make them pay for the boy's clothes that were ruined by the paint. Before the interview, the detective had decided to refer the boys to probation, a relatively severe disposition.

The important aspect of this case is that the disposition did not relate to the seriousness of the delinquent act. One of the boys involved had chased the victim down the street after the attack but had not participated in the attack. However, the detective almost referred this boy to probation because he insisted that the attack had never occurred. By not cooperating, the boy presented himself to the detective as a delinquent and to the other boys as a "tough guy"; and even though this boy's participation in the attack was minimal, in the encounter with the detective he came across as the "bad one."

Informal dispositions by detectives are of two distinct types. In the first type, the detectives issue a friendly, even parental warning to juveniles who have been in some kind of trouble, not so much in an effort to scare them into compliance with the law as to offer simple guidance on how to stay out of trouble. The following transcript (Sanders, 1974:232–33) illustrates an informal warning given to a boy accused of trespassing:

DETECTIVE: "Now also, ah legally, there is a law about trespass which is in the Penal Code, it is an offense. Before you go to one of these places, what were you guys doing? Collecting bottles or something like that?"

JUVENILE: "Yeah, old bottles."

DETECTIVE: "You are? Yeah, as a matter of fact one of my ex-sergeants I used to work for, he's a bottle collector himself, I can understand that. . . .

"The thing to do when you go up to one of these places is to go up to the house and explain what you're doing and get permission to do it. Okay?"

JUVENILE: (Nod)

DETECTIVE: "And that's the main thing."

The second kind of informal disposition is intended to threaten the juveniles with invocation of juvenile statutes, arrest, or referral to probation. If a juvenile is being especially troublesome but the detective does not want to make an arrest or refer the juvenile to probation, the warning can be given the necessary emphasis by calling the juvenile's parents. This is the most severe informal warning, and it is reserved for juveniles who are seen to be salvable but uncooperative. The following exchange (Sanders, 1974:234–35) between a detective and a juvenile's father illustrates this most severe informal disposition:

DETECTIVE: "Mr. Jones?"

FATHER: (Nod)

DETECTIVE: "I'm Detective Knight of the Sheriff's Department. Sorry to meet you under these circumstances. Wonder if you could come over here and talk to me a minute. Ah, this afternoon at approximately 3:15 we had a fight occur in this vicinity. We rolled units into the area. There were 50 to 60 juveniles gathered here who wouldn't break up. . . .

"There was a small group who were harassing the officers. We asked them on several occasions to leave the area. This they failed to comply with. Your daughter, Alice, was standing out here. She, ah, was talking back, to put in a blunt term, 'hassling' the officers around here. I asked her to move on several occasions. She said I didn't have any authority to tell her to, I couldn't tell her what to do. I asked her name several times. She refused to give me her name. I said, "What about your folks, what are they going to say about this?' And she said, 'I don't have any parents.' I said, 'Well, where's your home?' 'I don't have a home. You can't do this to me. My father's going to take care of you.'

"Ah, we had to fight tooth and nail to get any information out of her at all. . . . Ah, generally, she just tried to create a disturbance for the officers, and so it finally got to the point where she failed to obey our commands, and she was interfering with an officer in the performance of his duty and contributing to, ah, the fact, ah, what we call a public disturbance, a 415. So I just finally took her name and placed her in the car and decided to call you, rather than lock her up. So I'm going to release her in your custody. I thought you'd better hear about it."

FATHER: "Well, I'll take care of that."

As can be seen from this account, the detective called the girl's father because she did not honor his authority and refused to cooperate. In other studies of police discretion (cf. Westley, 1953; Piliavin and Briar, 1964) it has been found that such disrespect frequently leads to arrest or even police brutality. However, in dealing with juveniles, police officers have a greater choice of action. They can even take informal action, which, from the youth's subjective view, may be quite serious. In the case described above, the girl was extremely upset by the officer's call to her father. However, the detective chose this course rather than "making" the girl an official delinquent by invoking the law.

CONCLUSION

What distinguishes a delinquent from a nondelinquent is not necessarily that the former engages in delinquent activities while the latter does not. Not all actions that could be construed as delinquent are in fact defined as delinquent by observers. Of those actions that are considered delinquent, not all are reported to the police or observed by the police. Finally, not all actions that are considered to be delinquent and come to the attention of the police lead to the invocation of official sanctions. Only among those cases that entail the official use of the law do we find the great bulk of juvenile delinquents. To be sure, there are a number of juveniles who are seen to be "getting away with" delinquent acts, and some of these youths are no doubt considered to be juvenile delinquents by the community. But, as we have seen, to be a delinquent typically involves an *official* police record of delinquent actions.

It may seem at first that the police have enormous power in picking out the delinquents, but upon close analysis we find that community and parental definitions of delinquency have an equally great impact on what is and is not to be treated with official police action. The case of runaways, for example, shows that parental pressure on the police, not police discretion alone, is the primary factor leading to the delinquent label. Although the police certainly have power in deciding the fate of juveniles, their power is often no more than a reflection of community values, beliefs, and prejudices.

8 Dubious Salvation
Juvenile Justice

Unlike an adult, a juvenile who is brought to court for violation of a juvenile statute or criminal law is not charged with a criminal violation. Instead, a juvenile court petition is brought to compel the juvenile and his or her parents to appear before the court (Coffey, 1974:37). Even though, as we shall see, it was designed to have proceedings along the lines of a civil court, the juvenile court in practice resembles neither the criminal nor the civil court, and this fact has had important consequences in terms of the rights of due process.

JUVENILE COURT: THE CHILD-SAVERS

In the late nineteenth century, certain philanthrophic groups, backed by the general reform movement, came to see the problems of American society as largely the result of rapid urbanization (Platt, 1969). The reformers decided that something must be done to save the children who lived in the slums and labored in sweatshops, mines, and factories, where plentiful cheap unskilled labor was required. The reformers regarded the appalling conditions in the slums and work places as largely responsible for the increase in juvenile crime and the generally "immoral" behavior of lower-class children. To offset these debasing conditions, supporters of the child-saving movement began to look at the treatment of juvenile offenders. At the time, juvenile offenders were given the same treatment as adults by the criminal justice system. Young boys and girls were imprisoned together with adult criminals; there were no special accommodations for them.

A number of cities, notably Chicago, began developing special courts and procedures for juveniles around the turn of the century, although many felt that such benevolence would only spoil juveniles. In fact, under the zeal of reform, although the courts were supposed to protect them, juveniles were stripped of the constitutional right to due process in criminal matters enjoyed by adults, and several offenses that had previously been ignored or handled informally were brought under the jurisdiction of the newly formed juvenile courts (Platt, 1969). Not only did these courts handle all acts that would be criminal if committed by an adult and acts that violated city and county ordinances; they also became responsible for a residual category of juvenile conduct defined as "vicious or immoral behavior, incorrigibility, and truancy." As we noted in chapter 3, juvenile-status offenses make up a large proportion of what is considered juvenile delinquency, and these offenses were the product of the reform-minded juvenile court.

The "help" that was supposed to be provided by the juvenile court was forced like castor oil down the collective throats of the juveniles who came to the attention of the authorities. Those who were in control of the juvenile court system became increasingly authoritarian in deciding what the children needed, and the spirit of helping the juveniles was replaced by the spirit of "straightening them out." To do this, the child-savers sometimes engaged in procedures that denied children their civil rights. Since these actions were defined as "clinical treatment" and "moral development," they were not questioned (Platt, 1974:372). Moreover, since the juvenile court was defined as civil rather than criminal, the civil rights of juveniles were not protected. Just as medicine is seen to be only helpful, never harmful, so the juvenile court was not conceived of as an instrument of oppression, and the officialdom of the court did not see the due-process problems created by the "solutions" they offered.

To distinguish the proceedings of the juvenile court from those of the criminal court, much of the language was changed, but the consequences remained the same. Instead of a criminal complaint, a juvenile court petition was given, but the juvenile still had to appear in court. Similarly, arraignments came to be called "initial hearings," convictions were renamed "findings of involvement," and sentences were replaced by "dispositions" (Coffey, 1974:37). All these changes in nomenclature were supposed to restructure the proceedings along the lines of the new clinical ideal and to further the goal of investigation, diagnosis, and prescription of treatment rather than to adjudicate guilt or fix blame (President's Commission, 1967:3). The hearings were held in private, theoretically to protect the juvenile from the stigma of criminal involvement; the privacy of these hearings, however, allowed the judges to do what they wanted to do without being held accountable to the public.

The courts also went into business for themselves by identifying a group they called "predelinquents" or "PINS" (Persons in Need of Supervision)—children who had done nothing illegal but were believed to be on the path to becoming delinquent.

> The unique character of the child-saving movement was its concern for predelinquent offenders—"children who occupy the debatable ground between criminality and innocence"—and its claim that it could transform potential criminals into respectable citizens by training them in "habits of industry, self-control and obedience to law." This policy justified the diminishing of traditional procedures and allowed police, judges, probation officers, and truant officers to work together without legal hindrance. If children were to be rescued, it was important that the rescuers be free to pursue their mission without the interference of defense lawyers and due process. Delinquents had to be saved, transformed, and reconstituted. [Platt, 1974:378]

Thus, not only did the juvenile courts suspend the rights of juveniles who were brought before them for criminal activities;

they also established a whole new group subject to the med-
dling attention of the courts, and this group too had none of the
rights enjoyed by adult criminals. Had the members of this
group been adults, they could not legally have even been
brought before the courts.

It must be understood that the establishment of the juvenile
courts was not intended to be a backward move in criminal
justice, and, indeed, the reform movement accomplished a
number of improvements in the handling of juveniles. Juvenile
records were kept secret, far more so than were adult records.
Children were no longer thrown in with adult criminal suspects, and the dispositions were by and large more lenient than
were criminal sentences. But the reformers' juvenile court system was characterized by a lack of due process and the belief
that what the court decided was necessarily good. Sending a
child to a reformatory in the judges' view was not a punishment
but a treatment, intended to help the child. However, since this
disposition involved deprivation of freedom, there was not a
great deal of difference to the child between being sent to a
reformatory and to a penitentiary. In fact, being sent to a juvenile correctional facility has come to be regarded as a "more
serious" disposition than probation, and a number of those who
work in juvenile courts now see sending juveniles to state reformatories as equivalent to consigning them to prison. Moreover,
a court disposition to a reformatory carries an open-ended
term; the juvenile who is sent to such a facility thus has no idea
how long he or she must remain in confinement. The adult
prisoner at least knows the maximum period he or she must
serve.

"WE'RE ONLY HERE TO HELP YOU": THE ASSUMPTION OF GUILT

Perhaps the greatest problem with juvenile courts is the assumption of guilt in cases involving juveniles. Since the juvenile
courts are officially viewed as noncriminal, the issue of criminal
or delinquent culpability is not relevant. The court's function is

not structured around the adversary system, with innocence or guilt to be hammered out between the prosecutor and defense counsel, as in the criminal courts. Instead, under the philosophy of *parens patriae*, the court is supposed to act like a parent and attempt to help the children who come to its attention, whether or not they are guilty of a crime.

This is not to say that the juvenile courts put every juvenile who comes before them on probation or in a reformatory. In fact, the modal disposition in juvenile courts is dismissal. A juvenile's account means something in the court hearings, but since he or she is defined as "in need of assistance" in the first place, what the child has to say about the conduct in question carries very little weight. Instead, as we have stressed, the juvenile's rights are suspended. If the courts frequently dismiss cases, it is difficult to rationalize the suspension of rights on the ground that the courts are in existence to guide and assist juveniles (Lemert, 1967). How can juveniles be helped if their cases are dismissed?

Furthermore, when we look at the actual hearings in juvenile court, we find that juvenile cases are not handled in a wise and considered manner but rather are shuffled in and out as expeditiously as possible. In a study in Los Angeles in 1957, it was found that the larger juvenile courts spent an average of three minutes on each case. To some extent, this rapid handling is possible because the judge tends to rely on probation officers' reports. However, judges are not supposed to see these so-called social history reports until *after* there is an adjudicatory decision. It would seem, therefore, that more than a few minutes would be necessary to hear each case (Kerper, 1972:392).

In some states there are split hearings. During the first hearing the judge is supposed to determine jurisdiction; in the second hearing he or she is to decide what disposition is to be made, in part on the basis of the social history report. However, in a study of split hearings in New York and California, Lemert (1967 *b*) found that two-thirds of the judges used social history reports during the first hearing. Since these reports indicate a youth's previous delinquent involvement, those with a juvenile record were more likely to be seen as in need of the court's "guidance." In an adult court, a defendant's previous record cannot be entered during adjudication, and a judge and jury cannot use a criminal record as a resource in conviction. But since the determination of jurisdiction (i.e., the decision that the court should do something about a juvenile) is essentially the same as a conviction, juveniles with records suffer the same stigma the juvenile courts had been set up to abolish.

A further problem with the *parens patriae* philosophy of the juvenile courts is that it tempts the court to reach out ever further to involve itself in the lives of children who normally would not come to its attention. If the court sees itself as a "parent," and if parents are good for children, then the more children the court can reach the better. One judge went so far as to suggest:

> It seems to have been demonstrated that the broad powers of the juvenile court can be helpfully invoked on behalf of children whose maladjustment has been brought to light through juvenile traffic violations. A girl companion of a youthful speeder may be protected from further sexual experimentation. Boys whose only amusement seems to be joyriding in family cars can be directed to other, more suitable forms of entertainment before they reach the stage of "borrowing" cars when the family car is unavailable. [quoted in Lemert, 1967 b:92]

There seems to be no question in this judge's mind about what juvenile traffic violators are likely to be up to, even though such an assumption would appear absurd were it applied to adult drivers.

To refer to a traffic violation as an indicator of "maladjustment" stretches the limits of delinquency theory beyond both scientific and commonsense boundaries. Note also the judge's smug assumption that the juvenile court can be helpful in such cases. To date there is no evidence whatsoever that the juvenile court has helped juveniles who get into trouble. It has punished some and in this way may have frightened them and others into compliance with juvenile statutes and criminal law, but there is no evidence even for this. If anything, the evidence shows that the juvenile justice process sets up a delinquent identity and leads to secondary deviance (see chap. 2). The notion that one can be "killed with kindness" applies in the case of the juvenile courts. They believe that only good can come from their procedures and that therefore the greater their involvement the better. Certainly it is the intention of the juvenile courts to benefit children, but intentions and consequences do not always correspond.

Juvenile court judges, like just about everyone else in the criminal justice system, complain of an excessive volume of work. Because of the increasing number of cases they receive, they explain, there is not enough time to give each one the consideration necessary for a wise disposition. For some judges, it is undoubtedly true that the number of cases they receive precludes careful examination of each one. Table 10 provides a breakdown in caseloads of juvenile court judges.

As can be seen from table 10, more than half the full-time judges and more than three-fourths of the part-time judges hear 250 or fewer cases per year. These judges certainly appear to have sufficient time to make the necessary decisions in line with the intent of the juvenile courts. Perhaps it is true that judges who work in large urban areas and must deal with thousands of cases a year do not have enough time to handle all their cases

Table 10:   Number of Juvenile Cases Handled per Year

Caseload	Full-time Judges		Part-time Judges	
	Number	Percent	Number	Percent
100 or less	287	32.1	38	56.9
101–250	201	22.4	21	25.9
251–500	126	14.1	9	11.1
501–1,000	85	9.5	9	4.9
1,001–2,000	73	8.2	3	3.7
2,001–3,000	37	4.1	5	6.2
3,001–4,000	23	2.6	0	0
4,001–5,000	20	2.2	1	1.2
Over 5,000	37	4.1	1	1.2
Total	889	100.0	87	100.0

Source: Kenneth Cruce Smith, "A Profile of Juvenile Court Judges in the United States," *Juvenile Justice* 25 (Aug. 1974), p. 34.

properly. However, the majority of full-time judges and the greater majority of part-time judges in the juvenile court cannot use this excuse. Importantly, this situation raises a question as to the effectiveness with which the juvenile justice system *can* help juveniles. There is no evidence that the judges with few cases are making wiser decisions than the judges with overloads. That is, even if the judges had all the time they believe they need to make decisions in juvenile cases, there is no reason to think there would be a marked improvement in the dispositions made.

Furthermore, since the judges' decisions are based largely on the social history reports submitted by probation officers, there is not much for the judges to do. And because judges are typically trained in law schools and have little background in such fields as social work, psychology, or sociology, they may not be the best qualified people to determine dispositions. It appears that judges serve as rubber stamps for decisions made by others in the juvenile justice process, and the fact that some judges handle more than 5,000 cases annually suggests that their work can be done without a great deal of deliberation. If the judges' role is to be a viable one, they must make decisions on the basis of the law, not merely the probation officer's evaluation.

In the late 1960s a number of Supreme Court decisions held that *some* of the rights granted adults should also be granted to juveniles. In the landmark *Gault* decision, the Court ruled that juveniles must be given a number of protections enjoyed by adults and previously denied to youths, including the right to counsel, the right against self-incrimination, notice of charges, confrontation, and the right of cross-examination (Neigher, 1967). Several rights enjoyed by adults, including the right to a jury trial, are still denied to juveniles, but the *Gault* decision, along with the decision in *Kent* v. *United States* a year earlier, pointed to general dissatisfaction with the operation of the juvenile justice system. As Handler (1965) said, "There may be grounds for concern that the child receives the worst of both worlds: that he gets neither the protections accorded to adults nor the solicitous care and regenerative treatment postulated for children."

At the same time that these decisions established broader rights to be afforded to juveniles, they did not abolish the informality of the juvenile courts, which had always been seen as helpful to juveniles. The decisions did, however, provide a more compelling role for the judge, and as the spirit of these decisions was incorporated into state statutes governing juvenile procedures, the judge became a decision maker on legal requirements—a role that he was better equipped to perform than that of an expert on juveniles needs. Nevertheless, the juvenile court was not completely revamped by the *Gault* decision; juvenile-status offenses and other noncriminal activities are still handled by the court, caseloads are increasing, and dispositions are typically predetermined by probation officers.

THE PROCESS OF THE JUVENILE COURTS

Now that we have some understanding of the philosophy of the juvenile justice system, let us examine the process juveniles encounter as they come to the attention of the juvenile courts. The sequence presented here is by no means standard in all juvenile courts, but it is typical of fully developed urban juvenile courts (cf. Kerper, 1972:390–93).

Usually the police initiate the action that brings a juvenile to the attention of the court, but sometimes a child's parents will bring him in. The first contact a juvenile has with the court is an interview with an intake officer, who decides whether or not the juvenile should be referred to the court and, if so, what should be done with him until the court hearing. The intake officer may release the juvenile, refer him to a social agency, or hold him for a hearing before a judge. Another course of action is to turn the juvenile over to a probation officer, who will attempt to locate the child's parents and begin an investigation of the case.

If it is decided that the juvenile is to be detained, he is put in some kind of detention facility. Usually there is a special facility for juveniles, but often juveniles are put into jails with adults. The juvenile detention centers are different from jails only in that the children usually are permitted to spend more time outside their "rooms." During the day they are allowed to play outside or to watch television and play games indoors. In the evening, however, they are locked behind steel doors in concrete rooms with bars on the windows, for all intents and purposes exactly the same as adult jail cells. Detention is not supposed to exceed twenty-four hours, but in numerous cases, especially those involving juveniles whose parents cannot be located, detention is often much longer.

If a court hearing has been deemed the proper course of action in the case, charges against the juvenile are served to him or her and the parents. At this time both the child and the parents are advised of the right to counsel and other rights available to juveniles. A hearing is then held in which delinquent involvement is determined. Since the *Gault* and *Kent* decisions, such hearings supposedly resemble criminal court hearings, and a "conviction" is to be had only if the evidence shows delinquent involvement "beyond a reasonable doubt" (Kerper, 1972: 392). However, the cases involving juvenile-status offenses require only a "preponderance of evidence" for an adjudication of delinquency (i.e., conviction). Since juvenile-status offenses make up the great bulk of the cases, especially the cases involving girls, there is no necessity of proving guilt beyond a reasonable doubt, as is required in adult criminal court. Therefore, even though some claim that the *Gault* decision has transformed the juvenile court into a criminal court in terms of the requirements of proof, it is unlikely that the treatment of most of those brought before the court for juvenile-status offenses has changed significantly since *Gault.*

After the adjudicatory hearing, a probation officer makes up the social history report used by the judge as a resource for making a dispositional (and often an adjudicatory) decision. The social history report is based on investigation of the child's background and such artifacts as his school records, prior delinquent record, family relations, and mental and physical health history

(Kerper, 1972:392). Later we will consider how probation officers establish a particular juvenile's "social history." Here we wish to point out that the social history is not merely an objective set of facts but an organizationally produced document based on other organizationally produced documents (Cicourel, 1968). The reality of what a juvenile is or is not may not correspond to what he has done or is likely to do in the future. However, the reality of a juvenile as presented to the judge in a social history report is contingent on the organization of "facts" about the juvenile and those organizations which produce such facts. Once the judge decides what disposition should be made, the probation office or some other agency takes over, and the "court" aspect of juvenile justice is concluded.

Before examining the role of the probation officer, let us consider briefly the significance of what has been said thus far about the juvenile justice process. It has been shown that the juvenile justice system is not the benign institution envisaged at its inception. It is important to realize that the juvenile justice process is a socially organized phenomenon that serves *officially* to create delinquents. This is not to say that the system *causes* delinquency; in fact, it may even help to prevent delinquency, although we have no evidence to that effect. However, a great deal of activity that could be characterized as delinquency goes unnoticed by the juvenile justice system or, if noticed, unattended, and only those who go through the juvenile justice process are socially and legally considered to be delinquents. Moreover, this process can best be understood in terms of its organizational routines rather than its intentions and ideals. We have examined the juvenile justice process not so much in an attempt to condemn it as to point out what it actually is and does in terms of the phenomenon of juvenile delinquency. A reformed juvenile justice process might conceivably be more equitable or effective, but it would still operate to create official delinquents. Since some social agency and process will operate to create delinquents socially and legally, we need to understand the dynamics of such processes and structures.

"WHO'S YOUR P.O.?": JUVENILE PROBATION

Probation was created by the juvenile court system, and except
for dismissals, it is the most common juvenile court disposition
(Kassebaum, 1974:104–5). Officially, probation is a guidance
program to help juveniles overcome problems that may lead to
delinquency and to keep an eye on juveniles who have been
found to be in need of official supervision. However, the police
regard probation as something juveniles "get off with," and
many juveniles who receive probation instead of incarceration
view it in the same way. On the other hand, it can also be seen
as an infringement on the rights of juveniles to do what they
want to do, and very few see it as any "guidance" at all. The
dilemma between "guidance" and "control" is nicely summed
up by Emerson (1969:219):

> The formal goal of probation is to improve the delinquent's be-
> havior—in short, to "rehabilitate" him. This goal is short-cir-
> cuited, however, by a pervading preoccupation with *control.*
> Reflecting insistent demands that the court "do something"
> about recurrent misconduct, probation is organized to keep the
> delinquent "in line," to prevent any further disturbing and in-
> conveniencing "trouble." The ultimate goal of permanently "re-
> forming" the delinquent's personality and conduct becomes
> subordinated to the exigencies of maintaining immediate con-
> trol. Probationary supervision consequently takes on a decidedly
> short-term and negative character; probation becomes an essen-
> tially disciplinary regime directed toward deterring and inhibit-
> ing troublesome conduct.

From the point of view of the probation officer, something
must be done to stop a juvenile from persisting in delinquent
activities. Often by the time a juvenile is placed on probation,
he or she has a record of previous run-ins with the juvenile
justice system, usually the police. The courts attribute the juvenile's previous troubles to something wrong with the youth or
with his social milieu. It is inconceivable to them that the juvenile's problem may be due to the court's program for guidance
and control. They see the juvenile's record in terms of trouble

that he has caused or gotten into instead of as a formulation assembled by various people in the juvenile justice process. That is, they treat a juvenile's record as a set of relevant facts instead of as a social production created by an organization.

In a study of the juvenile justice system, Cicourel (1968) found that probation officers, like others in the system, constructed images of the juveniles they dealt with in terms of background expectancies for various particulars in a juvenile's past. Out of a vast array of previous activities, probation officers built up an account to explain the juvenile as someone who either was or was not in need of their attention. This was all accomplished in terms of some departmental rule or policy for handling juveniles (Cicourel, 1968:331). The probation officers saw themselves as merely employing a set of facts, but actually they elaborated the "facts" in terms of commonsense notions of what was "known" to accompany a "set of facts." In this way, they accomplished an orderly sense of what a juvenile had done and what he or she was. They were then in a position to use this "order" as a resource in decision making, following some policy for "offenders like this one." Instead of having an orderly procedure, either for evaluating juveniles or for administering policy, they established the order in an ongoing ad hoc process. Sometimes there was ambiguity as to what a juvenile "in fact" was and what was the proper course of action to take. However, by constructing an image of a juvenile in terms of rules and policies, they could define any juvenile who came before them in terms of whether he or she was "in need" of the probation officer's attention. This is not to say that the work accomplished by probation officers was slipshod or arbitrary. Instead, Cicourel points out that reality as seen by the probation officer is an ongoing social production, not a reaction to an objective set of facts somehow emanating from the juvenile's behavior.

In order to understand better the process a youth undergoes when in contact with a probation officer and the resources employed by the probation officer in the juvenile justice system, we will look at some of the reports, interviews, recommendations, and other resources employed by probation officers. These will provide insight into the production of an official delinquent. Our account is not intended as a criticism of what probation officers do but as a realistic picture of this aspect of juvenile justice.

Probation officers give a great deal of credence to the police record, which is used to determine whether a juvenile has been in trouble before. Actually, however, these "delinquent histories" reflect only those times when a juvenile has been judged officially to have been in trouble. Cicourel (1968:244) quotes the following police record of a middle-income youth who came to a probation officer's attention:

	ACT	DISPOSITION
4/27/60	Juvenile bothering	Warned & released by patrol
12/6/61	Shot BB gun in city	Witness only
1/6/63	Petty theft—shop-lifting	Warned & released to parents
1/21/63	Petty theft (purse and money)	Restitution—released to dad, pet. filed
2/14/63	Prob. office—informal prob. till 3/14/63	
5/28/63	Juvenile fight	Contacted & released by patrol
6/1/63	Petty theft—stepping stones (susp. only)	Not contacted
7/22/63	Burglary	Released to parents, pet. filed
8/9/63	Burglary (susp.)	Cleared
9/1/63	Burglary	Ref. on above
9/21/63	Burglary	Released to parents, pet. filed to include above

10/6/63	Burglary	Included on above
10/13/63	Suspicion juvenile	Talked to—warn. & rel.
12/26/63		Juv. court order: Declar. ward; rel. to parents; curfew: 8:00 P.M. weekdays; 10:00 weekends; restitution; am't. decided by P.O.
4/24/64	Petty theft—purse burglary (suspect only)	Dad will check out
10/6/64	Petty theft—purse from vehicle	Application for pet. filed
10/8/64	Prob. Dept. above not filed yet pending psycho. evalu- .ation	
11/23/64	Battery (Teacher at Jr. Hi); loiter at school	Pet. filed cont. ward: Rel. to parents.
12/28/64	Juv. ct. order	Curfew: 8 P.M. (10 P.M. Weekends)

Such a report is taken as a set of facts about the juvenile and used as a resource in determining what the youth "really" is. It should be noted that after the record began to develop this youth became a suspect in a number of thefts and burglaries. Such suspicions may be based on the youth's record, but at the same time they *add* to his record. On the one hand, they may be seen by police and probation officers as instances when the boy "got away with" something. On the other hand, they can be viewed as a result of his previous record. That is, since the boy had a record, he was more likely to be a suspect than a boy without a record, regardless of involvement.

The particulars of any given delinquent act categorized in the police record are provided in the individual police reports. These reports provide the context of what youth "really" is (cf. Daudistel and Sanders, 1974). A burglary, for example, is seen as serious or trivial depending on the context provided in the report. The following report might be used by a probation officer to "show" that the juvenile described was in need of psychiatric care:

> Subject admitted that he entered to use female clothing to excite his sexual desires and while in the house took 2 one-dollar bills. The victim later contacted and she stated that they were missing the 2 dollars but thought that it was on a later date. It appears possible that either the same boy was in the house twice or the money wasn't missed until later. . . . The subject later contacted and reported that he was in this house on three separate occasions. [Cicourel, 1968:249]

The reference to the use of "female clothing to excite his sexual desires" is the type of detail that typically leads a probation officer to conclude that a juvenile's activities are not merely burglary but reflect "a much greater problem." Had the report mentioned only the missing money and not the female clothing, a different set of assumptions would have been made concerning the "true nature" of the case.

Another resource used by probation officers in determining a youth's character is a personal interview with the juvenile and his parents. From such interviews, the probation officer makes inferences about what the youth is likely to do. In the following interview, the probation officer attempts to inquire into the sexual activities of thirteen-year-old Linda:

PROBATION OFFICER: How do you like school?
JUVENILE: I like school. I miss it.
PROBATION OFFICER: How are your grades?
JUVENILE: Not that bad. I usually get good grades, but since all this mess I haven't been able to do much concentrating.
PROBATION OFFICER: [Question about] best girlfriend or maybe one or two.

JUVENILE: Lisa Manson, we ditched once together. Bonnie Berner too.

PROBATION OFFICER: Who is your best boy, not for loving, but for friends?

JUVENILE: ... Charlie Dubay. (*The girl appears uneasy at this time.*)

PROBATION OFFICER: Who did you have intercourse with first?

JUVENILE: Ronnie Jones. I did it to keep him. He said he really didn't care. He wanted to just kiss me here and kiss me there.

PROBATION OFFICER: Have there been any other boys since the episode?

JUVENILE: No. That's all dropped.

PROBATION OFFICER: How did it all start?

JUVENILE: There was Robert Bean. We were talking about it at school and he said, "You gotta prove it." Well, I didn't want to lose him just like with Ronnie Jones. I was scared but didn't want them to think I was chicken. But I thought it was kinda cool.

PROBATION OFFICER: Did Gregg ever bother you?

JUVENILE: No, he just wanted to help me.

PROBATION OFFICER: You're not pregnant?

JUVENILE: No.

PROBATION OFFICER: Have you ever used anything to prevent pregnancy?

JUVENILE: Once he used one of those things.

PROBATION OFFICER: Did you ever feel scared about getting pregnant?

JUVENILE: No, I was always trying to get even with my parents.

PROBATION OFFICER: You sort of wanted to [get] even with them.

JUVENILE: Yes, I always wanted to get even with other people. My mother gets mad at me. I love my father. I know that's what's wrong with me. I talk about this with my parents. I don't know why. (*The manner of speaking appeared "sincere."*) [Cicourel, 1968:296]

Note that the probation officer begins with some questions about school to "determine" something about the girl's character, even though one might reasonably question what relationship there is between doing well in school and sexual activity. Apparently, the probation officer is working on the assumption that one who does well in school and likes school is a basically "good kid" whereas one who does not do well is potentially troublesome. The important point is that the probation officer can structure the questions so that the conclusions are predetermined (Cicourel, 1968:297). By asking certain kinds of questions and omitting others, he makes only certain types of responses possible. Therefore, what goes down on paper as the official record of delinquency is in a large part the result of actions of the probation officer, not just actions of the juvenile.

As we pointed out in chapter 2, some theories of juvenile delinquency center on the home life of the juvenile. Probation officers typically hold such theories, and as a result they interview the juvenile's parents to determine the character of the juvenile. Cicourel (1968:301) provides the following example of an interview with Linda's parents:

PROBATION OFFICER: How is she at home?

MOTHER: She's not wild. She just changes. She doesn't know why she's doing it. You say, "Why are you doing that?" and she doesn't know why.

PROBATION OFFICER: Does she feel sorry for what she did?

MOTHER: Always.

FATHER: What's happened to Linda is caused by an emotional factor. After these tests we should know what is wrong. She may need psychiatric help. Why this hearing if there is something wrong with her? We are more interested in her than the court.

MOTHER: She does this, but she doesn't know why.

PROBATION OFFICER: This [the hearing] is a legal proceeding, nothing more.

MOTHER: Then this is a routine thing?

PROBATION OFFICER: Yes. . . . that's all.

FATHER: Does she have to be a ward?

PROBATION OFFICER: I'll recommend that, and the judge may not agree. You can ask him to dismiss it.

Note how the parent's account can serve as a resource to the probation officer in constructing what the juvenile is. The parents define the situation as one in which the girl needs some kind of psychiatric help, some form of guidance. The probation officer says the occasion is a "legal proceeding" and ignores the parents' definition of the situation. This is significant in that the juvenile justice system is supposedly designed for guidance, as suggested by the parents, but the probation officer treats it as a merely "legal" situation. If it were that and "nothing more," it would seem unnecessary to elicit further information from the parents. The interview with the parents, then, appears to be merely a ritual that can be used to document the "interest" the juvenile justice system has in the child's welfare. These perfunctory interviews with both parents and child may have little actual bearing on the probation officer's decision even though their express purpose is to find out about the juvenile so that a proper disposition can be made.

Finally, the probation officer makes a recommendation based on his contacts with the juvenile and the parents, the psychiatric reports, and all other material gathered pertaining to the juvenile. The following recommendation was made:

> Linda's behavior is ... extreme. She is either very happy and lively and giddy, or she withdraws completely and is very moody. She is quite capable of stealing or lying according to whatever pressure is put upon her. Linda has an IQ overall of 100. Her reading scores are down in the fourth-grade level. Her arithmetic is around sixth grade. At the present time, Linda is in the eighth grade. ... She is not doing well and is constantly reminded by her teachers to get down to business. Dr. Moreau [psychiatrist] has stated that Linda has self-destructive impulses and fantasies to an alarming degree. He feels that this suggests a latent schizophrenic reaction, and intensive and prolonged psychotherapy is strongly recommended. The Officer has discussed with him his recommendation that this psychotherapy should be with her parents' participation and that institutionalization at this time could be harmful. The Officer in this discussion stated that the money factor here was going to be a problem. He, in turn, stated that the only other alternative would be to place Linda in an institutional setting, such as [the state mental hospital]. The Officer, in turn, talked this over with Mr. and Mrs. Peters, and, according to Mr. Peters, he felt that it would be best to place Linda under the Department of Mental Hygiene for a three- to six-month period with intensive therapy and then try her at home. [Cicourel, 1968:306]

From the interviews with Linda and her parents, the portrait of the girl is equivocal. To be "giddy" one moment and "moody" the next may indicate serious problems, but it could also describe behavior that is characteristic of thirteen-year-olds. However, the probation officer, with some urging from Linda's parents, agrees with the psychiatrist, in portraying the girl as in need of psychiatric help. This is not to say that the probation officer is incorrect but merely to point out that the picture of the girl's character is constructed from particulars that could be seen in an entirely different light. How any juvenile is viewed depends not so much on what resources are available for making sense out of the juvenile as on what interpretative schemes come to dominate the process. The information presented might be seen as pointing to a psychological problem, as in Linda's case, but it could be used to "see" evil, youthful revolt, a serious problem with the school system, or the blooming of a "flower child." All this is done not by following a set of prescribed rules but by interpreting the activities in terms of a set of prescriptions, policies, and theoretical guidelines (cf. Zimmerman, 1970:221–38). The probation officer's recommendation, then, is not a mere reaction to objective information about an offense or an offender but the product of a complex process of interpretation. It is neither right nor wrong, bad nor good, just nor unjust, and it is certainly not unreal. It is merely the way the judgmental function of the probation officer is performed.

There is another important point to note in the probation officer's recommendation. The officer states that there may be a financial problem in arranging for psychotherapy. The only alternative is to have the girl committed to some kind of public mental institution. In the United States the lack of private finances limits the possibility of private psychiatric attention. In most other modern societies, people's ability to pay for medical services does not determine their chance of receiving such services, and it remains one of the true anachronisms of American life that wealthy patients can receive private psychiatric attention while their poorer counterparts must be locked up in state institutions. A child whose parents have money may be sent to a private institution, where he will probably receive much better care than can be provided by the overworked staff of a state facility. However, since some of these "schools," as they are called, have a *monthly* "tuition" of a thousand dollars or more, the children of low- and moderate-income families have practically no chance of receiving their services. Thus, as Goffman (1961) points out, whether one is labeled and committed is often contingent on the available resources of both the individual and the society. In our society, whether a juvenile is labeled delinquent depends to a large extent on the ability of his parents to "buy" a nondelinquent disposition.

CONCLUSION

In this chapter we have attempted to show the character of the juvenile justice process as it developed historically and as it is socially operated. In comparison with the ideal, we find that juvenile justice is lacking in its actual operation. The juvenile justice process is not a reaction to delinquency but an interaction among various incumbents in the juvenile justice system, certain juveniles, their parents, the schools, and other societal and community resources. By understanding the process in this fashion, we can see the interconnection between delinquents and the institutional process for dealing with delinquents.

In the final chapter, we shall look at juvenile corrections examining both its dominant patterns and the various experimental alternatives. Much of what we have said in the present chapter relates to what we will discuss in the next, and while reading the next chapter the implications of this chapter should become more apparent.

9 Spare the Rod
Juvenile Corrections

In looking at correctional processes, we shall be concerned with the stated goals of the correctional system. We will then consider whether these objectives are being met by the system. Finally, we shall examine various approaches in society's efforts to correct youthful offenders.

Currently, there are three distinct views of what juvenile corrections are or should be doing (Garabedian and Gibbons, 1970:222–23). First, some believe that juvenile correctional facilities serve as warehouses in which young offenders are "stored" until someone decides to let them go. In this view, correctional institutions are neither good nor bad for the juveniles but simply serve to keep the kids out of trouble—"off the streets"—for a time. A second view, which is the official position of many juvenile correctional operations, is that juveniles should be "treated" for their delinquency as for an illness. According to this rehabilitative perspective, the correctional institution should be designed not merely to store juveniles and certainly not to punish them but instead to transform them into law-abiding citizens by providing a "rehabilitative milieu." A third perspective is that juvenile correctional institutions are nothing more than "crime schools," regardless of the good intentions of those who operate and administer them. In these institutions, juveniles are introduced to the delinquent population, tutored in delinquent perspectives, and come to develop a delinquent self-concept.

If we look at these perspectives in terms of the general objectives of incarceration, we can see certain relationships. Sutherland and Cressey (1974:497) identify four broad objectives of imprisonment: reformation, incapacitation, retribution, and deterrence. *Reformation* refers to socializing deliquents so that they will not break the law again. This is the thrust of the rehabilitative perspective of juvenile corrections. *Incapacitation*, in this context, has to do with protecting society from the delinquents by locking them up. The warehouse approach sees this as the primary objective of juvenile corrections. *Retribution* refers to "getting even" or the "revenge" society is to have on troublemakers. It is the ancient "eye for an eye" philosophy, which defines justice as making sure that the delinquent receives punishment equal in severity to the damage he or she has caused. None of the perspectives we have identified publicly advocates retribution as a goal of imprisonment, but the warehouse perspective might take credit for this kind of insight. Finally, corrections are supposed to act as a *deterrent* to others who might think of breaking the law. Locking up those who commit delinquent acts, it is believed, will discourage others from doing the same thing by making the probable consequences evident. Since juveniles do not want to be deprived of their freedom, locking up delinquents serves to deter other juveniles who might think of doing something wrong.

The "crime school" viewpoint runs counter to all these goals. In this view, the only positive function served by the juvenile corrections system is the temporary incapacitation of the delinquent. And even this does not really protect society, because when juveniles come out of the "crime schools" they are much more dangerous than when they entered. This is especially true of juvenile-status offenders, who have committed no crime for which an adult would be arrested. In the reformatories, they have opportunities to learn all the tricks of the criminal trade, which would probably have been denied them if they had not been locked up.

The viewpoints will serve as a frame of reference in our discussion of the disposition of juvenile offenders.

PROBATION

In chapter 8, we considered the role of the probation officer in the courts, which is mainly that of an information gatherer. Here we will look at the functions of the probation officer as he or she works with juveniles who have been placed on probation.

We have pointed out that, next to dismissal, probation is the most common disposition given in juvenile courts. In 1965 there were 62,773 juveniles in institutions and 285,431 juveniles on probation (President's Commission, 1967:161). First-time offenders and those judged guilty of relatively minor crimes were the most likely to receive probation (Cohn, 1963). Girls were far less likely than boys to be placed on probation and far more likely to be placed in institutions, especially for sex offenses, even though many people do not consider such offenses "serious." Our discussion of probation will therefore deal mainly with boys.

Probation consists mainly of periodic meetings between the juvenile and his probation officer in which the officer generally asks how the juvenile is doing. Sometimes counseling is done, either professionally or informally, by the probation officer, but typically the officer is so harried by other duties (for example writing social history reports and making contact with relatives of the juvenile) that this important part of probation cannot be accomplished. If the probation officer knows that the juvenile is having a specific problem at home, at school, or at work, he can serve as a mediator or he can attempt to change the actions of the youth or the source of the problem if it is not the youth. Because there is a good deal of variation among departments in the size of caseloads and the types of juveniles who are typically placed on probation, the time the probation officer has available for counseling activities varies widely (Carter and Wilkins, 1970).

The probation officer's ability to control the youth is pretty much limited to talk, whether it is counseling or threats. Probation can be rescinded on the recommendation of the probation officer, with the juvenile either freed or put into an institution, and this power certainly has the potential to compel the youth to respect the probation officer. But the promises of early release from probation and threats of incarceration are merely talk. As soon as the probation officer invokes the actions implied in his talk (i.e., release from probation), the juvenile is legally outside of the officer's control.

The conditions of probation and the ability of a probation department to make sure that these conditions are met depend on the available resources of the department. The following recommendation illustrates the problems involved in carrying out a probation sentence.

> It is respectfully recommended to the Court that if the allegations contained in the petition filed in behalf of Smithfield Elston are found to be true he be declared a ward of the Juvenile Court of County———, his care, custody and control to be placed with ———,who is authorized and directed to release the minor in the direct custody of his mother under the following terms and conditions of probation:
> 1. That he violate no law or ordinance;
> 2. That he obey the reasonable directive of his mother or the Probation Officer at all times;
> 3. That he attend school regularly and obey all school rules and regulations;
> 4. That he not be out after dark unless accompanied by his mother or some adult person approved by her;
> 5. That he report once each month to the Probation Officer, either in person or in writing. [Cicourel, 1967:212]

The first three of the five conditions of probation are simply a reiteration of what is required of all juveniles. The curfew and the monthly report to the probation officer are the only social requirements of a youth on probation. The degree of guidance that can come from a monthly meeting or letter to the probation officer is probably minimal, and judging from probation officers' common complaints of being overburdened with cases, it is often nil. This state of affairs is a continual source of frustration and despair to probation officers who still hope to help juveniles and a source of cynicism for those who have given up any pretense of helping juveniles.

JUVENILE JAILS

One of the problems in coming to terms with juvenile corrections is the language used to describe the institutions and the juveniles placed in them. We have used "correctional facilities" and other terms that suggest that some form of rehabilitation is supposed to take place. However, as we have pointed out, whether they are called "temporary holding facilities," "reformatories," "training schools," or whatever, these institutions are often nothing more than prisons in which juveniles are housed; therefore, they will be referred to here as "incarceratories." We do not wish to imply that juvenile incarceratories are good or bad or that no rehabilitation, correction, or reformation takes place in them. We simply want to avoid the implication that merely because they are designated in the official jargon by the process they are supposed to perform, they actually fulfill that function. The following account by the author of a visit to a Dutch juvenile incarceratory illustrates why this terminology is used:

The most striking thing about the juvenile prison, as the Dutch called it, was its setting. They had converted a Nazi concentration camp into what we would call a reformatory. The same barbed-wire fences used by the Nazis, with curved cement poles for holding the wires, were still in place. The buildings, including a crematorium outside the fence, were the same ones used to house Jews and other political undesirables by the Nazis in the Second World War. The interiors of the buildings were not bad, and indeed the Dutch had done a great deal to liven up the inside of these heinous structures. There was an abundance of trees and shrubs, and were it not for the fact that it had once been a concentration camp, the setting itself was quite pleasant. The director of the prison referred to the boys as "inmates," and even though they were treated more like students, it was refreshing to hear what I considered honest terminology. There were more staff than there were inmates, and there appeared to be a maximum effort to help the boys—mostly with vocational training—but since the director of the prison was a psychologist, there were counseling programs as well. There was an attempt to be democratic in some of the decision making; they held weekly meetings and discussions where complaints were aired, and the prisoners could vote on a number of alternatives. There was little emphasis on control, and some boys joked that they had to remind the guards, who stood near the entrance, to keep others *out*. If any of the boys wanted to escape, they would have had little difficulty. Had the prison been in the United States and were the setting not that of a former Nazi concentration camp, it would probably be seen as a greatly enlightened and progressive "reformatory."

As this description suggests, everything about the operation of the Dutch juvenile incarceratory belied its name. One who merely heard the name and knew of the setting might have concluded that the Dutch are unreasonably harsh in their treatment of juvenile offenders. Getting behind appearances and the official bureaucratic/psychiatric/social work jargon better enables us to understand what juvenile incarceratories are. In order to examine juvenile corrections, we need to look at additional examples and conceptualize what is taking place in terms of organizational routines.

For reasons that will become clear later, the custodial-oriented incarceratories for juveniles operate pretty much in line with the custodial goal they espouse. We will look first at an institution at the rehabilitative end of the continuum. The name of our example, the Fricot (California) Ranch School for Boys connotes the type of place the institution was designed to be.

In general, the Fricot Ranch School operates under the "training school" concept of rehabilitation, attempting to pro-

vide some form of educational and moral training so that boys
and girls who have gotten into trouble will be "cured" or
"rehabilitated." Moreover, this is done through understanding
and communication instead of control and repression. The daily
routine at the Fricot Ranch School is as follows:

Lights are turned on at 6:05 A.M. The group is on silence during
dressing and washing up, then the boys line up in the hallway,
where quiet talking is allowed until they leave for the dining
room at 6:35. On the dining-hall ramp the boys stand silent at
attention until the "At ease, quiet talking" order is given. In the
dining room low talking is allowed, but no horseplay or trading
of food. After breakfast the group is moved to the lodge yard,
where the supervisor takes a count and and runs a bathroom call.
He selects crews to sweep and mop the lodge washroom, locker
room, day room, dormitory, honor room hall and office, and
supervises the work. At 8:25 the boys are ordered into formation;
the supervisor takes another count and then accompanies the
group to the academic school building. When clases are let out
at 11:30 A.M., the boys go directly to the dining-hall ramp, met
by their supervisor, who takes count before the group enters.
After lunch the boys go to the lodge, usually for a quiet period
in the day room or on their beds, sometimes going on a short hike
or playing indoors. At 1:05 P.M. they are ordered into formation
for a count, then move again to the school building, followed by
the supervisor. School is dismissed for the day at 4:15, and the
boys go directly to their lodge yard, met by their supervisor, who
takes a count, then usually allows free play. By 4:30 P.M. the boys
are moved into the lodge to wash up before dinner, and they
leave the lodge about 5:05 P.M. to march to the dining hall. After
the meal the group moves back to the lodge for a count, a bathroom call, and a brief period of free play outdoors or in the lodge.
At 6:15 P.M. the group is split, following the preferences of the
boys, for the evening activities, which may include a hike, organized games, or supervised crafts. Activities end at 8:00 P.M.,
when the boys are returned to the lodge. They brush their teeth,
undress, put their shorts, socks, and T shirts into laundry bags,
and take showers by groups. As soon as they have showered, the
boys go to their beds, and there is "package call"—which means
that those who have received from home packages of cookies,
candy, and toys may enjoy these treats until 9:30, when all boys

must be in their beds. No boy is allowed out of bed after 10:30 unless it is to go to the bathroom, and during the night the supervisor quietly moves through the lodge to take a count of the boys three times every hour. [Jesness, 1965:9]

This routine is designed to provide close interpersonal relations between staff and the boys—the main emphasis of the "rehabilitation." However, there are a number of social forces working in the opposite direction. First of all, well-developed inmate groups form which exercise greater influence than the "therapeutic milieu" (Garabedian and Gibbons:1970:224). Indeed, at the Fricot Ranch School, the supervisors had what might be called an "exploitative truce" with the leaders of the various cliques (Jesness, 1965). The supervisors had to keep on the good side of the clique leaders if they hoped to maintain control. Boys who were given a choice between being ostracized or beaten by the powerful clique leaders or following the directions of the supervisors would generally succumb to the peer pressure.

Secondly, if we look carefully at the routine, we can see it more as a means of control than of therapy and rehabilitation. The lining-up and marching-off patterns are means of moving people in batches commonly used in total institutions (Goffman, 1961). By providing for some activity at all times, the authorities have maximal control. In custodial types of institutions, where there are fewer planned activities, there is actually less control. Additionally, the activities functioned both as punishments and as exhausting devices. Boys who got out of line were made to take strenuous hikes and to participate in "sports" (Jesness, 1965). In one incarceratory observed by the author, a supervisor explained that the purpose of the daily athletic schedule was not "therapy," nor did juvenile corrections professionals espouse the philosophy that there is a relationship between sports and character building. Instead, they believe that a hectic athletic program will tire the kids out and make them more easily controlable.

At this point the reader should be able to see the common thread running through all incarceratories regardless of the institutional policy. As we noted in passing, juvenile incarceratories are total institutions—that is, establishments that control all facets of the inmates' day-to-day existence (Goffman, 1961). Total organizations include prisons, the military, mental institutions, and convents. The emphasis in these organizations is on control of the clientele or membership. In institutions that admit to control as their primary end, such as those with a custodial policy, we are not surprised to find an emphasis on control. However, in institutions with a rehabilitative policy, we see a displacement of goals, for inevitably the goal of control comes to replace the goal of rehabilitation in the daily routine. At first, this would seem to contradict the benign policy of "guidance" and "rehabilitation," but in fact a treatment orientation, like traditional punishment, is nothing more than a form of control. The basic assumption behind any treatment program—necessarily, it would seem—is that the treaters are "right" and those who are to receive the treatment are "wrong." That is, the administrators of treatment see something wrong with those who are to be given treatment. In order to apply the treatment, those who are to receive it must be controlled, and the end of treatment is also control, in the form of self-control. Thus, both the means and the ends of treatment are control.

In order to have control, treatment-oriented incarceratories engage in manipulation of inmates by rewarding those who comply with institutional policy. Reciprocally, the inmates develop an "underlife" (Goffman, 1961) wherein they attempt to overcome the control of their keepers, whether it is custodial or treatment-oriented. The authorities' response to the inmate subculture is further control mechanisms, and the counterresponse is further inmate manipulation for the scarce and controlled goods and services. This cycle completely destroys the efforts at treatment as the staff comes to be more and more concerned with basic custodial control.

Part of the problem with the various treatment policies is the assumption that the inmates are inert and blind to the attempts to change them. No matter how good their intentions are, treatment orientations are always frustrated to some degree by their charges' lack of cooperation. Inmates, however, are very much aware of what is happening. One inmate pointed out that treatment programs measure the success of an inmate in terms of how far he has "progressed" from the time he entered the program. Inmates who were difficult as possible at the outset of treatment were able to demonstrate faster "progress" than inmates who immediately cooperated. Therefore, the inmates who at first "raised hell" and then later settled down and cooperated were regarded as "cured" much sooner. The con-wise inmates knew this while the novices did not; as a result, the treatment program was manipulated more effectively than it manipulated those who were being treated.*

Another problem with rehabilitation programs is in evaluating their effects. Improved postrelease behavior may be due merely to having been locked up, or it may be due to treatment or to changes in society. For example, a study in Florida found that after the introduction of a "guided group interaction" treatment program, there was a 44-percent reduction in delinquent recidivism (Grissom, 1974:62). At first it appeared that this might be due to the introduction of the new treatment program. However, in comparing Florida's rate of delinquent recidivism with that of Arkansas, it was found that the Arkansas rate was about 10 percent lower. Since the Arkansas training schools had no "guided group interaction" program, it was difficult to believe that the effect of the programs was the significant causal variable (Grissom, 1974:64–67). Different juvenile adjudicatory programs, different styles of law enforcement, or any number of other factors might have contributed to the different rates of recidivism in Florida and Arkansas. Without improved research and evaluation methods, we are in the dark as to the effectiveness of the various programs.

In summary, the effectiveness of juvenile incarceratories, whatever they are called and whether they are guided by a custodial or a rehabilitative policy, is often to be questioned. Evaluation procedures are very poor, and attempts to appraise what these institutions are doing suggest that the evidence is

---

*I am grateful to George Muedeking for this example.

equivocal not only as to their effectiveness but as to their actual operation. However, it is certain that incarceratories do not "cure" delinquency, and there is some evidence that they are more a part of the problem than of the solution.

In the following sections, we will examine two other approaches to handling delinquency. Neither involves locking up children, and both are responses to specific kinds of delinquency.

STREET WORK WITH GANGS

In chapter 6 we discussed the amount of delinquency generated in and around delinquent gangs. Because of the visibility of juvenile gangs and the public concern over gang activities (in addition, of course, to the very real problem of gang violence), gang delinquency has been recognized as a unique form of misconduct. One approach to the gang problem, which developed in the late fifties and was implemented in the sixties, was to intervene in the day-to-day lives of the gang members. Mobilization for Youth in New York, the Los Angeles Youth Project, the Chicago Area Project, and San Francisco's Youth for Service are some of the better-known examples of these "gang prevention" programs (Klein, 1971:44–45). Those who worked directly with the gang members were called "detached workers" or "street workers," and the gang-prevention programs were generally referred to as "street work" programs.

In the most general terms, the programs were designed as an alternative to juvenile corrections. It was hoped that sending detached workers to work with the gang on its own turf would decrease the amount of juvenile delinquency. According to Klein (1971:147–48), the rationales for this approach included the following:

1. Detached work is the only effective way to maintain contact with "hard-to-reach" gang membership.
2. Left to their own devices, gang members manage to mire themselves ever more deeply in a self-defeating netherworld of alienation and deprivation.

3. The societal costs, physical and financial, of gang activity require that special attention be paid to procedures that might reasonably be expected to decrease that activity.

A detached worker with delinquent gangs may accomplish the following goals:

1. Control (principally of gang fighting).
2. Treatment of individual problems
3. Providing access to opportunities
4. Value change.
5. Prevention of delinquency.

The general operation of these programs involved a detached worker "adopting" a gang and working with it—that is, helping to find jobs for gang members, encouraging them to stay in school, planning various social events such as dances, sports, trips, and other activities to keep them out of trouble, and acting as arbitrator or mediator in gang disputes.

The success of the programs was for the most part questionable. A number of the major projects had no evaluation program whatsoever, and it is difficult to say whether any observed change in the gang's behavior was due to the detached worker's presence or to some other factor. In those cases that were evaluated, most were not found to have reduced delinquency, and in at least one—the Group Guidance Project in Los Angeles—there was an *increase* in delinquency among gang members (Klein, 1971:50). Most programs simply did not work. A major exception was the Ladino Hills Project, which attempted to break up the gang's cohesiveness, regarded as the major contributing factor in the boys' delinquency. By doing so it reduced the overall number of gang offenses by 35 percent (Klein, 1971:51). However, the project did not reduce the number of offenses by individual gang members.

In some areas these projects were successful. Individual workers were able to stop a number of gang fights. In our discussion of gangs it will be remembered that gang members put a great deal of emphasis on appearing tough and brave; if they were ever put in a position where they had to fight or lose face, they would fight. The gang workers served as "face savers" (cf. Goffman, 1967:5–45), providing warring gangs with an "out" to fighting, and thus were often able to stop the fights. The following account illustrates how this was done:

> After several days of "hassling" between the Generals and the Red Raiders, it was clear that the Generals would be waiting for the Red Raiders at 3:15 near a local school. At the Red Raider's club meeting on the eve of the promised clash, approximately 80 members appeared in an unusual show of strength. One might have thought there would be no avoiding an all-out gang fight, but I watched worker H. put together his counseling skills with his knowledge that most members were fearful and would accept a face-saving alternative.
>
> It took two hours of discussion and harangue, but H. convinced the boys that they should all gather at 3:30 the next day at a playground some *six blocks* away from the school. I went to the school at 3:00 the next day and saw some of the Generals waiting. I then went to the playground and counted over 40 Red Raiders making a *show of strength which could not lead to a dangerous fight*. They were in "the wrong place at the right time," with some even claiming that the Generals were "chicken" and "poop-butts" because of their failure to make an appearance. No one, of course, had informed the Generals that the Red Raiders would be at the playground. The Red Raiders were thus able to convince themselves that they had acted nobly by being visible and available, but they had also avoided a serious fight. Worker H. had played a tricky game, and he had won. [Klein, 1971:149]

Other than occasional successes in stopping fights and breaking up gangs, though, these projects generally failed to make a significant dent on gang delinquency. Attempting to understand why they failed, Klein (1971:51–55) points out that most of the projects either lacked theoretical perspectives or were based on a hodgepodge of theories. Since theories are useful sources of direction when they are applied, the programs started without basic tools, or with such a motley assortment that they could never use them in a coordinated manner. Secondly, the scope of the problem was so great and the available resources so meager that the projects were doomed before they started. The conditions that led to the development and maintenance of the delinquent gangs could not be offset by a few workers in a few months. Thirdly, there was an absence of specifically appropriate techniques. Other than the techniques available for stopping gang fights (e.g., truce meetings), which themselves were initially ad hoc measures taken by detached workers, there were either vague techniques that were difficult to operationalize (e.g., talking to individual gang members) or none at all. Some of the techniques employed were inapporpriate and served to increase the problems instead of reduce them. Often assigning a worker to a gang would actually increase the gang's cohesiveness; what had been a fairly loose gang would be brought together by the gang worker. Furthermore, being assigned a street worker was a sign of status for the gang members, for only the "baddest," toughest gangs got to have a gang worker. (These unanticipated consequences, it might be noted, were generally caused by benevolent motives on the part of the agencies that were attempting to "help" the gang boys, but it should be remembered that the unanticipated consequences of a "get tough" policy equally serve to increase delinquency.) Finally, the workers lacked any way to elicit cooperation from the gang boys or other agencies in the community. The detached worker was literally *detached.* He was generally an alien in the gang community, in periodic conflict with other agencies such as the police, the YMCA, boys' clubs, and other institutions in his working milieu. If the boys did not voluntarily cooperate, there was little he could do to make them do so, and the same was true of the other community agencies.

Having reviewed the meager successes and massive failures of the gang prevention programs, we are tempted to dismiss the whole thing as a well-intentioned idea that did not work. By this token, however, we might also junk the police, the courts, and the correctional system, because they too have failed to reduce delinquency. Over the years attempts have been made to improve the police, the courts, and the correctional facilities, and the crime rates for both adults and juveniles have continued to climb. Nevertheless, because the gang programs did have some successes that may not have been realized without them, it would be wrong to throw out the good along with the bad. By grounding gang prevention programs in theory instead of the vague practicalities of street work, we would have a much better chance of success. Moreover, we need good evaluation research based on sociological and other social science methods to find out what does work as well as what does not. Only in this way can we hope for improvement.

DIVERSION FROM THE JUVENILE JUSTICE SYSTEM

The 1967 Report of the President's Commission on Law Enforcement and Administration of Justice, *The Challenge of Crime in a Free Society*, recommended that special programs and agencies be established as an alternative to normal processing in the juvenile justice system. In its 1973 report, *A National Strategy to Reduce Crime*, the National Advisory Commission on Criminal Justice Standards and Goals echoed this recommendation. If agencies were established that could deal with various forms of delinquency, especially juvenile-status and petty offenses, juveniles would not have to suffer the undesirable consequences of juvenile corrections. More importantly, these new agencies would be able to provide real help and guidance instead of punishment couched in the rhetoric of "rehabilitation" and "reformation."

The Commission therefore recommended the establishment of Youth Service Bureaus in the communities to provide services for juveniles who get into trouble. Instead of being taken to a juvenile incarceratory, such juveniles would be diverted to the Youth Service Bureau for professional help. Juveniles arrested for less serious offenses or for the first time would not be sent to "crime schools," where they would come into contact with juveniles who were committed to delinquent activities and identities.

The underlying theories that directed the establishment of the diversion programs were two we have discussed earlier. First, labeling theory, with its contention that individuals who are stigmatized as delinquent become what they are said to be, pointed to the juvenile justice process as a major contributor to the creation of a delinquent (Cressey and McDermott, 1973:2). Secondly, differential association theory showed that individuals became delinquent because of an abundance of associations and interactions with those already committed to delinquency. The juvenile correctional structure provided these associations and interactions (Cressey and McDermott, 1973:2). Thus, the establishment and implementation of diversion programs, unlike the gang prevention programs, were founded on and guided by theories. This is important, for not only do the programs provide a test of the diversion program per se. If properly administered, they also provide a test of two major theories.

Figure 1 is a diagram of the proposed juvenile justice system, with Youth Service Bureaus as an integral part. As can be seen from the diagram, direct referral to juvenile court is only one alternative, and not necessarily the primary one. The central agency is the Youth Service Bureau, which either offers services itself or refers the juvenile to an appropriate agency, which may or may not be juvenile court. The current system is not so much changed as it is bypassed, for the juvenile justice process itself remains intact. However, the expectation is that many youths will be diverted from the juvenile court to an agency or program that can help them more appropriately.

To date, little diversion research has been done, and what research has been attempted (Cressey and McDermott, 1973) has encountered massive problems.

The greatest problem related to the definition of "diversion" by the agencies that were supposedly carrying out diversion programs. Some considered diversion to be "informal probation," which was very much like formal probation except that the probation officers felt that those on informal probation had some chance of being rehabilitated and there was more frequent contact between the juvenile and the probation officer in informal cases. Moreover, informal probation was often characterized by poor records or none, in line with the philosophy of diversion that a juvenile record was possibly damaging to the juvenile. However, in order to have an idea of the program's effectiveness, it is necessary to record who succeeded after contact with the diversion program and who did not. Thus it was almost impossible to tell whether the juveniles placed in a di-

Figure 1

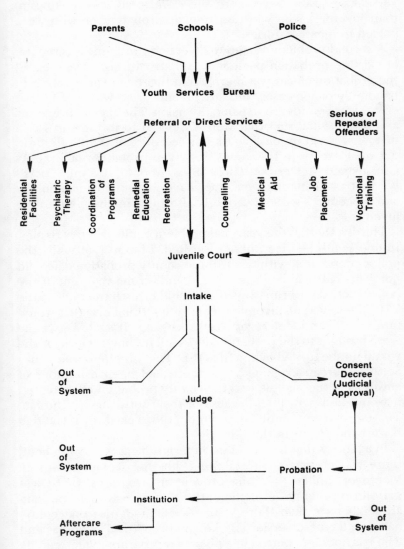

Source: President's Commission on Law Enforcement and Administration of Justice, *The Challenge of Crime in a Free Society* (Washington, D. C.: U. S. Government Printing Office, 1967), p. 89.

version program were more successful (had less recidivism) than juveniles who were on regular probation or who were placed in incarceratories.

A second problem related to diversion programs was the use of existing probation personnel and structure. In some cases, the probation officer was merely told that he or she was now to handle diversion cases, and any juvenile who was sent to that officer was considered to be on diversion. The special programs and professional staff that were supposed to use features of a diversion program or a Youth Service Bureau (YSB) often did not exist except in the new titles given probation officers. As Cressey and McDermott (1973:59) point out, "It is quite possible that participating personnel have revamped terminology and procedures without seriously altering what happens to the juvenile."

Thirdly, there is the very real problem of interagency rivalry. In one Youth Service Bureau I visited, I found that while the police cooperated with the YSB the county probation office did not. The YSB had been set up to handle runaways, and if the police picked up a runaway, they would bring him or her to the YSB. There was no juvenile record or anything else that would hint of a delinquent record or processing. If such a juvenile were brought to the probation department, however, he or she would not be turned over to the YSB. The director of the Youth Service Bureau explained that there had been a number of cutbacks in the budget, and the county probation office feared it would lose personnel because of the Youth Service Bureau. Therefore, the probation department did everything it could to thwart the efforts of the YSB.

In agencies that had a diversion program, as we pointed out, there was no way of determining whether it was successful. Moreover, unlike the gang prevention programs, there was very little program implementation. There was more bureaucratic rhetoric than there were specific activities that culminated in a true diversion. By keeping records of who has and who has not been placed in a diversion program (which can be done without giving the juvenile an official record), it will be possible to find whether or not the program is successful. Only

by actually setting up Youth Service Bureaus staffed by professional personnel who have been specifically prepared for *youth
service*, not merely for *control*, can we determine the program's success or failure.

CONCLUSION

We have now come full circle. Beginning with an overview of
the phenomenon of juvenile delinquency, we have examined
various theories of delinquency, the forms of delinquency, and
the societal reactions to delinquency. The phenomenon of delinquency begins and ends with some societal evaluation of a
juvenile's activities. In between there are numerous mitigating
elements, some of which are designed to control delinquency,
that in fact act to encourage certain patterns of delinquency.

The hope for the future lies not in more talk and rhetoric, but
instead, if we hope to understand and control delinquency, we
must develop and test theory. There is no paucity of ideas, but
ideas are not subject to the same rigors of serious theory and
empirical methodology. The basic research and theory development necessary in this area is the responsibility of sociology
students and practioners, and if there ever was a void to be
filled and an opportunity to add to human understanding, the
area of juvenile delinquency is that void.

References

ARNOLD, DAVID
1970 *The Sociology of Subcultures.* Berkeley, Calif.: Glendessary Press.

BECKER, HOWARD S.
1963 *Outsiders: Studies in the Sociology of Deviance.* New York: Free Press of Glencoe.
1967*a* "History, Culture, and Subjective Experience: An Exploration of the Social Bases of Drug-induced Experiences." *Journal of Health and Social Behavior* 8 (Sept.): 163–76.
1967*b* "Whose Side Are We On?" *Social Problems* 14 (Winter): 239–47.

BERGER, ARTHUR
1974 "Drug Advertising and the 'Pain, Pill, Pleasure' Model." *Journal of Drug Issues* 4 (Summer): 208–12.

BERNSTEIN, WALTER
1957 "The Cherubs are Rumbling." *The New Yorker* (Sept. 21).

BLACK, DONALD J., and REISS, ALBERT J., JR.
1970 "Police Control of Juveniles." *American Sociological Review* 35 (Feb.): 63–67.

BLUM, RICHARD H et al.
1970 *Students and Drugs.* San Francisco: Josey-Bass.

BLUMER, HERBERT
1969   *Symbolic Interaction: Perspective and Method.* Englewood Cliffs, N.J.: Prentice-Hall.

BOWERS, DON, and WHITE, LYNN
1974   "Behavior and Attitudes of Students: A Longitudinal Perspective." Turlock, Calif.: California State College, Stanislaus. Mimeographed.

CALIFORNIA, BOARD OF CORRECTIONS
1959   *Narcotics in California* (Feb. 18).

CALIFORNIA WELFARE AND INSTITUTION CODE
1972   Sacramento, Calif.: Department of General Services.

CAREY, JAMES
1968   *The College Drug Scene.* Englewood Cliffs, N.J.: Prentice-Hall.

CARTER, ROBERT M., and WILKINS, LESLIE T., eds.
1970   *Probation and Parole: Selected Readings.* New York: Wiley.

CAVAN, RUTH SHONLE
1962   *Juvenile Delinquency.* Philadelphia: Lippincott.

CAVAN, SHERRI
1963   "Interaction in Home Territories." *Berkeley Journal of Sociology* 8.

1970   "The Hippie Ethic and the Spirit of Drug Use." In *Observations of Deviance,* edited by Jack Douglas, pp. 314–26. New York: Random House.

CHAMBLISS, WILLIAM
1973   "The Saints and the Roughnecks." *Society* 11 (Nov.–Dec.): 24–31.

CHESNEY-LIND, MEDA
1974   "Juvenile Delinquency: The Sexualization of Female Crime." *Psychology Today* (July):43–46.

CICOUREL, AARON
1968   *The Social Organization of Juvenile Justice.* New York: Wiley.

CLOWARD, RICHARD A.
1959   "Illegitimate Means, Anomie, and Deviant Behavior." *American Sociological Review* 24 (Apr.): 164–76.

CLOWARD, RICHARD A., and OHLIN, LLOYD E.
1960   *Delinquency and Opportunity: A Theory of Delinquent Gangs.* New York: Free Press.

COFFEY, ALAN R.
1974   *Juvenile Justice as a System: Law Enforcement to Rehabilitation.* Englewood Cliffs, N.J.: Prentice-Hall.

COHEN, ALBERT
1955   *Delinquent Boys.* New York: Free Press.
1967   "Middle-Class Delinquency and the Social Structure." In *Middle-Class Juvenile Delinquency,* edited by Edmund W. Vaz. New York: Harper & Row.

COHEN, SIDNEY
1969   *The Drug Dilemma.* New York: McGraw-Hill.

COHN, YONA
1963   "Criteria for the Probation Officer's Recommendation to the Juvenile Court Judge." *Crime and Delinquency* (July): 262–75.

CONKLIN, JOHN E.
1972   *Robbery and the Criminal Justice System.* Philadelphia: Lippincott.

COOLEY, CHARLES HORTON
1902   *Human Nature and the Social Order.* New York: Scribner's.

COSER, LEWIS A.
1956   *The Functions of Social Conflict.* Glencoe, Ill.: Free Press.

CRESSEY, DONALD R.
1954   "The Differential Association Theory and Compulsive Crimes." *Journal of Criminal Law, Criminology, and Police Science* 45 (June): 29–40.
1971   *Other People's Money: A Study in the Social Psychology of Embezzlement.* Belmont, Calif.: Wadsworth.
1972   *Criminal Organization: Its Elementary Forms.* London: Heinemann.

CRESSEY, DONALD R., and MCDERMOTT, ROBERT A.
1973   *Diversion from the Juvenile Justice System.* Project Report for National Assessment of Juvenile Corrections (June). Ann Arbor: University of Michigan.

CRESSEY, DONALD R., and WARD, DAVID
1969   *Crime, Delinquency and Social Process.* New York: Harper & Row.

DAUDISTEL, HOWARD C., and SANDERS, WILLIAM B.
1974   "Police Discretion in Application of the Law," *et al.* 3: 26–40.

EMERSON, R. M.
1969   *Judging Delinquents: Context and Process in Juvenile Court.*
Chicago: Aldine-Atherton.

ENGLAND, RALPH W., JR.
1967   "A Theory of Middle-Class Juvenile Delinquency." In *Middle-Class Juvenile Delinquency*, edited by Edmund W. Vaz.
New York: Harper & Row.

ENGLISH, J.
1973   "Leaving Home: A Typology of Runaways." *Society* 10 (July–
Aug.): 22–24.

ENNIS, PHILLIP H.
1967   "Crimes, Victims, and the Police," *Trans-Action* 4 (June):
36–44.

ERIKSON, KAI
1962   "Notes on the Sociology of Deviance." *Social Problems*, 9
(Spring): 307-14.

EYNON, THOMAS G., and RECKLESS, WALTER C.
1961   "Championships at Delinquency Onset." *British Journal of
Criminology* 2 (Oct.): 167–68.

FEDERAL BUREAU OF INVESTIGATION
1972   *Uniform Crime Reports: Crime in the United States.* Washington, D.C.: U.S. Government Printing Office.

FINESTONE, HAROLD
1957   "Cats, Kicks and Color." *Social Problems* 5 (July): 3–13.

GARABEDIAN, PETER G., and GIBBONS, DON C., eds.
1970   *Becoming Delinquent: Young Offenders and the Correctional
System.* Chicago: Aldine.

GARFINKEL, HAROLD
1967   Studies in *Ethnomethodology.* Englewood Cliffs, N.J.: Prentice-Hall.

GEIS, GILBERT
1967   "Juvenile Gangs." From *Report of the President's Committee
on Juvenile Delinquency and Youth Crime*, pp. 1–16. Washington, D.C.: U.S. Government Printing Office.

GIBBONS, DON C.
1970   *Delinquent Behavior.* Englewood Cliffs, N.J.: Prentice-Hall.

GLUECK, SHELDON, and GLUECK, ELEANOR
1950   *Unraveling Juvenile Delinquency.* Cambridge: Harvard University Press.

GOFFMAN, ERVING
  1959   *The Presentation of Self in Everyday Life.* Garden City, N.Y.: Doubleday.
  1961   *Asylums.* Garden City, N.Y.: Doubleday.
  1963   *Stigma.* Englewood Cliffs, N.J.: Prentice-Hall.
  1967   *Interaction Ritual.* Garden City, N.Y.: Doubleday.

GOODMAN, PAUL
  1956   *Growing Up Absurd.* New York: Vintage Books.

GRISSOM, ROBERT J.
  1974   "The Effect of Guided Group Interaction Programs on Juvenile Delinquent Recidivism." Unpublished research paper, University of Florida, Gainesville.

HANDLER, JOEL
  1965   "The Juvenile Courts and the Adversary System: Problems of Function and Form," *Wisconsin Law Review* 54 (Winter): 7-51.

HARTJEN, CLAYTON A.
  1974   *Crime and Criminalization.* New York: Praeger.

HARTUNG, FRANK E.
  1965   *Crime, Law and Society.* Detroit: Wayne State University Press.

HASKELL, MARTIN R., and YABLONSKY, LEWIS
  1974   *Juvenile Delinquency.* Chicago: Rand McNally.

HOMER, LOUISE
  1973   "Juvenile Runaways." *Social Casework* 73 (Oct.): 473–79.

HOROWITZ, RUTH, and SCHWARTZ, GARY
  1974   "Honor, Normative Ambiguity and Gang Violence." *American Sociological Review* 39, No. 1: 238–51.

HUGHES, HELEN MACGILL
  1970   *Delinquents and Criminals: Their Social World.* Boston: Holbrook Press.

JACOBS, JANE
  1961   *The Death and Life of Great American Cities.* New York: Vintage Books.

JESNESS, CARL F.
  1965   *The Fricot Ranch Study.* Sacramento: State of California, Department of the Youth Authority.

JOHNSON, ELMER H.
  1974   *Crime, Correction and Society.* 3d ed. Homewood, Ill.: Dorsey Press.

KASSEBAUM, GENE
  1974   *Delinquency and Social Policy.* Englewood Cliffs, N.J.: Prentice-Hall.

KERPER, HAZEL B.
  1972   *Introduction to the Criminal Justice System.* St. Paul, Minn.: West.

KLEIN, MALCOLM
  1971   *Street Gangs and Street Workers.* Englewood Cliffs, N.J.: Prentice-Hall.

KNOCKE, PETER ANDREW
  1973   "The Economics of Marijuana: Current Estimates of Supply and Demand in an Illicit Market." Unpublished master's thesis, University of Florida, Gainesville.

KORBIN, SOLOMON
  1953   *Drug Addiction Among Young Persons in Chicago.* Illinois Institute for Juvenile Research (Oct.).

LEMERT, EDWIN
  1951   *Social Pathology.* New York: McGraw-Hill.
  1962   "Paranoia and the Dynamics of Exclusion." *Sociometry* 25 (Mar.): 2–20.
  1967*a*   *Human Deviance, Social Problems and Social Control.* Englewood Cliffs, N.J.: Prentice-Hall.
  1967*b*   "The Juvenile Court—Quest and Realities." In *Task Force Report: Juvenile Delinquency and Youth Crime,* by the President's Commission on Law Enforcement and Administration of Justice, pp. 91–97. Washington, D.C.: U.S. Government Printing Office.

LERMAN, PAUL
  1973   "Delinquents without Crimes." In *Law and Order: The Scales of Justice,* edited by Abraham S. Blumberg, pp. 241- 69. NewBrunswick, N.J.: Transaction Books.

LINDESMITH, ALFRED
  1947   *Opiate Addiction.* Bloomington, Ind.: Principia Press.

LUCKENBILL, DAVID
  1974   "Other People's Lives." Unpublished master's paper, University of California, Santa Barbara.

LYMAN, STANFORD, and SCOTT, MARVIN B.
  1970   *A Sociology of the Absurd.* New York: Appleton-Century-Crofts.

MCHUGH, PETER
1968   *Defining the Situation.* Indianapolis: Bobbs-Merrill.

MADISON, ARNOLD
1970   *Vandalism: The Not-So-Senseless Crime.* New York: Seabury Press.

MARTIN, JOHN M.
1961   *Juvenile Vandalism: A Study of Its Nature and Prevention.* Springfield, Ill.: Charles C. Thomas.

MARX, KARL
1910   *Poverty of Philosophy.* Translated by H. Quelch. Chicago: Charles H. Kerr.

MARX, KARL, and ENGELS, FRIEDRICH
1888   *Manifesto of the Communist Party.* Chicago: Charles H. Kerr.

MAYHEW, HENRY
1861   *London Labor and the London Poor.* London: Griffin, Bohn, and Co. (Reference from excerpt in *The Heritage of Modern Criminology,* edited by Sawyer F. Sylvester, Jr., pp. 47–62. Cambridge, Mass.: Schenkman, 1972).

MERTON, ROBERT K.
1957   *Social Theory and Social Structure.* New York: Free Press.

MILLER, WALTER
1966   "Violent Crimes in City Gangs." *Annals of the American Academy of Political and Social Sciences* 343 (Mar.): 97–112.

1969   "White Gangs." *Trans-action* (Sept.): 11–26.

MILLS, C. WRIGHT
1940   "Situated Action and the Vocabulary of Motives." *American Sociological Review* 6 (Dec.): 904–13.

NATIONAL ADVISORY COMMISSION ON CRIMINAL JUSTICE STANDARDS AND GOALS
1973   *A National Strategy to Reduce Crime.* Washington, D.C.: U.S. Government Printing Office.

NEIGHER, ALAN
1967   "The Gault Decision: Due Process and the Juvenile Courts." *Federal Probation* (Dec.): 8–18.

NETTLER, GWYNN
1974   *Explaining Crime.* New York: McGraw-Hill.

NEWSWEEK
1970   "The New Gangs" (May 8).

PACKER, HERBERT L.

1968 *The Limits of the Criminal Sanction.* Stanford: Stanford University Press.

PARKER, T., and ALLERTON, R.

1962 *The Courage of His Convictions.* London: Hutchinson & Co.

PENNSYLVANIA, COMMONWEALTH OF

1953 Public Law 1433.

PILIAVIN, IRVING, and BRIAR, SCOTT

1964 "Police Encounters with Juveniles." *American Journal of Sociology* 70 (Sept.): 206–14.

PLATT, ANTHONY

1969 *The Child-Savers: The Invention of Delinquency.* Chicago: University of Chicago Press.

1974 "The Triumph of Benevolence: The Origins of the Juvenile Justice System in the United States." In *Criminal Justice in America: A Critical Understanding,* edited by Richard Quinney. Boston: Little, Brown.

POLSKY, NED

1969 *Hustlers, Beats and Others.* Garden City, N.Y.: Doubleday.

PRESIDENT'S COMMISSION ON LAW ENFORCEMENT AND ADMINISTRATION OF JUSTICE

1967 *The Challenge of Crime in a Free Society.* Washington, D.C.: U.S. Government Printing Office.

QUICKER, JOHN

1974 "The Chicana Gang: A Preliminary Description." Paper presented at the annual meetings of the Pacific Sociological Association, San Jose, Calif. Mimeographed.

RECHY, JOHN

1961 "A Quarter Ahead." *Evergreen Review* 5 (July–Aug.).

REISS, ALBERT, JR.

1960 "Sex Offenses: The Marginal Status of the Adolescent." *Law and Contemporary Problems* 25 (Spring).

1961 "The Social Integration of Queers and Peers." *Social Problems* 9 (Fall): 102–20.

1971 *The Police and the Public.* New Haven, Conn.: Yale University Press.

REISS, ALBERT J., JR., and RHODES, A. LEWIS

1964 "An Empirical Test of Differential Association Theory." *Journal of Research in Crime and Delinquency* 1 (Jan.): 5–18.

REISS, IRA L.
  1970   "Premarital Sex as Deviant Behavior: An Application to Current Deviance." *American Sociological Review* 35 (Feb.): 78–87.

ROBIN, GERALD D.
  1963   "Patterns of Department Store Shoplifting." *Crime and Delinquency* 9 (Apr.): 163–72.

RODMAN, HYMAN, and GRAMS, PAUL
  1967   "Juvenile Delinquency and the Family: A Review and Discussion." Appendix L of *Task Force Report: Juvenile Delinquency and Youth Crime*, by the President's Commission on Law Enforcement and Administration of Justice, pp. 188–221. Washington, D.C.: U.S. Government Printing Office.

ROSENBERG, BERNARD, and SILVERSTEIN, HARRY
  1969   *The Varieties of Delinquent Experience*. Waltham, Mass.: Blaisdell.

ROSSI, PETER H., et al.
  1974   "The Seriousness of Crimes: Normative Structure and Individual Differences." *American Sociological Review* 39 (Apr.): 224–37.

RUBINGTON, CARL, and WEINBERG, MARTIN S.
  1968   *Deviance: The Interactionist Perspective*. New York: Macmillan.

RUBINSTEIN, JONATHAN
  1973   *City Police*. New York: Farrar, Straus & Giroux.

SANDERS, WILLIAM B.
  1970   "Drug Use Among Suburban Midwest High School Students." Unpublished consultant paper prepared for Palos Township Youth Council.

  1974   "Detective Story: A Study of Criminal Investigations." Ph.D. diss. University of California, Santa Barbara.

SANDERS, WILLIAM B., and LUCKENBILL, DAVID
  1974   "Occasions: Criminal Investigations and Criminal Homicide." Working paper presented at the annual meetings of the American Sociological Association, Montreal, Canada (Aug.).

SCHEPSES, ERVIN
  1961   "Boys Who Steal Cars." *Federal Probation* (Mar.): 56–62.

SCHUB, CHRISTINE CAROL
1973   "A Comparison of Social and Personality Characteristics of Incarcerated Drug Users and Non-Users." Master's thesis, University of Florida.

SCOTT, MARVIN B., and LYMAN, STANFORD M.
1968   "Accounts." *American Sociological Review* 33: 46–62.
1970   *The Revolt of the Students.* New York: Charles Merrill.

SELLIN, THORSTEN
1938   "Culture Conflict and Crime." Bulletin 41, Social Science Research Council.

SELLIN, THORSTEN, and WOLFGANG, MARVIN E.
1964   *The Measurement of Delinquency.* New York: Wiley.

SHAW, CLIFFORD R.
1933   "Juvenile Delinquency: A Group Tradition." Bulletin of the State University of Iowa, no. 23, N.S. no. 700.

SHAW, CLIFFORD R., and MCKAY, HENRY D.
1931   "Social Factors in Juvenile Delinquency: A Study of the Community, the Family, and the Gang in Relation to Delinquent Behavior." In *Report on the Causes of Crime* by the National Commission on Law Observance and Enforcement, vol. 2, no. 13, chap. 6. Washington, D.C.: U.S. Government Printing Office.

SHERIDAN, WILLIAM H.
1967   "Juveniles Who Commit Noncriminal Acts: Why Treat in a Correctional System?" *Federal Probation* 31 (Mar.): 26–30.

SHIRLEY, DAVID L.
1972   "Semi-Retired Graffiti Scrawlers Paint Mural at C.C.N.Y. 133." *New York Times* (Dec. 8): 49.

SHORT, JAMES F., JR.
1968   *Gang Delinquency and Delinquent Subcultures.* New York: Harper & Row.

SHORT, JAMES F., JR., and NYE, F. IVAN
1958   "Extent of Unrecorded Juvenile Delinquency: Tentative Conclusions." *Journal of Criminal Law, Criminology, and Police Science* 49 (Nov.–Dec.): 296–302.

SIMMEL, GEORG
1950   *The Sociology of Georg Simmel.* Edited by Kurt H. Wolff. New York: Free Press.

SIMMONS, JERRY, and WINOGRAD, BARRY)
1966   *It's Happening.* Santa Barbara, Calif.: Marc-Laird.

SIMON, WILLIAM, and GAGNON, JOHN H.
    1968   "Children of the Drug Age." *Saturday Review* 51 (Sept. 21):
            60–78.

SLOCUM, WALTER, and STONE, CAROL L.
    1963   "Family Culture Patterns and Delinquent-type Behavior."
            Marriage and Family Living 25: 202–8.

SMITH, KENNETH C.
    1974   "A Profile of Juvenile Court Judges in the United States."
            Juvenile Justice 25 (Aug.): 27–38.

SPERGEL, IRVING
    1964   *Racketville, Slumtown and Haulburg.* Chicago: University of
            Chicago Press.

SPRADLEY, JAMES
    1970   *You Owe Yourself a Drunk.* Boston: Little, Brown.

STINCHCOMBE, ARTHUR L.
    1963   "Institutions of Privacy in the Determination of Police Ad-
            ministrative Practice." *American Journal of Sociology* 69
            (Sept.): 150–60.

STUMBO, BELLA
    1973   "Spector of Houston Haunts Parents." *Los Angeles Times*
            (Sept. 16).

SUTHERLAND, EDWIN H., and CRESSEY, DONALD R.
    1974   *Criminology.* 9th ed. Philadelphia: Lippincott.

SYKES, GRESHAM, and MATZA, DAVID
    1957   "Techniques of Neutralization: A Theory of Delinquency."
            American Sociological Review 22 (Dec.): 664–70.

TENENBAUM, S.
    1947   *Why Men Hate.* New York: Beechhurst Press.

THOMAS, W. I.
    1923   *The Unadjusted Girl.* Boston: Little, Brown.

THRASHER, F. M.
    1936   *The Gang.* Chicago: Chicago University Press.

TIME
    1969   "Zapping Zap." (May 16).
    1970   "Kids and Heroin: The Adolescent Epidemic." (Mar. 16).

TOBY, JACKSON
    1957   "The Differential Impact of Family Disorganization." *Ameri-
            can Sociological Review* 22 (Oct.): 502–12.

WALLACE, THOMAS
1972 "Culture and Social Being." Unpublished masters paper, University of California, Santa Barbara.

WATTENBERG, WILLIAM W., and BALISTRIERI, JAMES
1952 "Automobile Theft: A 'Favored Group' Delinquency." *American Journal of Sociology* 57 (May): 575–79.

WEINER, NORMAN
1970 "The Teen-age Shoplifter: A Microcosmic View of Middle-Class Delinquency." In *Observations of Deviance*, edited by Jack Douglas. New York: Random House.

WERTHMAN, CARL
1967 "The Function of Social Definitions in the Development of Delinquent Careers." *Task Force Report: Juvenile Delinquency and Youth Crime.* Washington, D.C.: U.S. Government Printing Office.

WERTHMAN, CARL, and PILIAVIN, IRVING
1967 "Gang Members and the Police." In *The Police: Six Sociological Essays*, edited by David J. Bordua. New York: Wiley.

WESTLEY, WILLIAM A.
1953 "Violence and the Police." *American Journal of Sociology* 49 (July): 34–41.

WHEELER, STANTON, and COTTRELL, LEONARD S.
1966 *Juvenile Delinquency: Its Prevention and Control.* New York: Russel Sage Foundation.

WHITTEN, PHILIP, and ROBERTSON, IAN
1972 "A Way to Control Heroin." *Boston Globe Magazine* (May 21).

WHYTE, WILLIAM H., JR.
1956 *The Organization Man.* New York: Simon & Schuster.

WIEDER, D. LAWRENCE
1973 *Language and Social Reality: The Case of Telling the Convict Code.* The Hague: Mouton.

WILSON, JAMES Q.
1968 "The Police and the Delinquent in Two Cities." In *Controlling Delinquents*, edited by Stanton Wheeler, pp. 9–30. New York: Wiley.

WINICK, CHARLES
1961 "Physician Narcotic Addicts." *Social Problems* 9 (Fall): 174–86.

WISEMAN, JACQUELINE
1970   *Stations of the Lost.* Englewood Cliffs, N.J.: Prentice-Hall.

YABLONSKY, LEWIS
1962   *The Violent Gang.* Baltimore: Penguin Books.
1965   *The Tunnel Back: Synanon.* New York: Macmillan.
1968   *The Hippie Trip.* Indianapolis: Pegasus.

YANKELOVICH, DANIEL
1974   *The New Morality: A Profile of American Youth in the 70's.*
New York: McGraw-Hill.

ZIMMERMAN, DON H.
1970   "The Practicalities of Rule Use," In *Understanding Everyday Life,* edited by Jack Douglas, pp. 221–38. Chicago: Aldine.

ZORBAUGH, HARVEY W.
1929   *The Gold Coast and the Slum.* Chicago: University of Chicago Press.

Index

advertising, 112-13,114, 115
age, 46-47; gangs and, 137; generation gap and, 40, 41-45, 111; homosexual activity and, 71, 72; incarceration and, 177, 184-85; misrepresentation of, 25; offenses defined by, 3-8 (*See also* juvenile-status offenses); property crime arrest rates and, 12, 84, 87-88, 92-93, 104; psychiatric commitment and, 194-95
alcohol, 22, 32, 60, 75, 113, 128; class and, 135, 166; juvenile status and, 4, 21, 64, 66, 82, 83, 89; liquor law violations, self-reported, 16 (*tab.*), 17(*tab.*), 25, 81; situational use of, 121
alienation, 95, 101, 103, 207
Allerton, R., cited, 53
amphetamines, 18(*tab.*), 22, 126, 146
Ann Arbor, Michigan, 131
antifornication laws, 65n
anti-Semitism, 41, 101-102, 201
Arkansas, 206
Arnold, David, cited, 41
arrest, 64; class and, 11-12; drugs and, 109; false arrest risks, 87; group crimes and, 12, 105, 144; police discretion in, 157, 158-68, 170-73, 174, 175, 184, 187; for property crimes, 84, 88-89, 90, 92-93, 104; self-reported offenses compared, 15, 16(*tab.*), 17 (*tab.*); victim reports compared, 13-14, 19
arson, 53, 95

assault and battery, 15, 22, 38, 66, 151, 166, 169 (*tab.*); for profit, 143; self-reported rates of, 16(*tab.*), 17(*tab.*), 20
association, *see* differential association
auto theft, 10, 20, 24, 30, 92-95, 105, 145; arrest rates, 12, 13, 15-18, 84; as character test, 57, 58, 144; court anticipation of, 181; residual vandalism and, 97-98

Balboa, California, 99
Balistrieri, James, cited, 92, 93
barbiturates, 22, 112
Beat movement, 110, 113
Becker, H.S., 23, 53-54, 114, 115
behavior: advertising and, 112-13, 114, 115; in arrest, 158-61, 162, 165, 166, 167, 170, 171-72; association and, 46-47, 48-49, 50; conformity or deviance in, 23-24, 25, 30-35, 51-54, 182; drugs and, 120-21; labeling and, *see* labeling; nonutilitarian, 38-41, 60-61, 93, 94, 95-96, 97
Berger, Arthur, quoted, 112
Bernstein, Walter, quoted, 142
birth control, 82
Black, Donald J., cited, 11, 161, 162
blacks, 11, 70, 114, 160, 161, 162
Blum, Richard H., cited, 118
Blumer, Herbert, cited, 8
Boston, Massachusetts, 96, 135
Bowers, Don, cited, 50

231

Briar, Scott, 11, 157, 158, 159(tab.),
  162, 165, 174; quoted, 160
Brooklyn, New York, 134-35
burglary, 53, 143, 144, 189-90, 191;
  juvenile status and, 4, 65, 84;
  police time on, 169(tab.); skills,
  45-46, 85, 145; vandalism and,
  96, 97
California, 95, 99, 147-48; 180;
  juvenile status in, 4-5, 20; surfing
  in, 19; training school in, 202-204
California Board of Corrections,
  quoted, 148
California Welfare and Institutions
  Code, 4-5, 6
Carey, James, quoted, 108
Carter, Robert M., cited, 200
Cavan, Ruth, 70-71, 93, 101
Cavan, Sherri, cited, 115-16, 118, 153
Chambliss, William, 135, 165-68
character, 55-61, 62-63, 76, 85. See
  also identity; status; values
Chesney-Lind, Meda, 69; quoted, 82
Chicago, Illinois, 147, 153, 207;
  courts, 177; gang violence in, 148;
  Oldtown, 42; vandalism in, 101,
  103
Cicourel, Aaron, 27, 89, 101, 186, 188,
  189-94, 200
civil rights, 42, 58-59; due process,
  81, 177-78, 179, 180, 183-84, 185
class, 22, 43, 44-45; arrest records
  and, 11-12, 165-68; associations
  and, 50-51, 53; character tests and,
  56-58; gangs and, 135-36, 138, 146,
  150-51, 155; opportunity and, 28,
  29-30, 31, 32-34, 35-36, 38-40, 149,
  167, 176-77; sexual mores and, 70,
  71, 72. See also middle class;
  poverty
Cloward, R., 32-35, 38, 39, 138, 147-
  48
cocaine, 18(tab.), 132
Coffey, Alan R., cited, 176, 178
Cohen, Albert, 38-40, 97, 98, 138
Cohen, Sidney, 107, 123, 124
Cohn, Yona, cited, 199
Columbia University, 103
compulsive crimes, 49-50
condemnation device, 36, 37
conflict, 40, 43-45, 61; community
  stability and, 34-35; unrealistic,
  41. See also violence
conflict gangs, 38, 141-43, 145, 146,
  148

conformity, 30, 31, 33, 115; in subcultures, 23-24, 25, 32, 34, 35
Conklin, John E., cited, 93
Cooley, Charles Horton, cited, 52
correctional institutions, 1, 164, 165,
  177, 197-215; diversion program
  alternative to, 211-15; gangs and,
  144; homosexuality in, 72; inmate
  and high school self-report groups
  compared, 15, 16(tab.), 17(tab.),
  67, 86; mental, 195-96; probation
  as alternative to, 179, 187, 199,
  200; sentences, 65-66, 72, 78, 83,
  178, 179; stigmatization and, 53,
  158; street work as alternative to,
  207-11
Coser, Lewis A., cited, 41
Cottrell, Leonard S., cited, 31
counterculture, 31, 42-43
courage, 33, 35, 56, 150; drugs and,
  59-60; property crimes and, 57-58,
  85, 88, 100, 144; runaways and, 79.
  See also honor; status
Cressey, Donald R.: cited, 46, 47-48,
  49, 50, 77, 88, 92, 96, 198; on diversion programs, 211, 212,
crime, 1, 25, 45-46, 83; incarceration
  rates for, 65-66; police investigative time on, 169(tab.), 170.
  See also delinquency
"criminal gangs," 142-45, 146
criminalization process, 26-63, 82;
  shoplifting and, 88-90
curfew violations, 25, 64, 200
custody, as institutional goal, 197,
  198, 202, 204, 205
Daudistel, Howard C., cited, 92, 191
delinquency, 33, 174-75; anticiapted,
  178-79, 181; character theory of,
  55-61; frequency estimates, 12-19,
  54, 186; intention and, 8-9, 100-
  101; juvenile status and, 3-8, 15,
  20-22, 24-25, 64-83; records and,
  10-11, 12, 13, 51-54, 168-70, 175;
  rehabilitation, 187, 197
demeanor, 159-61, 162, 165, 170, 171-
  72; class and, 166, 167
detention centers, 1, 2, 7, 184-85. See
  also correctional institutions
deterrence, as incarceration goal,
  198
deviance: defined, 23-24, 25; labeling and, 51-54; secondary; 52, 53,

deviance (cont.)
54, 182; structural frustration and, 31, 32
differential association, 40, 44-51, 55, 61-62; diversion programs and, 211-12; labeling and, 52-53, 54; runaways and, 76; vandalism and, 99, 100, 105-106
discipline: gang, 146, 147, 208, 210; home, 28, 128; institutional, 203-205; by the judicial system, 58, 59, 163, 187. See also laws, enforcement severity
"double failures," 32, 35, 36, 147-48
dress, 154-55, 160
drop-outs, 30-31, 36; drug culture and, 111, 126, 147
drugs, 2, 3, 19, 22, 75, 85, 107-33; character testing and, 59-60; gangs and, 146-48, 156; laws on, 41-42, 108, 111, 112; property crimes and, 86; retreatism and, 30, 31, 32, 35-36, 39; self-reported rates of use, 16(tab.), 17(tab.), 18, 50
due process of law, 81, 177-78, 179, 180, 183-84, 185

education, 20, 21, 45; auto theft and, 93, 94; class and, 29-30, 36; in criminal skills, 1, 45-46, 47-48, 50, 83, 85, 98-99, 145, 198-99, 211; of judges, 183; official focus on, 191, 192, 194; "predelinquent," 178; in prison schools, 202, 203; sexual, 82; of social workers, 212, 214-15; vandalism and, 95, 104-105
embezzlement, 49, 50
Emerson, R.M., cited, 187
employment, 3, 20, 21, 44, 176; prostitution as, 70-71, 72, 73; social goals and, 29, 36, 39-40
Engels, Friedrich, cited, 43
England, Ralph W., Jr., cited, 40
England, 130, 134
English, J., cited, 76-80
Ennis, Phillip H., cited, 13, 14
Erikson, Kai, cited, 10
"erosive vandalism," 102-104
ethnic groups, 11, 24, 42, 160, 161, 162; auto theft and, 93, 94; gangs and, 114, 139-40; Nazi persecution of, 41, 201; sexual mores and, 70; vandalism and, 101-102, 104
excitement, 59-60; gangs and, 143,

144; property crimes and, 85, 91, 92, 93, 94, 99-101, 105; running away for, 75, 79, 80
Eynon, Thomas G., cited, 50

family, 10-11, 184; "broken homes," 27, 36; "control" in, 2, 4-5, 7-8, 21, 27-28, 39, 42, 64, 66, 73-75, 82; defiance (self-reported) of, 16(tab.), 17(tab.); drugs and, 113, 128, 129; gang model of, 137-38; probation interviews, 193-95, 199; runaways and, 73, 74-75, 76, 77, 79, 170, 175; theft from, 86; value conflicts in, 40, 41-45, 68, 82; wealth and, 29-30, 75
fashion, 15, 18-19, 26, 42, 120
Federal Bureau of Investigation, 11, 14, 109
Federal Narcotics Bureau, 108, 111, 113-14
Finestone, Harold, cited, 60
floaters, 76-78, 80
forgery, 169(tab.)
Fort Lauderdale, Florida, 99
Fricot Ranch School, 202-204

Gagnon, John H., cited, 113
game laws, 6-7, 8, 16(tab.), 17(tab.)
gangs, 3, 22, 35, 36-37, 134-56; arrest rates and, 12, 144, 160-61; character testing in, 56-58, 60-61, 156, 208-209; criminal subculture rejection of, 34, 142; drugs and, 114, 146-48, 156; fight participation (self-reported), 16(tab.), 17(tab.); invidual roles in, 9, 25, 26, 32, 33, 47, 55-56, 137, 143, 144, 146, 150; "street work" with, 207-11, 212, 214
Gerabedian, Peter G., 197, 204
Garfinkel, Harold, 89, 123, 167
Gault decision, 81, 183, 184, 185
Geis, Gilbert, cited, 134
Germany, 41, 134
Gibbons, Don, 6, 19, 67, 93, 135, 197, 204
girls 17(tab.); arrest rates, 15, 25; gangs and, 137-38, 139-40; incarceration rates, 64, 65; runaways, 70-71, 75-76, 77-78; sexual "immorality" and, 21, 43, 64-65, 67, 68-69, 70-71, 72-73, 82, 83, 181, 191-96, 199
Glueck, S. and E., 27, 28

Goffman, E., 52, 122, 196, 204, 205, 209; character theory of, 55-61, 62, 76, 94, 100, 150
Goodman, Paul, cited, 81
graffiti, 102-104
Grams, Paul, cited, 28
Great Britain, 130, 134
Grissom, Robert J., cited, 206
guilt, 179-84, 185; rationalizations of, 36-38, 91-92
guns, 98, 99, 142, 151-52

halfway houses, 131
Handler, Joel, quoted, 183
hangouts, 154-55
hard-road freaks, 79-80
Hartjen, Clayton A., cited, 7, 26
Haskell, Martin R., cited, 103, 126, 138, 140, 141, 143-44
hearings, 178, 179-86, 193
hepatitis, 129
heroin, 18(tab.), 30, 60, 86, 110, 113; addiction to, 128-32; gangs and, 146, 147; marijuana and, 108, 111, 121, 127-28
high school students: drugs and, 109, 116-17, 120; training school groups compared with, 15, 16(tab.), 17(tab.), 18, 20, 67, 86
hippies, 3, 19, 31, 36; drugs and, 2, 110, 111-12, 113, 114, 115-16, 118-20, 122-25, 126, 133, 146
Hitler, Adolf, 41
Holland, 201-202
Homer, Louise, cited, 75, 77, 78
homosexuality, 37, 71-73, 165; self-reported practice of, 16(tab.), 17(tab.)
honor, 149-50, 160-61; drugs and, 148, 156; rumbles and, 60-61, 151, 152. See also courage; status
Horowitz, Ruth, 60, 148-49, 151
housing, 35
Houston, Texas, 74
Hughes, Helen MacGill, cited, 92

identity: gang membership and, 137-41, 146, 150, 156; incarceration and, 198; labeling and, 51-54, 62, 63, 135-36, 181-82; performance and, 55-61, 62, 76; property crime and, 85, 94, 144; runaways and, 79, 80
incapacitation, 197, 198

Indiana, University of, 108
individual, the: criminal training and, 1, 46, 85; gang leadership and, 139, 144, 150-51; media stereotypes and, 80-81; police cooperation and, 159-61, 171-74; property crimes and, 85-86, 94; self-image of, see identity; social milieu and patterning, 46-49; structural frustration and, 26-32, 35, 61, 70-71, 76, 208; subculture conflicts and, 43, 61, 206
interactionist theory, 62-63, 212; arrest and, 159-60; justice system and, 196; symbolic, 51-54, 55; vandalism and, 105-106
Italians, 70
Jacobs, Jane, cited, 153
Japan, 134
Jesness, Carl F., quoted, 203-204
Jews, 41, 101-102, 201
Johnson, Elmer H., cited, 27
judges, 179; case loads, 182-83; conduct of hearings, 178, 180-81, 184, 186
juvenile courts, 15, 81, 176-96, 210, 212; homosexual activity and, 72-73; juvenile-status offenses and, 2, 5, 7-8, 20, 42-43, 44, 65-66, 67, 78, 80, 82, 83, 177-79, 184; police attitudes toward, 158, 163, 164-65; records, 13, 14, 19, 22, 89-90, 92, 163, 187-88; sentencing patterns of, 27, 64, 65-66; women's treatment in, 69-70, 181, 185, 193, 199
juvenile-status offenses, 3-8, 20-21, 24, 30, 64-83, 177, 179, 184; generation gap and, 42-43; hearings, 185

Kassebaum, Gene, cited, 187
Kent v. United States 183, 185
Kerper, Hazel, 180, 184, 185, 186
Klein, Malcolm, quoted, 207-208, 209
Knocke, Peter, 120, 132
Korbin, Solomon, cited, 147
Ku Klux Klan, 24

labeling, 51-54, 55, 62; court hearings and, 180-82, 186, 187-88; diversion programs and, 211-12; gangs and, 135-36; police "delinquent histories" and, 157, 189-91; probation disposition and, 191-96; runaway records and, 80, 170, 175; shoplifting records and, 88-90

larceny, 21, 57-58, 84-106,169(*tab.*);
justice system responses to, 65-66,
135, 164-65, 168, 170, 189, 190; for
profit, 71, 85, 143-44, 145; rates of,
13-14, 16(*tab.*), 17(*tab.*), 20. *See
also specific forms of larceny,
e.g., burglary*
laws: attitudes toward, 1, 21-22, 23,
24, 33, 40, 43, 46, 48, 73, 159, 183-
84; on auto theft, 92, 93; drugs
and, 41-42, 108, 111, 112, 115, 126,
129, 130, 131, 132, 133; enforcement severity, 58, 59, 65-66, 72-73,
81, 88-90, 108, 130, 157-59, 162-63,
164, 174-75, 210; juvenility defined
by, 3-7, 20, 45; offenses defined by,
2, 6-9, 15, 21, 40, 64, 177; social
goals and, 29, 30, 32, 176-79, 181
Leary, Timothy, quoted 111
Lemert, Edwin, 52, 140, 180, 181
Lerman, Paul, cited, 65, 66
Lindesmith, Alfred, 108
Los Angeles, California, 42, 74, 103,
180; street work in, 207, 208
LSD, 18(*tab.*), 59, 111, 113, 116, 122-
25, 147
Luckenbill, David, 49
Lyman, S. M., 24, 56, 59, 153

McDermott, R.A., 211, 212, 214
McHugh, Peter, 140
McKay, Henry D., cited, 50
Madison, A., 99, 100, 101, 102
malevolent vandalism, 101-102
malicious mischief, 5, 8. *See also* vandalism
marijuana, 22, 60, 110, 113, 116-21,
146, 147; decriminalization of, 41-
42, 131; high school use rates
(1970), 18(*tab.*), 50; physiological
effects of, 107-108, 111, 114-15,
119, 127-28
marriage, 20, 42, 68, 70
Martin, J., 96, 97, 98, 99, 101, 104
Marx, Karl, cited, 43
mass media: drugs and, 110, 111-12,
113, 114, 115, 130, 133; social
values and, 28-29, 40, 59, 80, 82,
113
materialism, 28-29, 116; responses
to, 30-31, 36, 39-40, 42, 111, 125,
150-51
Matza, David, cited, 36, 37, 40, 91
Mayhew, Henry, 134
mental institutions, 195-96, 205

Merton, Robert, cited, 28-29, 30, 31,
32, 35, 147
mescaline, 18(*tab.*), 110
methadone, 131
methedrine, 111, 126
Mexicans, 139-40
middle class, 35, 36, 38, 39, 56, 110;
arrest records and, 11-12, 165-68;
associations and, 50-51; auto theft
and, 93-94; drugs and, 117-18,
128-29, 131-32, 146; gangs and,
135-36, 146, 150-51, 155;
materialist goals and, 28-29, 30,
39-40; runaways and, 75, 80; sexual mores of, 70, 72-73; shoplifting
and, 90-91, 92; vandalism and, 95
Miller, Walter: quoted, 153-54; on
gang structure, 47, 60, 134, 135,
136, 137-38, 139, 144; on gang
violence, 148, 150, 151, 152
minorities, labeling and, 54. *See also*
ethnic groups
Montana, 96
Muedeking, George, 206*n*
murder, 2, 5, 49-50, 158; gang
violence and, 151; of runaways, 74

National Advisory Commission on
Criminal Justice Standards and
Goals, 211
Nazis, 201-202
neighborhoods, 34-35, 37, 70, 131-32;
gangs and, 42, 47, 134-36, 138, 140,
142-43, 145, 146, 150, 151, 153-55,
156, 167; vandalism and, 97, 103
Neigher, Alan, cited, 183
Nettler, Gwynn, cited, 49
neutralization techniques, 36-38;
shoplifting and, 91-92
Newsweek (periodical), 147, 150
New York City, New York, 42, 69, 73,
207; gang violence in, 148; heroin
deaths (1969) in, 129; vandalism
in, 102-103
New York City Transit Authority,
103
New York State, 103, 180
non-utilitarian behavior, 38-41, 60-
61; auto theft, 93, 94; vandalism,
13, 38, 95-105
norms, 23-24, 25, 41; collective
frustration and, 33, 35, 44; guilt on
violation of, 36-38; rejection of,
30-31, 32. *See also* values
North Dakota, 99

Nye, F. Ivan, cited, 16(*tab.*), 17(*tab.*), 18, 20, 67, 81, 86, 109

Ohlin, Lloyd E., cited, 32-35, 38, 39, 138, 147-48
opium, 18(*tab.*), 132
opportunity, 29-30, 80, 167; for character testing, 56-58; subculture alternatives to, 32-34, 35-36, 38-41, 144, 145, 149-50

Packer, Herbert L., cited, 132
parens patriae philosophy, 180, 181, 183-84
Parker, T., cited, 53
"pass system," 164-65
peer groups, 40, 41-45, 63; drugs and, 50, 85, 115, 118, 128, 129, 130-31, 132; gangs, 47 (*See also* gangs); prison cliques, 204; property crimes and, 84-86, 88, 91-92, 93, 94, 97-98, 99, 102, 103, 104-105, 106; runaways and, 75, 76, 78-79, 83
Pennsylvania, 5-6
peyote, 18(*tab.*), 110
Philadelphia, Pennsylvania, 87, 97; gangs, 135, 136-37
Piliavin, I., 11, 154, 157, 158, 159(*tab.*), 162, 165, 174; quoted, 160
"PINS" (Persons in Need of Supervision), 178
Platt, Anthony, cited, 176, 177
police, 1, 2, 7, 8, 9, 24, 46, 157-75, 178, 184; drugs and, 109, 110, 118, 127, 129, 132; gangs and, 135, 136-37, 145, 152, 153, 155, 160-61; juvenile detective work of, 168-74; proeprty crimes and, 88-89, 92, 94, 97, 101; records of, 10-11, 12, 13, 14, 19, 54, 89, 94, 158, 168-70, 187, 189-91; runaway caseloads and, 73-75, 168-70, 214; severity of, 58, 59, 151, 158-61, 162-63, 164, 165, 210
Polsky, Ned, 110; quoted, 108
poverty, 29, 31, 56, 176-77; arrest rates and, 11-12, 22, 165-68; drugs and, 131, 132; labeling and, 53, 54; neighborhood and, 34-35, 167; property crimes and, 85, 90-91, 94, 98; psychotherapy and, 195-96; runaways and, 75; sexual trade and, 70, 71-72; violence and, 149-50

"predelinquents," 178
President's Commission on Law Enforcement and Administration of Justice, 14, 178, 199; on diversion programs, 211, 213(*fig.*); on property crime rates, 11, 12, 84
prison, *see* correctional institutions
probation, 53, 178, 187-96, 199-201; diversion programs and, 212, 214; interrogation techniques of, 191-95; juvenile status and, 7, 79; records of, 89, 101, 180, 183, 184, 185-86, 188; referral discretion, 172, 173, 179, 180, 184, 187 .
property crimes, 11, 30, 84-106; class and, 28, 90-91, 92, 93-94, 95, 96; gangs and, 144; self-reported rates of, 16(*tab.*), 17(*tab.*). *See also* larceny; vandalism
prostitution, 71-72, 73
psychology, 26, 27, 28; psychotherapeutic access, 193-96
Puerto Ricans, 104, 114

Quicker, J., 137, 138, 139, 140

racketeers, 33-34, 142, 145
rape, 65, 66, 83, 158; statutory, 21
rebellion, defined, 31
Rechy, John, quoted, 71
recidivism, 90, 158, 212, 214; "pass system" and, 164-65
Reckless, Walter C., cited, 50
recordkeeping, 10-11, 12, 163; auto theft and, 94; diversion programs and, 212, 214; estimates of unreported delinquency, 13-19, 22, 54; labeling process of, 51-54, 158, 168-71, 175, 180-81, 183, 187, 189-91; probation reports, 89, 101, 180, 183, 184, 185-86, 188, 191-95; secrecy in, 179; shoplifting charges and, 88-90, 92
reformatory, 179, 180, 201-202. *See also* correctional institutions
Reform Movement (19th century), 176-79, 186, 196
rehabilitation, as correctional goal, 179, 187, 197, 198, 201-207, 211
Reiss, Albert J., Jr., cited, 11, 12, 50, 71, 161, 162; quoted, 68
residual vandalism, 96-99, 102
responsibility, denial of, 36
retreatism, 30-31, 32, 35-36, 39; gangs and, 147-48

retribution, as goal, 198
Rhodes, A. Lewis, cited, 12, 50
ritualism, 30, 31
robbery, 29, 32, 48-49, 144, 158, 164; associations and, 51; incarceration for, 1, 65, 66, 83
Robertson, Ian, cited, 130
Robin, Gerald, cited, 87-88, 90
Rodman, Hyman, cited, 28
Rosenberg, B. 85-86, 88, 98
Rossi, Peter H., cited, 66, 169
Rubington, Carl, cited, 62, 97
runaways, 2, 5, 6, 7-8, 42, 164-65; age definition of, 3, 20, 64; girls as, 70-71, 75-76, 77-78; police caseloads, 73-75, 168-70, 175, 214; punishment of, 65, 66, 83; types of, 76-80

safecracking, 45-46
Sanders, William B., 49; on drug use, 18, 25, 50, 74, 81, 109, 115, 120, 127, 128; on police, 13, 53, 89, 92, 168, 172-74, 191
San Francisco, California, 42, 73, 207
San Francisco State College, 59
Santa Monica, California, 131
Schepses, Ervin, cited, 92, 93
schools: vandalization of, 95-96, 101. See also education
Schub, Christine Carol, cited, 118
Schwartz, G., 60, 148-49, 151
Scott, M., 24, 56, 59, 153
self-report surveys, 13, 14-15, 16(tab.), 17(tab.), 20, 22; on class and delinquency, 31; on drugs, 18(tab.), 50, 81, 109, 116-17; on property crimes, 86
Sellin, Thorsten, cited, 3, 4, 44
sentencing, 65-66, 72, 89, 178, 181; indeterminate, 179, 194
sex comparisons: arrest rates, 15, 25; auto theft and, 93; double standard attitudes, 68-70, 71, 73, 80, 82; gang membership, 137-38, 139-40, 147; incarceration rates, 64, 65; probation disposition, 199; self-reported delinquencies, 16(tab.), 17(tab.), 20, 31, 67, 86; shoplifting, 90, 92; vandalism, 104
sex experience, 39, 60; juvenile status and, 21, 25, 42-43, 64-65, 66, 67-73, 81-82, 83; official focus on, 181, 191-92, 199; runaways and, 70-71, 75-76, 77-78; self-reported rates of, 16(tab.), 17(tab.), 67

Shaw, C., 34, 50, 84-85
Sheridan, William H., cited, 65
Shirley, David L., cited, 103
shoplifting, 13, 32, 46, 52, 86-92, 105, 164; arrests of women for, 69, 90, 92; juvenile status and, 9, 10-11; turf and, 154
Short, James F., 84, 137, 141, 142, 144; on self-reported delinquencies, 16(tab.), 17(tab.), 18, 20, 67, 81, 86, 109
Silverstein, H., 85-86, 88, 98
Simmel, Georg, cited, 41, 120
Simmons, Jerry, cited, 122, 123
Simon, William, cited, 113
skills, 45-46, 47-48, 198-99; of vandalism, 98-99, 102-103
Smith, Kenneth Cruce, cited, 182
social deprivation, 26-32. See also class; opportunity; poverty
"social history" reports, 89, 101, 180, 184, 185-86; construction of, 188, 191-95, 199
social workers, 145, 152, 207-15
Spanish, 70
Spergel, Irving: cited, 142, 143(tab.); quoted, 85, 145
splitters, 78-79, 80
sports, 19, 56; prison, 203, 204
Spradley, James, cited, 121
state laws, 3-4, 65, 87
status: 1, 33, 35, 43, 149; drugs and, 146-48, 156; juvenile, 20-21 (See also juvenile-status offenses); non-utilitarian action and, 38, 57-58, 60-61; occupational, 29; runaway, 78-79, 80; sexual roles and, 68-69; symbolic, 15, 39, 40, 94, 150-51, 208-209, 210.
Stinchcombe, Arthur L., cited, 155
street work, 207-11, 212, 214
structural frustration, 26-38; defined, 29; non-utilitarian behavior and, 38-41, 60-61, 95-96, 97; runaways and, 80; of women, 70-71, 76
Stumbo, Bella, 74
subcultures, 23-24, 40-45, 61; of conflict, 33, 34-35, 38, 141-43, 146; "criminal," 1, 25, 32-34, 37-38, 46, 50, 85, 104-105, 139-40, 142-45, 146; drug use and, see drugs; institutionalization and, 204, 205-206; retreatist, 33, 35-36, 39, 147-48

surfers, 19, 56, 95, 120
Sutherland, Edwin H., cited, 46, 47-48, 92, 198
Sykes, Gresham, cited, 36, 37, 40, 91
symbolic interactionist theory, 51-54, 55
Synanon, 131

Tenenbaum, S., quoted, 102
theft, *see* larceny
Thomas, W.I., 140; quoted, 51
Thrasher, F.M., cited, 97
Time (periodical), 99, 128, 129
Toby, Jackson, cited, 27-28
training schools, *see* correctional institutions
trashing, 95-105. *See also* vandalism
trespass, 6-7, 8, 20, 172-73
trial, 178, 183. *See also* hearings
truancy, 3, 5, 6, 15, 64, 66; class and, 135, 166; formal castigation of, 177; subculture norm of, 25. *See also* runaways
turf, 153-56
Turkey, 132

Uniform Crime Reports (FBI), 11, 109
United States National Guard, 99
United States Supreme Court, 81, 183, 184, 185
urban areas, 94, 176-77, 182; gangs and, 134-35, 138, 151

values: advertising and, 112-13, 114; class and, 29, 33, 35, 39, 70, 135-36, 165-68; criminal subcultural, 33, 34, 35, 38, 46-47, 48, 145, 146-47, 150, 208; generation gap in, 40, 41-45, 68, 82, 83, 195; hippie, 110, 116, 118, 119-20, 122-25, 126, 133, 147; materialist, 28-29, 36, 39-40, 111, 125; prison, 197-98, 202-203, 204-205; professional police, 163-64, 175; sexual mores and, 67-68, 70, 71, 72-73, 80, 181, 191; vandal, 100; youth gang performance and, 56-58, 60-61, 145, 147

vandalism, 8, 13, 38, 95-105, 135, 166, 168; police case-time on, 169; sentencing for, 5, 65
venereal disease, 69, 70, 78, 81-82
victims, 11, 13-14, 19, 161; delinquent denial of, 37, 53, 91
Vietnam War, 42, 44, 58-59, 111, 149
violence, 35, 36-37; gangs and, 138, 140, 141-43, 148-55, 156, 166, 208-209, 210; status and, 38, 57-58, 60-61. *See also specific crimes*

Wallace, Thomas, 121; quoted, 119
warfare: gang model of, 22, 141-43, 149, 151-52, 208-209
Watergate scandal, 44
Wattenberg, W. W., 92, 93
Weber, Max, 115-16
Weinberg, Martin S., cited, 62
Weiner, Norman, cited, 90-91
Werthman, C., 56, 58, 154, 160
Westley, William A., cited, 174
West Philadelphia, Pennsylvania, 135
West Virginia, 96
Wheeler, Stanton, cited, 31
White, Lynn, cited, 50
Whitten, Philip, cited, 130
Wieder, D. Lawrence, cited, 131
Wilkins, Leslie T., cited, 200
Wilson, James Q., cited, 163-64, 165
Winick, Charles, cited, 130
Winograd, Barry, cited, 122, 123
Wiseman, Jacqueline, cited, 121
Wolfgang, Marvin E., cited, 3, 4
World War II, 39, 93, 101-102; concentration camps of, 201-202

Yablonsky, L., 103, 125, 126, 131, 137, 138, 140, 141; quoted, 143-44
Yankelovich, Daniel, cited, 42, 67
Youth Service Bureaus, 211-15

Zap, North Dakota, 99
Zimmerman, Don H., cited, 195
Zorbaugh, Harvey Warren, cited, 153